ASIAN ECONOMIC AND POLITICAL ISSUES, VOLUME 11

Asian Economic and Political Issues, Volume 11

Harvey E. Roth
Editor

Nova Science Publishers, Inc.
New York

For permission to use material from this book please contact us:
Telephone 631-231-7269; Fax 631-231-8175
Web Site: http://www.novapublishers.com

LIBRARY OF CONGRESS CATALOGING-IN-PUBLICATION DATA

Available upon request.

ISBN: 978-1-60021-192-8
ISBN: 1-60021-192-5

Published by Nova Science Publishers, Inc. ✦ New York

CONTENTS

PREFACE

It is predicted by some observers that the 21st century will be remembered as the "Asian Century." Many of the countries in the region seem to be able to take the economic and trade baton when one of the others experiences problems. the region, in general, continues to grow economically, politically and militarily.

The articles presented in this book examine the current political and economic situations in nations across Asia, particularly focusing on economic developments.

Chapter 1 - This chapter discusses the role of FDI in the economic growth and development of Southeast Asian economies. It analyzes the various theories that relate to FDI, namely, the theory of the firm, the theory of factor endowment, and FDI-cum-trade approach. It also analyzes the geographical and industrial patterns of FDI in each of these economies. It also discusses the various motives and determinants of FDI in the context of the theories discussed.

Chapter 2 - In response to the crisis, various policies were adopted by the international organizations and by the respective economies in the region. This chapter evaluates each of these policies. The differences in their policy actions are highlighted and explained. This chapter also examines the various strategies aimed at improving the global financial architecture.

Chapter 3 - The 1997/98 economic crisis faced by the Southeast Asian economies was linked to the interactions between the households, corporate and government sectors in the pursuit of their three main activities such as production, demand and income. The first section of this chapter investigates the various conditions which existed before the crisis and which contributed to the crisis. These include rising income expectations, worsening current account deficits, rising external indebtedness, and rapid expansion of domestic credit. The second section analyzes the impacts of the crisis on the four sectors such as the external (trade and financial capital flows), production, labor and financial sectors.

Chapter 4 - It is well-known internationally that Japan has been experiencing serious economic and financial difficulties since the 1990s. This chapter aims to explain the current important issues regarding the Japanese monetary policy and financial system. Struggling with unprecedented deflation, the Bank of Japan has employed unusual policy tools, such as reducing target interest rates to zero and buying stocks. The financial system of Japan is having trouble with financial intermediation, risk sharing and liquidity services. It is notable that the Japanese financial system is quite different from that of a decade ago. In recent years, the Japanese household and business enterprise sectors as a whole are lenders, and the government and foreign sectors are borrowers. As a result, the business model of Japanese banks during the high growth period when banks collected money from households as deposits and lent it to large enterprises is no longer sustainable. In terms of households' portfolio investments, safe assets such as bank deposits and traditional insurance make up substantial shares and risky assets such as stocks are marginal. A bank-centered financial system like Japan's faces financial difficulties when the risk taking ability of financial institutions decreases, which actually occurred due to the huge non-performing loans of the 1990's. The government initiated the Japanese Big Bang to vitalize the financial market in Japan, but a satisfactory outcome has yet to be seen.

Chapter 5 - This chapter analyzes the industrial sector and its significance in the transformation process of Southeast Asian economies. These economies have different industrial patterns and development experiences. They have different modes of industrial development including import-substitution, export-promotion and export-substitution policies. The Philippines had the longest import-substitution policy while Singapore, the shortest. Malaysia, Thailand and Indonesia are in between. Country experiences, problems and policies are discussed.

Chapter 6 - South Korea is a major economic partner for the United States. In 2004, trade between the two countries was over $70 billion, making South Korea the United States's seventh-largest trading partner — ahead of France and Italy — and its seventh-largest export market. In 2005, the U.S. was Korea's third-largest trading partner, second-largest export market, and its largest supplier of foreign direct investment (FDI).

Bilateral economic relations have advanced to the point that the two sides in February 2006 announced their intention to negotiate a bilateral free trade agreement (FTA), which they hope to complete by 2007. The announcement followed South Korean concessions in four areas: beef, automobiles, pharmaceuticals, and "screen quotas" limiting the amount of screen time that foreign films could be shown. The United States had said an FTA could not be launched unless Seoul demonstrated its ability to deliver compromises in these sectors. If an agreement is reached, it would be the United States's largest FTA since the completion of the North American Free Trade Agreement. To go into effect, FTAs must be approved by Congress and the Korean National Assembly. The FTA negotiation and ratification processes are likely to politicize bilateral trade disputes and produce spillovers between the economic and strategic aspects of the relationship, particularly if there are dramatic developments in the crisis over North Korea's nuclear weapons program.

Increased U.S.-South Korean economic interaction has been accompanied by numerous disagreements over trade and economic policies. The intensity of the disputes has diminished considerably since the late 1980s and early 1990s, in part because South Korea has enacted a set of sweeping market-oriented reforms as a *quid pro quo* for receiving a $58 billion package from the International Monetary Fund (IMF) following the near collapse of the South Korean economy in 1997. In recent years, the United States and South Korea appear to have become more adept at managing their trade disputes, so that they tend to be less acrimonious than they were in the 1980s and 1990s. This is due in part to the quarterly, working-level bilateral trade meetings that have been held since early 2001. Strategic factors, including South Korea's increased economic integration with North Korea, have become issues on the bilateral U.S.-South Korea economic front. In the FTA talks, South Korean officials have said they will try to secure preferential tariff treatment for goods made by South Korean firms in the Kaesong industrial zone, located inside North Korea. In 2003, China surpassed the United States as South

Korea's largest trading partner. Many South Korean exports to China are believed to be intermediate goods that are incorporated into products sent to the United States.

This report summarizes the main issues in U.S.-South Korean economic relations, including South Korea's economic prospects and economic reforms, major bilateral economic disputes, and the pros and cons of a U.S. -South Korean FTA. The report will be updated periodically.

Chapter 7 - This chapter examines the regional integration process that has taken place in Southeast Asia through the ASEAN regional grouping. It analyzes the initiatives that have been undertaken by ASEAN to foster closer regional economic integration. It also identifies and explains the different factors which have affected the ASEAN integration process. Finally, it identifies ASEAN's linkages with the global economy at the multilateral, regional and bilateral levels including the present and future schemes which may impact on the ASEAN regional grouping.

Chapter 8 - This chapter examines the trade sector in Southeast Asian economies. It discusses the theories of trade including the absolute advantage, comparative advantage, Heckscher-Ohlin model, and competitive advantage. Some illustrations of these concepts in the context of Southeast Asia are discussed. This is followed by a discussion of the various trade policies including tariffs and non-tariff barriers. This chapter also analyzes the geographical and industrial patterns of Southeast Asia's exports and imports. Finally, it discusses the trade liberalization schemes followed by the Southeast Asian economies including the creation of the ASEAN Free Trade Area (AFTA).

Chapter 9 - This article begins by summarizing President Putin's petroleum-and-pipelines strategy to revitalize Russia and, possibly, the country's imperial ambitions. It then shifts its focus to Azerbaijan, which once made Russia the world's largest petroleum producer. The article reviews key developments there during the czarist, Soviet, and post-independence periods. Next, it describes Baku's second oil and natural gas revolution, together with various pipeline alternatives for exporting Azerbaijani energy. The article goes on to consider several threats to these energy exports. In doing so, it pays particular attention to dangers resulting from the stolen presidential election of 2003 and the establishment of a political dynasty by the Aliyev clan in Baku. After taking note of the international reaction to this situation, the article concludes with a discussion of its consequences for Azerbaijan, Russia, the European Union, and the United States.

In: Asian Economic and Political Issues, Volume 11
Editor: Harvey E. Roth, pp. 1-24
ISBN: 1-60021-192-5

Chapter 1

FOREIGN DIRECT INVESTMENT IN SOUTHEAST ASIA: TRENDS, PATTERNS AND DETERMINANTS

Teofilo C. Daquila

ABSTRACT

This chapter discusses the role of FDI in the economic growth and development of Southeast Asian economies. It analyzes the various theories that relate to FDI, namely, the theory of the firm, the theory of factor endowment, and FDI-cum-trade approach. It also analyzes the geographical and industrial patterns of FDI in each of these economies. It also discusses the various motives and determinants of FDI in the context of the theories discussed.

INTRODUCTION

Foreign direct investment (FDI) has both positive and good points. On the positive front, FDI accelerates host countries' growth by augmenting domestic savings and investment, helping transfer of technology from the "leaders," increasing competition in the host country's domestic market, increasing exports and earning foreign exchange, and imparting several other types of positive externalities (spillovers) to the economy at large.[1] Moreover, FDI has given the global integration process a major impetus by helping link markets for capital and labor and raise relative wages and productivity of capital in recipient countries.[2] Indeed, the optimism associated with the prospects for capital flows, technology transfer,

---

[1] Rati Ram and Kevin Honglin Zhang, "Foreign Direct Investment and Economic Growth: Evidence from Cross-Country Data for the 1990s," *Economic Development and Cultural Change,* Vol.51, No.1, 2002, p.205. See also Stephen Thomsen, *Southeast Asia: The Role of Foreign Direct Investment Policies in Development,* Working Papers on International Investment, Paris: Organization for Economic Cooperation and Development (OECD), 1999.

[2] IFC, "Foreign Direct Investments," *Lessons of Experience*, No.5, 1997, Washington DC, USA: International Finance Corporation, p.14.

management know-how, access to export markets, and faster economic growth has given birth to renewed interest in the role of transnational corporations (TNCs) as engines of economic growth.[3] According to UNCTAD, some 40,000 parent firms and approximately 270,000 foreign affiliates controlled an FDI stock of US$2.7 trillion, equivalent to 10% of the world GDP in 1995.[4] This gives recognition to the enormous benefits brought by FDI.

However, FDI may repatriate funds almost to the same extent as it brings funds, transfer technologies that are inappropriate for the host country's factor proportions, kill indigenous enterprise through an intense competition, especially due to the strong economic power of large foreign companies that bring FDI, primarily target the host country's domestic market and thus not increase exports, cause distortions in the host country's policies so as to benefit the foreign investors, and create distortions in the host country's social and economic structures by infusing inappropriate social and cultural norms and behavior patterns.[5]

As IFC (1997:20) stated, the largest economies naturally attract FDI, but experience shows that it can be an important part of even the smallest, poorest economies. There is no doubt that FDI has played a significant role in the economic development of Southeast Asia, particularly in small economies like Singapore. Since its independence in 1965, Singapore has explicitly and pragmatically relied on an outward-oriented industrialization policy by encouraging FDI and promoting trade. Singapore's heavy dependence on FDI was due to its lack of natural resources, small domestic market, lack of domestic entrepreneurs, and lack of domestic savings.[6] Other countries such as Indonesia, Malaysia, the Philippines and Thailand have relied on FDI to a lesser extent than Singapore because of their bigger domestic markets and the presence of natural resources that they can depend on. However, having realized the significant contribution of FDI in the economic transformation of Singapore, the other Southeast Asian countries have increasingly relied on the inflows of FDI into their economies. From a poor, underdeveloped country with a per capita GNP of less than US$500 and a 14 percent unemployment rate in 1960, Singapore has become a newly industrialized economy with a per capita income of about US$25,000 in the year 2000.

This chapter provides an analysis of FDI in Southeast Asia. In the next section, the theories of FDI are discussed to understand the conceptual framework that governs FDI – why FDI takes place. The third section discusses the three types of FDI which include natural-resource investment, investment to serve the host market, and export-oriented investment. The fourth section identifies the various government institutions in the respective countries in Southeast Asia which are responsible for investment promotion and facilitation activities. The fifth and sixth sections analyse the geographical and industrial patterns of FDI in the five Southeast Asian countries. Because of the inconsistency in the reporting of the data

---

[3] Momtaz Uddin Ahmed, "Foreign Direct Investment and Technology Flows in Asia and the Pacific Region in the 1990s: An Analysis of Trends, Patterns and Policies," in Behrman, J.R, M.Dutta, S.L. Husted, Sumalee, C. Suthiphand, and P. Wiboonchutikula, *Restructuring Asian Economics for the New Millenium,* JAI – Elsevier Science, 2001, p.643.

[4] Ahmed, "Foreign Direct Investment …, p.643.

[5] Rati Ram and Kevin Honglin Zhang, "Foreign Direct Investment and Economic Growth …," p.205.

[6] When a domestic resource gap exists, that is, when gross domestic investment exceeds gross domestic savings, this can be financed by foreign borrowings or foreign direct investment. The main difference between the two forms of external financing is that the former involves repayment of principal and interests. FDI involves the transfer of, not only financial capital but also physical resources (eg. machineries and equipment) from the investing countries. While FDI does not require repayment of principal and interest in the case of foreign loans, it involves payment and remittance of dividends to foreign investors.

on FDI by geographical and sectoral basis, analysis is done on an individual country basis. The seventh section explains the motives and determinants of FDI in Southeast Asia.

THEORIES OF FDI

Several explanations have been put forward to analyse the three tasks related to FDI; namely, the determinants (why investment takes place), the impact on the host country, and the impact on the investing country. However, as what most studies have done, this section focuses on the first task, that is, to explain the determinants of FDI. Among the various theories of FDI, three theories are discussed here; namely, the factor endowment approach, the profit maximization approach, and the FDI-cum-trade approach.[7]

Factor Endowment Approach

The motive for foreign direct investment is a higher rate of return to the factor (i.e. capital) transferred through FDI. This model assumes that that capital moves from capital-abundant countries with relatively low returns to capital-scarce countries with relatively high returns to capital. However, this approach is constrained by the fact that it cannot explain the investment flows between capital-abundant countries such as those between the United States and Japan, and between Europe and Japan. Moreover, this model blurs the differences between FDI and other types of capital flows.

Theory of the Firm Approach

This approach focuses on the profit maximization behavior of the firm. Among the various theories that fall under this category, Dunning's eclectic theory (1977) has been the most comprehensive approach that integrates both international trade and production theories.[8] It assumes that there are three sets of determinants; namely, the ownership advantages, locational advantages, and advantages that would arise from internalization. In general, this approach argues that these advantages must outweigh the costs of operating in foreign markets.

Firstly, what do foreign investors have or what can they offer? Foreign investors should possess some form of ownership advantages over their competitors or potential competitors in the host country, which may take the form of either a monopoly over a product or a brand name, a patent on a production process or technology, superior knowledge of the host market, management skills or marketing expertise.

---

[7] For a very comprehensive survey of these theories, see Udom Kerdpibule and Eric Ramsetter, "Foreign Investment Theories and Policy Issues," in Seiji Naya (ed.), *Direct Foreign Investment and Export in Asia,* Kuala Lumpur: SEACEN, 1987, pp.1-23. See also ADB, 'Foreign Direct Investment: An Explanation," *Asian Development Outlook,* Manila: Asian Development Bank, p.47.

[8] For further discussion, see John Dunning, *International Production and the Multinational Enterprise*, London: Allen & Unwin, 1981, chapters 2-4.

Secondly, what do the host countries offer? The foreign investors should be able to derive benefits from the locational advantages that are available in the host country which include their ability to access the host market or to make the host country a production and/or export platform for their products or services. A host country can provide a comparative advantage over the other countries in terms of abundance of high-quality low-wage labor, low transport costs, excellent infrastructure, a strategic geographical location, and favorable investment incentives, among others. In the absence of these locational advantages, the foreign investor would choose exporting the product instead of direct investment for him to exploit his ownership advantage.

Lastly, aside from ownership and location advantages, there should be an internalization advantage which encourages the foreign investors to choose direct investment over other types of arms-length arrangements such as production licensing and franchising. Foreign investors usually bring technology with them as part of FDI package, which host countries would like to be unbundled. However, unbundling becomes difficult because of problems related to the definition of the technology component to be sold and the price of the component.

FDI-Cum-Trade Approach

The trade-oriented nature of FDI has been very important for many countries including Japan, the newly-industrialized economies (NIEs) of South Korea, Hong Kong, Taiwan and Singapore, and the more developed countries of Southeast Asia like Malaysia and Thailand. With FDI, trade is stimulated. In this case, FDI is viewed as a complement to trade. This view is explained in two ways. First, according to the factor endowments theory, foreign direct investment is viewed as complement to trade if trade volume increases after the inflow of FDI takes place. This is true as long as differences in technologies exist between the investing country and the recipient country. Thus, the trade-oriented nature of this type of FDI exists.

The second view is according to the product cycle hypothesis.[9] Both Akamatsu and Vernon suggested that, in the context of the product cycle hypothesis, leading economies typically develop new products and export them to lesser developed countries (LDCs). As production becomes standardized, it is transferred to 'host' LDCs via FDI, until the production of the goods is carried out mainly in the LDCs. The goods are then exported back to the investing countries, known as the boomerang effect.

Kojima analysed the trade-oriented nature of Japanese FDI. There is a progression from industries in which Japan loses its comparative advantage, and the host country gains an advantage, presumably while new products and industries generate new areas of competitiveness for Japan. This process would result in Japanese FDI being 'trade-oriented'.

---

[9] For full discussion, see Kaname Akamatsu, ''A Historical Pattern of Economic Growth in Developing Countries,'' *The Developing Economies*, The Preliminary Issue, No.1, 1962a, p.3-25; Kaname Akamatsu, "A Theory of Unbalanced Growth in the World Economy," *Weltwirtschafliches Archiv*, Heft 86, Band 2, 1962b, pp523-544; Raymond Vernon, "International Investment and International Trade in the Product Cycle", *Quarterly Journal of Economics,* Vol.80, No.2, 1966, pp.190-207; Kiyoshi Kojima, *Direct Foreign Investment: A Japanese Model of Multinational Business Operations*, New York: Praeger, 1978; and Kiyoshi Kojima, "A Model of Trade-Oriented Foreign Investment," in Seiji Naya (ed.), *Direct Foreign Investment and Export Promotion Policies: Policies and Experiences in Asia,* Kuala Lumpur: Southeast Asia Central Banks Research and Training Center and Hawaii: East-West Resource Systems Institute, 1987, pp. 159-183.

Japan, the investing country, would benefit if it disinvests from a comparatively disadvantaged, marginal domestic industry, in order to produce the same product in a host country at costs much lower than in Japan. The product can then be exported to the investing country (Japan) as well as to other markets.

Types of FDI

There are basically three types of FDI particularly in developing countries; namely, (a) investment in natural resources, (b) investment to serve the domestic market of the host country, and (c) investment in export-oriented industries. An example of natural-resource investment is British investment in the oil and gas sector in Brunei. The locational advantage is present in Brunei because of the abundance of oil and gas there. The ownership advantage of the British is also present because they have the high capital and technology requirements of natural resource extraction. The internalization advantage is also present but not as strong as in other sectors.

The second type of investment to serve the host country market took place during the 1950s and 1960s when developing countries followed import-substitution policies to protect their domestic industries. As imports of consumer goods of the protected industries were restricted, FDI became a means to circumvent import restrictions. More recently, FDI to serve the host markets include those in the services sectors like banking and finance, insurance and tourism. In these sectors, both ownership and locational advantages are present.

The third type of investment in export-oriented industries has occurred since the 1970s and 1980s when massive FDI from Japan and the United States came into Asia particularly the NIEs and then to Southeast Asia making these countries the production and export bases for the products of the foreign investors. The locational advantage was present in the form of low-cost labor and investment incentives. The ownership advantage was also present as foreign investors had inside knowledge of the labor-intensive consumer products like electronics products. One significant impact of this type of investment was the ability of the host countries, like the NIEs, to become foreign investors themselves in other host countries in Southeast Asia like Malaysia, Thailand and Indonesia as locational advantages and ownership advantages were both present.

Investment Agencies in Southeast Asia

Generally, there are two types of lists which many developing countries have utilized in restricting FDI. First, there is a positive list which specifies sectors open to FDI. Second, there is a negative list which specifies the industries closed to FDI. The sectors permitted or banned were sometimes specified in concrete terms and sometimes imprecisely that "threaten the economic interests of the state."[10] There also geographical restrictions as specified in these lists, that is, which regions or areas will ban or allow FDI.

In many countries, including Southeast Asia, FDI are usually subject to official approvals by government agencies. We can classify the investment agencies in Southeast Asia into two

[10] IFC, "Foreign Direct Investments…, p.30.

groups. The first group consists of Indonesia's BKPM and Thailand's BOI given that these agencies primarily perform their conventional functions of investment promotion and facilitation. The second group consists of Malaysia's MIDA, the Philippines' BOI and Singapore's EDB. Not only these agencies perform their traditional functions, but also they are involved significantly in shaping the industrial development of their economies.

In Indonesia, the Badan Koordinasi Penanaman Modal (BKPM), known as the the Investment Coordinating Board, is the main government agency which handles the statistics and other information on foreign direct investment in Indonesia. It was created in 1973 to effectively implement the enactment of law on foreign and domestic investment.[11] It has been operating directly under the Office of the President. Its main functions include investment promotion, facilitation and policy formulation. It grants investment incentives, circumscribe investment areas and assist investors in setting up their businesses.

The Malaysian Industrial Development Authority (MIDA)[12] is the principal government agency which promotes and coordinates industrial development and investment in Malaysia. Since its establishment in 1965, it was primarily engaged in protecting and promoting industries before it assumed a larger role of investment promotion with the passage of the Promotion of Investments Act in 1986. Having been under the Ministry of International Trade and Industry, MIDA recommends trade policies and strategies relevant to the promotion and development of industries.

The Board of Investment (BOI)[13] is the main government agency which is responsible for the promotion of investments in the Philippines. It is a unit under the Ministry of Trade Industry, whose functions include investment promotion and industry planning. It also undertakes sectoral analysis, industry planning, and preparation of the annual Investment Priorities Plan. It also facilitates investment application, processing and approval through a "One Stop Action Centre." It also provides traditional services like granting incentives and project monitoring.

The Singapore Economic Development Board (SEDB)[14] was one of the oldest investment agencies in Southeast Asia, having been set up in 1961 as a statutory board under the Ministry of Trade and Industry. Since then, the SEDB has been mainly responsible for steering the growth of domestic industries particularly in the manufacturing and trade services. Its activities have been guided by its main focus which is to ensure a conducive and competitive business environment and to work with the government so that relevant infrastructure and manpower capabilities for the industries and businesses would be met. It has also provided a one-stop investment facilitation – from assisting investors to establish their businesses in Singapore, securing infrastructure and manpower, to connecting with regional business partners. Thus, SEDB has performed not only its conventional investment promotion and facilitation role, but also its economic developmental role.

The Board of Investment of Thailand (BOI)[15] is the principal investment agency in Thailand. Having been established with the passage of the Investment Promotions Act of 1977, it reports directly to the Prime Minister of Thailand. Its main functions include the

[11] For more information, see Indonesia's BKPM website, http://www.bkpm.go.id
[12] For more information, see MIDA's website: http://www.mida.gov.my.
[13] For more information, see Philippine BOI website: http://www.boi.gov.ph.
[14] For more information, see Singapore's EDB website: http://www.sedb.com.
[15] For more information, see Thailand's BOI website: http://www.boi.go.th.

promotion of investment in Thailand and providing business-related services to prospective investors.

Geographical Patterns of FDI

As a general guiding principle, FDI is defined as 'investment that is made to acquire a lasting interest in an enterprise operating in an economy other than that of the investor.'[16] For statistical purposes, the International Monetary Fund defines foreign investment as direct (FDI) when the investor holds 10 percent or more of the equity of an enterprise, which as a rule of thumb, is usually enough to give the investor a say in the management of the enterprise.[17]

Indonesia

Table 1. shows the approved foreign investment projects in Indonesia by sources of origin as reported by Indonesia's Investment Coordinating Board called Badan Koordinasi Penanaman Modal (BKPM). By region, Europe is the largest investing group with a share of 39.4 percent in 1998, followed closely by Asia with a share of about 34 percent. A far third is North America whose share was about one-tenth of Europe's share. In 1999, we observe a significant decrease in Europe's and North America's shares while Asia's share markedly increased to about 60 percent. In 2000, we have a completely different picture as Europe's share rebounded more than five times, while Asia's share dropped to about half of its share in 1999. An important observation from Table 1 is the significant contribution of Northeast Asia mainly because of Japan, Taiwan and Korea. As a group, it accounted for about a fifth of FDI in Indonesia during the 1998-2000 period. By country sources, UK was the largest investor in 1998 whose share was even a lot more than the combined shares of the other three top investors, namely, Japan, Singapore and the US. But in 1999, both UK and the US were out of the top four investors, as Australia and Taiwan took the top two positions. In 2000, UK again took the top spot but Singapore and the US dropped to lower positions as the Netherlands and Germany garnered the third and fourth ranks.

Malaysia

Table 2 shows the approved foreign investments in Malaysia as reported by the Malaysian Industrial Development Authority (MIDA). By region, North America was the leading investor during the 1998-1999 period, with an average share of about 46 percent. However, its share fell in the year 2000 to about 38 percent. Asia was the second largest investing group in both 1998-99 period, but managed to take the lead in the year 2000 as it accounted for about two-fifths of the total FDI. Europe was consistently the third placer with

[16] Hal Hill, "Foreign Investment and East Asian Economic Development," *Asian-Pacific Economic Literature,* Vol.4, No.2, 1990, p.23.

[17] IFC, "Foreign Direct Investments," ... p.9.

an average share of about 18 percent during the 1998-2000 period. It even showed an increasing trend as its share more than doubled in the year 2000 relative to that of 1998. Within Asia, it is again interesting to note that Northeast Asia was a significant player as it accounted for about a quarter of the total FDI in 1998 and 2000. However, its share had more than halved in 1999 because of the reductions in Japanese and Taiwanese investments. As for country sources, the United States was the top investor accounting for about 40-50 percent during the 1998-2000 period. Japan took the second position with an average share of about 12 percent during the same period. The other top investors during this period were Taiwan (1998), Singapore (1998-2000), Netherlands (1999-2000) and Germany (2000).

Table 1. Geographical Distribution of Approved FDI in Indonesia (in mil USD)

Country	**1998**	**% share**	**1999**	**% share**	**2000**	**% share**
Total	**13563**	**100**	**10890**	**100**	**15413**	**100**
Asia	**4594**	**33.9**	**6486**	**59.6**	**3820**	**24.8**
- ASEAN	**n.a.**	**-.**	**n.a.**	-	**n.a.**	-
Malaysia	n.a.	-.	n.a.	-	n.a.	-
Philippines	n.a.	-	n.a.	-	n.a.	-
Singapore	1267	9.3	731	6.7	536	3.5
- Northeast Asia	**2247**	**16.5**	**2473**	**22.7**	**2878**	**18.7**
Hong Kong	549	4.0	77	0.7	105	0.7
Japan	1331	9.8	644	5.9	1954	12.7
Taiwan	165	1.2	1489	13.7	131	0.8
South Korea	202	1.5	263	2.4	688	4.5
China	n.a.	-	n.a.	-	n.a.	-
-Other Asia	**1079**	**8.0**	**3282**	**30.1**	**405**	**2.6**
Europe	**5346**	**39.4**	**773**	**7.1**	**5980**	**38.8**
- European Union	**5311**	**39.1**	**731**	**6.7**	**5938**	**38.5**
Belgium	12	0.1	10	0.1	0.5	...
France	8	0.1	23	0.2	65	0.4
Germany	71	0.5	87	0.8	960	6.2
Netherlands	412	3.0	49	0.4	1159	7.5
United Kingdom	4745	35.0	507	4.7	3645	23.6
- Switzerland	35	0.3	42	0.4	42	0.3
North America	**576**	**4.2**	**140**	**1.3**	**244**	**1.6**
Canada	8	...	3	...	2	...
United States	568	4.2	137	1.3	242	1.6
Australia	**85**	**0.6**	**2458**	**22.6**	**48**	**0.3**
Other countries	**2718**	**20.0**	**1006**	**9.2**	**4776**	**31.0**

Source of basic data: Badan Koordinasi Penanaman Modal as cited *in Indikator Ekonomi (Economic Indicators*), Busan Pusat Statistik, Jakarta -Indonesia, March 2001, p.58.

Table 2. Geographical Distribution of Approved FDI in Malaysia (in mil RM)

Country	**1998**	**% share**	**1999**	**% share**	**2000**	**% share**
Total	**13063**	**100**	**12274**	**100**	**19819**	**100**
Asia	**4427**	**33.9**	**2366**	**19.3**	**8142**	**41.1**
- ASEAN	**1028**	**7.9**	**934**	**7.6**	**1861**	**9.4**
Indonesia	55	0.4	32	0.3	66	0.3
Brunei	1	...	...	...	...	...
Philippines	2	0.01	...	...	...	...
Singapore	968	7.4	902	7.3	1778	9.0
Thailand	2	0.01	...	...	16	0.08
- Northeast Asia	**3328**	**25.5**	**1383**	**11.3**	**4897**	**24.7**
Japan	1868	14.3	1006	8.2	2879	14.5
Taiwan	1001	7.7	267	2.2	916	4.6
South Korea	76	0.6	35	0.3	723	3.6
China	361	2.8	74	0.6	379	1.9
Hong Kong	22	1.7	-	-	-	-
-Other Asia	**71**	**5.4**	**49**	**0.4**	**1384**	**7.0**
Europe	**1543**	**11.8**	**2104**	**17.1**	**4847**	**24.4**
- European Union	**1382**	**10.6**	**1335**	**10.9**	**4755**	**24.0**
France	14	1.1	8	0.07	3	0.01
Germany	152	1.2	187	1.5	1655	8.4
Netherlands	628	4.8	772	6.3	2174	11.0
United Kingdom	479	3.7	192	1.6	747	3.8
- Switzerland	141	1.1	708	5.8	91	0.4
North America	**6475**	**49.5**	**5273**	**43.0**	**7494**	**37.8**
Canada	42	0.3	115	0.9	2	0.01
United States	6433	49.2	5159	42.0	7492	37.8
Australia	**117**	**0.9**	**52**	**0.4**	**130**	**0.7**
Other countries	**501**	**3.8**	**2479**	**20.2**	**793**	**4.0**

Source of basic data: MIDA, *Statistics on the Manufacturing Sector*, Kuala Lumpur: Malaysian Industrial Development Authority, 1994-98 issue; and MIDA, *Report on the Performance of the Manufacturing Sector* 2000, Kuala Lumpur: Malaysian Industrial Development Authority, February 6, 2001, p.124.

Philippines

Table 3 provides the data on approved foreign investments in the Philippines as reported by its Board of Investments. By region, Europe, North America and Asia were the top investors in the Philippines during the 1997-1999 period. While Europe accounted for bulk of FDI in 1997, its share fell drastically to 32 percent in 1998 and to 9 percent in 1999. The complete opposite was shown by North America as its share more than tripled in 1999 relative to 1997. As for Asia, its share more than tripled in 1998, but dropped to about a third in 1999. Table 3 also shows that Africa had substantial investment in the Philippines during the 1997-98 period. As for country sources, no country breakdown was available. However, it has been known that the United States has been a major investor in the Philippines historically. Japan was also one of the top investors.

Table 3. Geographical Distribution of Approved FDI in Philippines (in mil pesos)

Country	1997	% share	1998	% share	1999	% share
Total	**58716**	**100**	**37299**	**100**	**21180**	**100**
Asia	7498	12.8	14571	39.1	2869	13.5
North America	10522	17.9	7998	21.4	13921	65.7
Central America	-	-	-	-	-	-
South America	-	-	-	-	1920	9.1
Europe	32335	55.1	11968	32.1	1990	9.4
Australia	296	0.5	267	0.7	3	0.01
Africa	4366	7.4	2198	5.9	39	0.2
Middle East	-	-	87	0.2	-	-
Others	3698	6.3	209	0.6	438	2.1

Source of basic data: NSCB, *Philippine Statistical Yearbook,* Manila: National Statistical Coordinating Board, 2000, p.6-17

Singapore

The EDB reports the amount of approved FDI in Singapore. However, the analysis here is based on the stock of FDI at end-1980, end-1990 and end-1999 (latest data available) as reported by the Department of Statistics in Singapore. By region, Europe, Asia and North America were the top three investing groups in Singapore during the 1980-99 period. While Europe and Asia accounted for about a third each, North America shared about a fifth of the total FDI in Singapore. Within Asia, the Northeast Asian group was been a significant investor as it accounted for about a quarter of FDI in Singapore.

On a country basis, the United Kingdom was the leading investor in Singapore in 1980 as it accounted for about a quarter of total FDI, followed closely by the US. A far third was Japan with a share of about one-tenth. However, in 1990, Japan overtook both the UK and the US as its share almost doubled relative to 1980. In 1999, Japan and the US maintained the first two positions, but their shares dropped to about 15 percent each. During the 1980-99 period, the other significant investors were Malaysia (about 4-6 percent), Hong Kong (but its share dropped from 12 percent in 1980 to about 3 percent in 1999), the Netherlands (whose share rose more than 7 times in 1999 relative to 1980), and Switzerland (whose share more than doubled in 1999 relative to 1980).

Table 4. Geographical Distribution of FDI In Singapore (S$ Million)

Country	1980	% share	1990	% share	1999	% share
Total	**11,201.7**	**100.0**	**49,830.6**	**100.0**	**150,451.9**	**100.0**
Asia	**3,659.1**	**32.7**	**17,301.6**	**34.7**	**40,367.1**	**26.8**
- ASEAN	**827.2**	**7.4**	**3,002.7**	**6.0**	**8,028.0**	**5.3**
Brunei Darussalam	33.8	0.3	71.4	0.1	202.6	0.1
Indonesia	71.1	0.6	245.1	0.5	1,441.3	1.0
Malaysia	684.3	6.1	2,109.7	4.2	4,956.7	3.3
Philippines	11.3	0.1	159.3	0.3	638.4	0.4
Thailand	26.6	0.2	417.3	0.8	762.0	0.5
-Northeast Asia	**2718.7**	**24.2**	**14154.8**	**28.5**	**31812.8**	**21.2**
Hong Kong	1,357.4	12.1	3,267.1	6.6	4,044.7	2.7
Japan	1,311.8	11.7	10,662.7	21.4	23,102.1	15.4
China	-	-	61.5	0.1	877.6	0.6
South Korea	-	-	-61.7	-0.1	724.0	0.5
Taiwan	49.5	0.4	225.2	0.5	3,064.4	2.0
Europe	**4,286.3**	**38.3**	**13,465.2**	**27.0**	**57,220.9**	**38.0**
- European Union	**3,709.4**	**33.1**	**10,564.3**	**21.2**	**40,255.4**	**26.8**
Germany	416.5	3.7	884.1	1.8	1,554.7	1.0
Netherlands	217.4	1.9	4,072.3	8.2	21,433.8	14.2
United Kingdom	2,947.7	26.3	4,639.0	9.3	10,479.9	7.0
- Switzerland	506.1	4.5	2,262.4	4.5	15,362.3	10.2
North America	**2515.7**	**22.5**	**11096.4**	**22.2**	**25895.7**	**17.2**
Canada	-	-	2,506.2	5.0	4,127.9	2.7
United States	2,515.7	22.5	8,590.2	17.2	21,767.8	14.5
Australia	**269.3**	**2.4**	**2,953.1**	**5.9**	**2,687.7**	**1.8**
Other countries	**471.3**	**4.2**	**5014.4**	**10.2**	**24280.5**	**16.1**

Source: Department of Statistics, *Foreign Equity Investment in Singapore*, Singapore: Department of Statistics, Various Issues

Thailand

The Board of Investments report the data on the approved FDI in Thailand. However , the analysis here is based on the actual investments as reported by the Bank of Thailand on a net flow basis (inflows minus outflows) given its availability. This is seen in Table 5. By region, Asia has been a significant investing group as it accounted for bulk of FDI in Thailand. From 51 percent in 1998, its share fell to about 40 percent in 1999, but rose to 67 percent in the year 2000. North America and Europe were the other leading investing groups in Thailand. Europe's share, however, dropped significantly to almost 7 percent in 2000 from a high of 40 percent in 1999. On the other hand, the North American share almost doubled in 2000 relative to 1999. Like in other Southeast Asian countries, the Northeast Asian group has been a major investing group as it accounted for about 25-40 percent during the 1998-2000 period, which was mainly due to huge investments coming from Japan, Hong Kong and Taiwan.

By country sources, Table 5 reveals that the top investors in Thailand were Japan, the United States and Singapore. After falling from about a quarter of total FDI in 1998 to about 18 percent in 1999, the US share of investment almost doubled in 2000. Japan's share showed a similar trend: falling from about a third in 1998 to about 14 percent in 1999 and then rising to about a quarter in 2000. Singapore's share more than doubled in 2000 relative to 1998. The other significant players in Thailand were Hong Kong (4th in 1998 and 2000) and Netherlands (1st in 1999).

Table 5. Geographical Distribution of Actual Foreign Investment in Thailand (on a net flow basis, million baht)

Country	1998	% share	1999	% share	2000	% share
Total	**209,888**	**100**	**134,592**	**100**	**107,281**	**100**
Asia	**107955**	**51.4**	**53385**	**39.7**	**72304**	**67.4**
- ASEAN	**23817**	**11.3**	**21260**	**15.8**	**24587**	**22.9**
Indonesia	111	0.1	46	0.03	37	0.03
Malaysia	711	0.3	1044	0.8	742	0.7
Philippines	320	0.2	123	0.1	0.9	...
Singapore	22674	10.8	20047	14.9	23807	22.2
- Northeast Asia	**84138**	**40.1**	**32125**	**23.9**	**47447**	**44.2**
Hong Kong	16571	7.9	8862	6.6	13645	12.7
Japan	60478	28.8	18558	13.8	26318	24.5
Taiwan	4073	1.9	4581	3.4	7466	6.9
South Korea	2799	1.3	205	0.2	-169	-0.2
China	217	0.1	-81	-0.1	187	0.2
Europe	**40648**	**19.4**	**54209**	**40.3**	**6960**	**6.5**
- European Union	**37570**	**17.9**	**51941**	**38.6**	**7201**	**6.7**
Belgium	1297	0.6	-1380	-1.0	-987	-0.9
France	10926	5.2	8983	6.7	-133	-0.1
Germany	4073	1.9	10973	8.2	2603	2.4
Netherlands	13836	6.6	24584	18.3	-3898	-3.6
United Kingdom	4815	2.3	7009	5.2	8248	7.7
- Switzerland	3078	1.5	2268	1.7	-241	-0.2
North America	**51928**	**24.7**	**24250**	**18.0**	**33396**	**31.2**
Canada	128	0.06	113	0.1	190	0.2
United States	51800	24.7	24137	17.9	33206	31.0
Australia	**1526**	**0.7**	**490**	**0.4**	**693**	**0.6**
Other countries	**7829**	**3.7**	**2256**	**1.7**	**-5802**	**-5.4**

Source: Bank of Thailand, *Quarterly Bulletin*, Bangkok: Bank of Thailand, Dec 2000, p.90

INDUSTRIAL PATTERNS OF FDI

Indonesia

Table 6 shows that the industrial sector was the major recipient of FDI in Indonesia as it had accounted for about three-quarters of the total FDI. Among all the economic sectors, the manufacturing sector is the most dominant having received about 50-70 percent of total FDI during the 1996-2000 period. Investments in the electricity, gas and water industry had been significant particularly during the 1996-99 period, but it dropped markedly in the year 2000. The services sector accounted for about a fifth of total FDI.

Table 6. Approved Foreign Investment Projects in Indonesia (US$ million)

	1996	1997	1998	1999	2000
Total Investment	**29,929**	**33,833**	**13,563**	**10,891**	**15,413**
Agricultural sector	**1522 (5.1)**	**464 (1.4)**	**998 (7.3)**	**491 (4.5)**	**443 (2.9)**
Industrial sector	**21784 (73.1)**	**25165 (74.4)**	**10381 (76.5)**	**9406 (86.4)**	**10930 (70.9)**
Mining, quarrying	1697 (5.7)	2 (...)	0.3 (...)	14 (0.1)	2 (0.01)
Manufacturing	16072 (53.7)	23017 (68.0)	8388 (61.8)	6929 (63.6)	10703 (69.4)
Electricity, gas and Water	3808 (12.7)	1839 (5.4)	1795 (13.2)	2310 (21.2)	0.4 (...)
Construction	297 (1.0)	307 (0.9)	198 (1.4)	153 (1.4)	225 (1.4)
Services Sector	**6533 (21.8)**	**8204 (24.2)**	**2183 (16.1)**	**993 (9.1)**	**4040 (26.2)**
Wholesale, retail trade, restaurants, Hotels	1762 (5.9)	472 (1.4)	673 (5.0)	508 (4.7)	1671 (10.8)
Transport, storage, communications	695 (2.3)	5900 (17.4)	79 (0.6)	103 (0.9)	1219 (7.9)
Finance, insur., real estate, business services	3000 (10.0)	1398 (4.1)	1271 (9.4)	179 (1.6)	302 (1.9)
Community, social and personal services	1076 (3.6)	434 (1.3)	160 (1.2)	203 (1.9)	848 (5.5)

Note: Figures in the parentheses refer to percentage share of each sector to total FDI for each year.
Source of basic data: *Economic Indicators*, Badan Pusat Statistic, Indonesia, March 2001, p.55.

Malaysia

There is no sectoral breakdown of FDI in Malaysia. Table 7 only shows the industrial breakdown of the actual FDI in the manufacturing sector based on manufacturing surveys at end-1997 compared with that at end-1993. These data were collected from the 1990-94 and

1994-98 data series. The 1998-2002 data are not yet available at the time of writing. To make the data more meaningful for analysis, the sectoral classification based on capital intensity was adopted. It is interesting to observe that the bulk of FDI in Malaysia had been in high-capital intensive industries particularly in the electrical and electronics industry, and petroleum and coal products. The low- and medium-capital intensive industries shared about 20 percent and 25 percent, respectively. The more significant sectors were food manufactures, non-metallic products, and fabricated metal products within the medium-capital intensive group. The textiles and textile products, wood and wood products, and plastic and plastic products were the more significant sectors within the low-capital intensive sectors.

Table 7. Industrial Distribution of FDI (paid-up capital) in Malaysia

	End-1993		**End-1997**	
	Mil RM	**% share**	**Mil RM**	**% share**
Total	**13500**	**100**	**20665**	**100**
High -capital intensive	**6890**	**51.0**	**11329**	**54.8**
Electr. and electronic prods.	4207	31.2	6686	32.3
Scientific and measuring inst.	255	1.9	357	1.7
Chemicals and chem prods.	885	6.6	1202	5.8
Petroleum and coal products	883	6.5	1877	9.1
Basic metal products	660	4.9	1208	5.8
Medium-capital Intensive	**4025**	**29.8**	**5088**	**24.6**
Transport Equipment	539	4.0	675	3.3
Machinery manuf'ging	390	2.9	896	4.3
Food Manufactures	1,251	9.3	1185	5.7
Beverages and tobacco	472	3.5	578	2.8
Fabricated metal products	635	4.7	780	3.8
Non-metallic mineral prod.	738	5.5	974	4.7
Low -capital Intensive	**2585**	**19.2**	**4247**	**20.6**
Rubber products	455	3.4	552	2.7
Plastic products	433	3.2	568	2.7
Textile and textile products	825	6.1	1914	9.3
Leather and leather products	35	0.3	22	0.1
Wood and wood products	469	3.5	698	3.4
Furnitures and fixtures	95	0.7	103	0.5
Paper, printing and publish'g	131	1.0	217	1.0
Miscellaneous	142	1.0	174	0.8

Source of basic data: Malaysian Industrial Development Authority, *Statistics on the Manufacturing Sector,* Kuala Lumpur: MIDA, 1990-94 and 1994-98 issues.

Philippines

Table 8 shows that, in 1997, the services sector received about two-thirds of FDI in the Philippines because of the enormous investments in the public utilities for a share of about 57 percent. However, investments in the services sector fell drastically to about a third in 1998 and then to 6 percent in 1999. On the other hand, the industrial sector experienced a marked increase as its share rose by about three times to 94 percent in 1999. This was mainly due to a hefty increase in manufacturing investments which accounted for about 84 percent in 1999.

Table 8. Industrial Distribution of Approved FDI in the Philippines(mil pesos)

	1997		1998		1999	
Grand Total	**58737**	**100**	**37299**	**100**	**21180**	**100**
Agricultural Sector	**337**	**0.6**	**182**	**0.5**	**24**	**0.1**
Industrial Sector	**19385**	**33.0**	**28912**	**77.5**	**19844**	**93.7**
-Mining	4379	7.4	1332	3.6	161	0.8
-Manufacturing	8136	13.9	16380	43.9	17709	83.6
-Energy-related	6726	11.4	11006	29.5	1928	9.1
-Motor vehicle program	144	0.2	12	0.03	46	0.2
Service Sector	**39014**	**66.4**	**8386**	**22.5**	**1310**	**6.2**
-Public Utilities	33435	56.9	-	-	24	0.1
-Export traders	68	0.1	3	...	-	-
Service exporters	65	0.1	-	-	6	0.02
-Tourism-oriented	376	0.6	140	0.4	-	-
-Infrastructure/ individual services	4903	8.3	7845	21.0	517	2.4
- R and D projects	9	0.01	-	-	-	-
-Environment protection	122	0.2	350	0.9	736	3.5
-Regional Headquarters	36	0.06	48	0.1	27	0.1

Source of basic data: Philippine Board of Investments, as cited in NSCB, *Philippine Statistical Yearbook* Manila: National Statistical Coordination Board, 2000, p.6-16.

Singapore

Table 9 shows the sectoral classification of FDI as reported by the Department of Statistics. While the industrial sector accounted for the bulk of FDI in 1980, its share showed a declining trend: falling to about 41 percent in 1990 and to about 37 percent in 1999. This was due mainly to the declining share of the manufacturing sector from about 57 percent in 1980 to about 36 percent in 1999. On the other hand, the share of the services sector reflected an increasing trend: from 42 percent in 1980 to 59 percent in 1990 and to 63 percent in 1999. The significant increase was experienced in the financial and business services sectors as their combined shares more than doubled in 1999 relative to 1997. This pattern is consistent with the long-term target of transforming Singapore into a financial and business hub in the region. It can be recalled that the services sector has accounted for about 60 percent of Singapore's GDP.

Table 9. Industrial Distribution of FDI In Singapore (S$Million)

Industry	1980		1990		1999	
Total	11202	100	49831	100	150452	100
Agricultural sector	5	0.04	117	0.02	48	0.03
Industrial sector	6517	58.2	20317	40.8	55316	36.8
Mining and Quarrying	11	0.1	-44	-0.08	-14	...
Manufacturing	6340	56.6	19760	39.7	53893	35.8
Electricity, gas and water	-	-	-	-	-	-
Construction	165	1.5	601	1.2	1437	1.0
Services Sector	4680	41.7	29398	58.9	95159	63.3
Commerce	1800	16.1	6517	13.1	21996	14.6
Transport, Storage and Telecommunications	385	3.4	1230	2.4	4323	2.9
Financial, insurance, real estate, business services	2457	21.9	21531	43.2	68840	45.8
Social and Personal services	38	0.3	120	0.2	-70	-0.04

Source: Department of Statistics, *Foreign Equity Investment in Singapore*, 1980-89, 1990-92, 1998-99 (latest issue), Singapore: Department of Statistics.

Thailand

Table 10 shows that the service sector has accounted for the bulk of FDI in Thailand for a share ranging from 52 percent in 2000 to about 70 percent in 1999. This was due to the large contributions of the trade and services sectors. Investment in financial institutions was about 20 percent in 1998, but its share dropped in the two subsequent years. The industrial sector accounted for about two-fifths of the total FDI in 1998 and 2000, dropping to 31 percent in 1999. The manufacturing sector continued to be the dominant sector during the 1998-2000 period.

Table 10. Industrial Distribution of Approved FDI in Thailand (on a net flow basis, in billion bahts)

	1998	% share	1999	% share	2000	% share
Total	**182.8**	**100**	**134.0**	**100**	**111.1**	**100**
Agricultural sector	**0.002**	**...**	**0.069**	**0.05**	**0.016**	**0.01**
Industrial sector	**80.6**	**44.1**	**41.6**	**31.0**	**52.3**	**47.1**
- Mining andquarrying	3.3	1.8	2.7	2.0	0.3	0.3
- Manufacturing	74.1	40.5	43.2	32.2	52.2	47.0
- Construction	3.2	1.8	-4.3	-3.2	-0.2	-0.2
Service Sector	**102.2**	**55.9**	**92.4**	**69.9**	**58.9**	**52.9**
-Financial institution	34.5	18.9	9.3	6.9	2.8	2.5
-Trade	34.1	18.7	38.8	29.9	22.8	20.5
-Real Estate	0.6	0.3	5.6	4.2	3.5	3.1
-Services	11.9	6.5	17.9	13.4	31.9	28.7
-Others	21.1	11.5	20.8	15.5	-2.1	-1.9

Source of basic data: Bank of Thailand, *Quarterly Bulletin*, Bangkok: Bank of Thailand, December 2000, p.90

MOTIVES AND DETERMINANTS OF FDI

From the analysis of geographical trends in the fifth section, we can conclude that FDI in Southeast Asia has come mainly from Japan, the United States, and the United Kingdom. The other significant players are Singapore, Germany, the Netherlands, and Switzerland. Table 11 also reveals that the top 10 foreign affiliates in the five Southeast Asian countries by sales were mainly Japanese companies (39 out of the top 50 TNCs). This is followed by the EU(5 companies)[18], US (3 companies), Singapore (2 companies), and USA/Hong Kong (1 company).

The question then is: what are the factors that can explain the inflows of FDI from these investing countries? We can use the various approaches discussed in section 2 of this chapter. The theory of the firm states that foreign firms want to maximize profits. The factor endowment approach states that foreign capital, through FDI, will flow from capital-abundant to capital-short countries where the rate of returns to capital would be higher. According to the eclectic approach, foreign investors certainly have ownership advantage as they possess monopoly over brand names, products, production processes, technology, excellent knowledge of the market and marketing techniques.

These leading investors have certainly generated an enormous amount of revenues and profits. Evidence is seen, for example, in the returns on foreign equity. However, Singapore is the only country which reports this kind of data as shown in Table 12. In 1980, the Dutch investors had the highest return of about 56 percent on their equities in Singapore, followed by the Americans (about 35 percent), Germany (26 percent), UK (24 percent) and Switzerland (19 percent). Japanese investors had a return of about 10 percent lower than Hong Kong investors' return of 17 percent. In 1990, the returns on equities of these foreign investors remained high particularly for the American and European investors. However, in 1998, the returns on their equities fell significantly. However, in 1999, while some investors experienced an improvement in their returns such as the Germans, Dutch, Swiss, and Americans, other investors continued to suffer lower returns. By industrial classification, foreign equity investments in the manufacturing sector generated higher returns particularly the electronics and the machinery sectors a shown in Table 12.

Table 11. The Ten Largest Foreign Affiliates in SE Asia By Sales (million US$)

Company	Home Economy	Industry	Sales	Year
Indonesia				
.Japan Indonesia Oil Co. Ltd	Japan	Petroleum	1127	1992
.Lasmo Oil (Malacca Strait) Ltd.	United Kingdom	Petroleum	361	1991
.Indomobil Suzuki International,	Japan	Transport Equipment	356	1991
.International Nickel Indonesia,	Japan	Chemicals	223	1991
.Tembaga Mulia Semanan	Japan	Electrical Equipment	134	1991
.Mitsubishi Krama YudhaMotors	Japan	Transport Equipment	132	1991
.Panen Lestari Internusa (Sogo),	Japan	Distributive Trade	121	1992
.Bridgestone TireIndonesia	Japan	Rubber	110	1992
.Yamaha Indonesia Motor Mfg.	Japan	Electrical Equipment	108	1991
.Teijin Indonesia Fibre Corp.	Japan	Textiles	107	1992

[18] These were mainly from UK, Netherlands and Denmark.

Table 11. (Continued)

Company	Home Economy	Industry	Sales	Year
Malaysia				
.Perusahaan Otomobil Nasional	Japan	Transport Equipment	1180	1993
.Shell Refining Co. Bhd	UK/Netherlands	Petroleum	882	1992
.Amalgamated Steel Mills Bhd	Singapore	Metals	656	1992
.Esso Malaysia Bhd	United States	Petroleum	635	1992
.Nissho Iwai Corp.	Japan	Distributive Trade	630	1992
.Marubeni Corp.	Japan	Distributive Trade	560	1992
.Genting Bhd.	Singapore	Diversified	444	1992
.Oriental Holdings Bhd.	Japan	Motor Vehicles	422	1992
.Rothmans Pall Mall (Malaysia)	USA/Hong Kong	Tobacco	373	1992
.HitachiSemiconductor Malaysia	Japan	Electrical Equipment	367	1993
Philippines				
.Pilipinas Shell Petroleum Corp.	UK/Netherlands	Petroleum	1159	1992
.Philippines Automotive Mfg.	Japan	Motor vehicles	244	1992
.Shell Gas Eastern Inc.	UK/Netherlands	Coal and petroleum	199	1992
.Philippine Automotive Mfg.Co.	Japan	Transport Equipment	166	1991
.Toyota Motor Philippines Corp.	Japan	Transport Equipment	161	1991
.Texas Instruments Philippines	United States	Diversified	159	1992
.Matsushita Communication	Japan	Electrical Equipment	140	1992
.Matsushita Electric Philippines	Japan	Electrical Equipment	127	1992
.Nissan Motor Philippines, Inc.	Japan	Transport Equipment	101	1990
.Sharp (Philippines) Corp.	Japan	Electrical Equipment	88	1992
Singapore				
.Nissho Iwai Petroleum Spore	Japan	Distributive trade	3064	1993
.Cosmo Oil International PteLtd	Japan	Petroleum	2187	1992
.Itochu Petroleum Co.(Spore)	Japan	Petroleum	1728	1992
.ITOCHU Petroleum co.(Spore)	Japan	Distributive trade	1512	1993
.Marubeni Singapore Pte Ltd	Japan	Distributive trade	1506	1993
.Hitachi Asia Pte Ltd	Japan	Distributive trade	1495	1993
.Marubeni International Petrol	Japan	Distributive trade	1300	1993
.Hitachi Asia Pte Ltd	Japan	Distributive trade	1155	1992
.Kanemasu Oil Singapore Pte	Japan	Petroleum	1037	1992
.Takashimaya (Singapore) Ltd	Japan	Distributive trade	905	1993
Thailand				
.Toyota Motor Thailand Co. Ltd.	Japan	Transport Equipment	1893	1993
.Marubeni Thailand co. Ltd	Japan	Distributive Trade	1704	1993
.Thai Oil Co. Ltd	UK/US/Netherlds.	Petroleum	1554	1992
.Mitsiam International Ltd.	Japan	Distributive Trade	1442	1992
.MMC Sittipol co., Ltd.	Japan	Transport Equipment	1188	1993
.Seagate Technology (Thailand)	United States	Motor Vehicles	826	1992
.Thai Honda Mfg Co. Ltd.	Japan	Motor Vehicles	434	1992
.Minebea Thai Ltd.	Japan	Electrical Equipment	381	1992
Thai Arrow Products Co. Ltd.	Japan	Transport Equipment	320	1993
Sukosol and Mazda Co. Ltd.	Japan	Transport Equipment	317	1993

Source: UNCTAD

We can also apply the eclectic approach considering the locational advantages of the host countries made available to the foreign investors. These investors have been able to access the Southeast Asian market whose population has risen from 160 million in 1960 to 202 million in 1970. Currently, the combined Southeast Asian market has a population of about 550 million. Moreover, the rising per capita incomes of the Southeast Asian economies has been an important incentive for the foreign investors. The Southeast Asian region also offers other locational advantages or 'pull' factors including abundance of high quality, low-wage labor,

Table 12. Returns on Foreign Equity Investments in Singapore, %

	1980	1990	1998	1999
	By investing countries, %			
United States	**34.7**	**20.7**	**6.2**	**11.4**
Europe	**25.6**	**24.5**	**8.7**	**17.3**
-UK	23.7	25.5	22.5	11.8
-Germany	25.5	23.1	-108.7	36.4
-Netherlands	56.4	19.8	11.3	21.6
-Switzerland	18.5	26.2	18.8	26.4
Asian	**15.2**	**15.2**	**-8**	**2.3**
-Japan	9.6	17.4	-3.5	6.6
-ASEAN	17.1	12.7	-4.5	1.9
-Taiwan	6.6	5.3	-14.2	-7.7
-Hong Kong	16.8	12.3	-14.6	1.0
	By sectoral investment, %			
Manufacturing	21.0	18.3	17.4	15.6
-Electronics	28.4	20.8	20.1	21.0
-Electricals	-	-	10.2	14.2
-Machinery	25.9	11.9	12.0	16.5
-Chemicals	19.5	27.9	21.9	10.0
-Food products	11.1	12.3	4.8	15.4
-Textiles	0.3	5.0	2.6	7.0
Financial Service	16.4	9.4	-8.5	5.0
Business Services	8.2	10.3	-5.5	5.0
Commerce	15.9	16.4	0.8	11.6
Construction	-13.8	-9.2	-23.2	-3.6

Note: (a)Returns on equity investment is a measure of the profitability of the equity investment, and is calculated as the ratio of the current year's earnings to the average of the stock of equity capital invested in the current year and the preceding year. See Department of Statistics, *Foreign Equity Investments in Singapore*, 1980-89, pp.14. Source: Department of Statistics, *Foreign Equity Investment in Singapore*, Singapore: Department of Statistics, Various Issues

low transportation costs, generous investment incentives and political regional stability. However, some of these pull factors have begun to affect some foreign investors like the Japanese manufacturers. According to the Straits Times, 13 September 1996 issue, a survey of 977 firms revealed that most Japanese manufacturers cited labor-related issues and rising wage levels as the most pressing problem they had faced in the region. The survey was done by the Japan External Trade Organization (JETRO), which sent out 2200 questionnaires to Japanese- owned or joint venture manufacturers and received 977 replies. Respondents were involved in electronics and electrical equipment, metal, chemical, and pharmaceutical products, textiles and transport equipment. A tabulation of the results of this survey is presented in Table 13. These results are consistent with the study by Tham (1998).[19] Moreover, in order to attract FDI into the Southeast Asian region, their governments have initiated or sponsored the so-called "growth triangles" which include the SIJORI (involving Singapore, Johor in Malaysia and Riau in Indonesia), the IMT (Indonesia, Malaysia and Thailand), and the EAGA (East ASEAN Growth Area, involving Eastern Malaysia, Southern Philippines, Brunei and Eastern Indonesia).[20] In addition, the creation of the ASEAN Free Trade Area (AFTA) is another incentive to attract FDI into the region.

Table 13. Results of JETRO's Survey

INVESTMENT FACTORS		
Here are the key factors influencing Japanese investment decisions in the ASEAN region (in order of importance)		
	Positive factors	**Negative factors**
Singapore	political and social stability, infrastructure, quality of labor force, foreign investment incentives, potential of domestic market, low labor cost	rise in wages, labor-related problems, exchange rate fluctuations, competition with other manufacturers and suppliers, unfavorable market conditions
Indonesia	low labor cost, potential of domestic market, political and social stability, quality of labor force, foreign investment incentives, infrastructure	bureaucracy/red tape, exchange rate fluctuations, tariff and customs procedures, taxes, rise in wages
Malaysia	political and social stability, infrastructure, foreign investment incentives, low labor cost, quality of labor force, potential of domestic market	labor-related problems, rise in wages, exchange rate fluctuations, difficulty in obtaining visas or work permits, competition with other manufacturers
Thailand	political and social stability, low labor cost, quality of labor force, potential of domestic market, foreign investment incentives, infrastructure	rise in wages, labor-related problems, tariff and customs procedures, exchange rate fluctuations, quality control
Philippines	quality of labor force, low labor cost, foreign investment incentives, potential of domestic market, political and social stability, infrastructure	labor-related problems, rise in wages, exchange rate fluctuations, poor infrastructure, tariff and customs procedures

Source: The Straits Times, September 13, 1996.

[19] Tham Siew Yean, "Competition and Cooperation for Foreign Direct Investment: An ASEAN Perspective," *Asia-Pacific Development Journal,* Vol.5, No.1, 1998, p.9.

[20] Hadi Soesastro, "Policies Towards Foreign Direct Investment – New Challenges Facing Asian Developing Countries," *The Indonesian Quarterly,* Vol.24, No.2, 1996, p.166. See also G. Naidu, "Johor-Singapore-Riau Growth Triangle: Progress and Prospects," in Myo Thant, et.al. 1994, pp.218-242.

In the context of the FDI-cum-trade approach, since the 1970s, the Southeast Asian region has become, not only a production base to serve the domestic markets, but also a distribution base for export-oriented FDI. The domestic costs of production in Japan rose significantly as the yen appreciated strongly in 1985.[21] Japanese manufacturers then exported their industries by relocating their factories outside Japan including Southeast Asian countries where costs of production were lower. As Fukushima and Kwan (1995) stated, the three main factors that made this shift to the Southeast Asian region are as follows: (a) Japanese firms have already established themselves in the region, particularly in Singapore, (b) there has been successful technology transfer from Japanese electronic companies to the region since the 1980s, and (c) Southeast Asian countries are ready to receive the transfer of higher technology products and production process through investment in social infrastructures such as transportation network and the development of supporting industries for FDI firms.[22] Southeast Asian affiliates have produced manufactured goods, mostly intermediate parts and components which are then exported to parent companies in Japan for the final assembly of high value products and hence indicates an international division of labor. This process generates what has been known as 'boomerang effect.'[23]

Conclusion

This chapter discusses the geographical and industrial distribution of foreign direct investments in Southeast Asia. The top leading investors in the region are the Japanese, Americans, and British. The other significant investors are the Singaporeans, Dutch, Germans, and Swiss. In terms of the industrial analysis, the manufacturing sector has been the dominant sector as it receives bulk of FDI in Southeast Asia, except in Singapore, where the services sector has increasingly hosted more foreign investments. The various determinants of FDI are discussed including the profit maximization approach, factor endowment approach, the eclectic approach, and FDI-cum-trade approach. All these models were found to be highly relevant in explaining FDI in Southeast Asia.

Questions for Discussion

1. Why do foreign direct investments (FDI) take place? Discuss.
2. To what extent are FDI concepts relevant to the developing world? Discuss your answer with reference to Southeast Asia?

---

[21] Because of rising production costs in the newly industrializing economics (NIEs) triggered by higher wages and currency appreciation in the late 1980s, the NIEs were no longer the major target for Japanese FDI.

[22] Kiyohiko Fukushima and C.H.Kwan, "Foreign Direct Investment and Regional Industrial Restructuring in Asia," in NRI and ISEAS (compilers), *Foreign Direct Investment in Asia,* Tokyo: Tokyo Club Foundation for Global Studies and Singapore: Institute of Southeast Asian Studies, 1995, p.7.

[23] The 'boomerang' effect is a term to describe the impact on the Japanese economy of increased imports of goods resulting from Japanese overseas investment in manufacturing (Shinohara 1982 as cited in Meng Kng Chng and Ryokichi Hirono, *Asean Japan Industrial Cooperation: An Overview*, Jakarta: ASEAN Secretariat, Japan Institute of International Affairs, and Singapore: Institute of Southeast Asian Studies, 1987, pp.87.

3. Among the Southeast Asian economies, Singapore is the most dependent on FDI. Why?
4. Would it be possible for Southeast Asian economies to grow and develop without FDI? Discuss.

SUGGESTED MATERIALS FOR CASE STUDIES:

Soesastro, Hadi, 1996, "Policies Towards Foreign Direct Investment – New Challenges Facing Asian Developing Countries," *The Indonesian Quarterly,* Vol.24, No.2, pp.161-180.

Ram, Rati and Kevin Honglin Zhang, 2002, "Foreign Direct Investment and Economic Growth: Evidence from Cross-Country Data for the 1990s," *Economic Development and Cultural Change,* Vol.51, No.1, pp.205-215.

REFERENCES

ADB, 'Foreign Direct Investment: An Explanation," *Asian Development Outlook,* Manila: Asian Development Bank.

Ahmed, Momtaz Uddin, 2001, "Foreign Direct Investment and Technology Flows in Asia and the Pacific Region in the 1990s: An Analysis of Trends, Patterns and Policies," in Behrman, J.R, M.Dutta, S.L. Husted, Sumalee, C. Suthiphand, and P. Wiboonchutikula, *Restructuring Asian Economics for the New Millenium,* JAI – Elsevier Science, pp.643-668.

Akamatsu, Kaname, 1962a, ''A Historical Pattern of Economic Growth in Developing Countries,'' *The Developing Economies*, The Preliminary Issue, No.1, pp.3-25.

Akamatsu, Kaname, 1962b, "A Theory of Unbalanced Growth in the World Economy," *Weltwirtschafliches Archiv*, Heft 86, Band 2, pp.523-544.

Chng, Meng Kng and Ryokichi Hirono, 1987, *Asean Japan Industrial Cooperation: An Overview*, Jakarta: ASEAN Secretariat, Japan Institute of International Affairs, and Singapore: Institute of Southeast Asian Studies.

Dunning, John, 1981, *International Production and the Multinational Enterprise*, London: Allen and Unwin.

Fukushima, Kiyohiko and C.H.Kwan, 1995, "Foreign Direct Investment and Regional Industrial Restructuring in Asia," in NRI and ISEAS (compilers), *Foreign Direct Investment in Asia,* Tokyo: Tokyo Club Foundation for Global Studies and Singapore: Institute of Southeast Asian Studies, pp.3-39.

Hill, Hal, 1990, "Foreign Investment and East Asian Economic Development," *Asian-Pacific Economic Literature,* Vol.4, No.2, pp.21-58.

IFC – International Finance Corporation, 1997, "Foreign Direct Investments," *Lessons of Experience*, No.5, Washington DC, USA: International Finance Corporation.

Ismail Md Salleh, 1995, "Foreign Direct Investment and Technology Transfer in the Malaysian Electronics Industry," in NRI and ISEAS (compilers), *Foreign Direct*

Investment in Asia, Tokyo: Tokyo Club Foundation for Global Studies and Singapore: Institute of Southeast Asian Studies, pp.133-159.

Kerdpibule, Udom and Eric Ramsetter, 1987, "Foreign Investment Theories and Policy Issues," in Seiji Naya (ed.), *Direct Foreign Investment and Export in Asia,* Kuala Lumpur: Southeast Asia Central Banks Research and Training Center (SEACEN) and Hawaii: East-West Resource Systems Institute, pp.1-23.

Kojima, Kiyoshi, 1978, *Direct Foreign Investment: A Japanese Model of Multinational Business Operations*, New York: Praeger.

Kojima, Kiyoshi, 1987, "A Model of Trade-Oriented Foreign Investment," in Seiji Naya (ed.), *Direct Foreign Investment and Export Promotion Policies: Policies and Experiences in Asia,* Kuala Lumpur: Southeast Asia Central Banks Research and Training Center and Hawaii: East-West Resource Systems Institute, pp. 159-183.

Naidu, G., 1994, "Johor-Singapore-Riau Growth Triangle: Progress and Prospects," in Myo Thant, Min Tang, and Hiroshi Kakazu (eds.), *Growth Triangles In Asia:A New Approach To Regional Economic Cooperation*, Hong Kong: Oxford University Press, pp.218-242.

Ram, Rati and Kevin Honglin Zhang, 2002, "Foreign Direct Investment and Economic Growth: Evidence from Cross-Country Data for the 1990s," *Economic Development and Cultural Change,* Vol.51, No.1, pp.205-215.

Soesastro, Hadi, 1996, "Policies Towards Foreign Direct Investment – New Challenges Facing Asian Developing Countries," *The Indonesian Quarterly,* Vol.24, No.2, pp.161-180.

Tham, Siew Yean, 1998, "Competition and Cooperation for Foreign Direct Investment: An ASEAN Perspective," *Asia-Pacific Development Journal,* Vol.5, No.1, pp.9-36.

Thomsen, Stephen, 1999, *Southeast Asia: The Role of Foreign Direct Investment Policies in Development,* Working Papers on International Investment, Paris: Organization for Economic Cooperation and Development (OECD).

Vernon, Raymond, 1966, "International Investment and International Trade in the Product Cycle", *Quarterly Journal of Economics,* Vol.80, No.2, pp.190-207.

INTERNET SOURCES

Indonesia's Investment Coordinating Board, Badan Koordinasi Penanaman Modal (BKPM) website, http://www.bkpm.go.id

Malaysian Industrial Development Authority (MIDA's website: http://www.mida.gov.my.

Philippine Board of Investment (BOI) website: http://www.boi.gov.ph.

Singapore's Economic Development Board (EDB website: http://www.sedb.com)

Thailand's Board of Investment (BOI website: http://www.boi.go.th)

In: Asian Economic and Political Issues, Volume 11
Editor: Harvey E. Roth, pp. 25-46
ISBN: 1-60021-192-5

Chapter 2

POLICY RESPONSES TO THE CRISIS[1]

Teofilo C. Daquila

ABSTRACT

In response to the crisis, various policies were adopted by the international organizations and by the respective economies in the region. This chapter evaluates each of these policies. The differences in their policy actions are highlighted and explained. This chapter also examines the various strategies aimed at improving the global financial architecture.

INTRODUCTION

In response to the crisis, the respective governments in Southeast Asia have adopted various policy responses which include, among others, reliance on international financial assistance, demand-management policies (fiscal, monetary and exchange rate policies), supply-side policies and capital controls, bank restructuring, and privatization. The differences in their policy responses manifest (i) the extent and nature of the crisis (e.g. Malaysia's relatively smaller foreign debt vs. Indonesia's huge foreign debt), (ii) the pervasiveness and severity of the impact of the crisis (e.g. Singapore's banking and financial sector being less affected than in Thailand and Indonesia), (iii) the governments' priorities, in terms of achieving either a move towards internal balance (less severe impact on unemployment) or a move towards external balance (trade surplus) or both, and (iv) the government leaders' willingness to subscribe to international financial order and its conditionalities (Thailand and Indonesia following the IMF conditions which required painful

[1] Earlier versions of this chapter include guest lectures and seminar presentations at the following institutions: El Colegio de Mexico (1998), Nordic Institute of Asian Studies (Copenhagen, 1999), Ludwig-Maximilians Universitaet Muenchen (Munich, 1999), University of Sweden's Center for Pacific and Asian Studies and Stockholm School of Economics (1999), and the University of Paris Sciences-Po Asia-Europe Program (1999); and invited conference papers presented at Chulalongkorn University (1999) and the Center for the Study of International Institutions (Austria, 2003).

and immediate reforms versus Malaysia's non-subscription to IMF's conditionalities and instead adopt a 'pragmatic' approach).

POLICY RESPONSES

International Financial Assistance

Thailand and Indonesia availed of the international financial assistance organized by the IMF and the World Bank with funds coming from them and various countries led by the US, Japan and the European Union (EU). In August 1997, the Thai government accepted an international financial package which consisted of a medium-term loan of US$17.2 billion to shore up Thai's foreign exchange reserves.[2] It also obtained US$1 billion trade assistance from the Asian Development Bank (ADB) to help Thai exporters. This came in the form of ADB-guaranteed export-financing facility involving 9-10 commercial banks from the US, Japan and EU. The ADB's move followed the IMF's relaxation of the budget surplus requirement from a target of 1 percent of the country's GDP to a modest deficit in the region of 1-2 percent due to the changed circumstances including slowing down of Thailand's economic growth.[3]

On October 8, 1997, Indonesia sought IMF assistance and on November 5, 1997, the IMF announced a US$43 billion financial package for Indonesia. This package consisted of a combined loan of US$18 billion from the IMF, World Bank and Asian Development Bank (ADB); US$20 billion from bilateral donor countries; and, US$5 billion from Indonesia's own reserves.[4] The bilateral donor countries include Singapore, Malaysia, Japan and Australia which had offered an additional US$11 billion financial rescue package to Jakarta since these countries have traded heavily with Indonesia and have long-term investments that they understandably want protected.[5]

However, the size of the total international package was exaggerated for two reasons.[6] First, some of the loans from the ADB, World Bank and other governments which contributed to the package would have been provided under the normal lending programs to Indonesia. Second, the US$5 billion of Indonesia's own foreign assets, which had not previously been counted as part of its official foreign exchange reserves, was also included. It is to be noted that Indonesia's call for the IMF support was rather slow in contrast to Thailand due to two factors. First is the optimistic assessment of Indonesia's growth fundamentals and

[2] Key elements of the financial package included financial restructuring measures (such as closure of insolvent financial institutions); fiscal adjustment measures equivalent to some 3 percent of GDP to bring the fiscal balance back into surplus and contribute to shrinking the current account deficit; and control of domestic credit. For full discussion, see Timothy Lane and Marianne Schulze-Ghattas, *IMF-Supported Programs in Indonesia, Korea and Thailand: A Preliminary Assessment,* Occasional Paper No.178, Washington D.C.: International Monetary Fund, 1999, p.2.

[3] *The Straits Times, "Thailand gets reprieve with fresh financing plan from ADB," February 14, 1998, p.53.*

[4] Soedradjad Djiwandono, "Bank Indonesia and the Recent Crisis," Bulletin of Indonesian Economic Studies, Vol.36, No.1, 2000, p.56.

[5] Leif Roderick Rosenberger, "Southeast Asia's Currency Crisis: A Diagnosis and Prescription," Contemporary Southeast Asia, Vol.19, No.3, p.244.

[6] George Fane, "Indonesian Economic Policies and Performance," The World Economy, Vol.22, No.5, July 1999, p.661.

economic prospects provided by the IMF and World Bank. Moreover, on May 30, 1996, the World Economic Forum ranked Indonesia 15th in terms of its economic competitiveness, an improvement from its 30th rank a year ago.[7] Second, former President Suharto was reluctant to adhere to the stringent IMF conditions as it could significantly erode his power and strength. In February 1998, the Suharto government even proposed the establishment of a currency board but gave up the idea due to strong pressures from various sectors, compounded with political uncertainties and civil unrest. On May 21, 1998, President Suharto resigned amidst Indonesia's economic, political and social problems.

The IMF-arranged financial assistance to Indonesia was subject to various stringent conditions and reforms. These include (a) a revision of the 1998/99 budget to start in April 1998 with the following targets – zero economic growth, 20 percent inflation, rupiah pegged at 5000 to US$ and budget deficit of 1 percent of GDP, (b) a gradual phasing out of government subsidies for domestic fuels and electricity, (c) giving autonomy to Bank Indonesia to set interest rates, and (d) encouraging banks to merge and adhere to requirements and rules. One of the additional reforms would have been the dismantling of the National Logistics Agency (Bulog) as it was accused of monopolizing the commodity markets to the detriment of the consumers and the protectors. However, a United Nations report stated that Bulog is what stands in the way of mass starvation for millions in the remote parts of Indonesia due to its price-stabilizing role. The report projected that there will be a shortage of 3.5 million tons of rice in 1998 and hence called on the international community to donate 2 million tons either in kind, cash or credit.[8]

Malaysia succumbed to the crisis with only a little foreign debt exposure and this had enabled Malaysia to muddle through without an IMF-sponsored rescue package.[9] Moreover, former PM Mahathir did not want to follow a "high-interest rate and reduced-spending" strategy imposed by the IMF. While high interest rates could lead to exchange rate stability in the short-run, it would certainly be detrimental to banking and industries in the medium to long run. Certainly, the Malaysian government had placed a stronger preference for a 'low interest rate and increased spending policy' as it would generate less severe impact on the larger proportion of its population. The Philippines, which was supposed to exit from over three decades of economic stewardship by the IMF, was given extension to do so provided that the government passed a new oil deregulation law and boost government revenues. It entered into a precautionary arrangement which was has less stringent conditions than the full-fledged standby arrangement that Indonesia and Thailand entered into with the IMF.[10] The IMF agreed to extend the US$1.3 billion aid package to the Philippines and effectively put an end to the planned graduation from the IMF program in the meantime.[11] Singapore did not need to resort to IMF funding because of its healthy financial position. Singapore was in a position to lend a helping hand instead as illustrated by its assistance to Indonesia, Thailand and Malaysia.

---

7 Mohammad Sadli, "The Indonesian Crisis," ASEAN Economic Bulletin, Vol.15, No.3, 1998, pp.272-289.

8 The Straits Times, "Jakarta agency wards off starvation," April 21, 1998, p.20.

9 Prema-chandra Athukorala, "Swimming against the Tide: Crisis Management in Malaysia," *ASEAN Economic Bulletin,* Vol.15, No.3, 1998, pp.281-289.

10 Soedradjad Djiwandono, "Bank Indonesia...," 2000, p.52.

11 Gerardo Sicat, "The Philippine Economy in the Asian Crisis," *ASEAN Economic Bulletin,* Vol.15, No.3, 1998, p.292.

As for international financial assistance, there are a number of relevant issues. First, has the IMF done its role properly? There has been a growing debate on whether the IMF has prescribed the correct policies or not. Based on its practice, the IMF has imposed its orthodox policies of restrictive fiscal and monetary policies (cutbacks in government spending and high interest rates) and closures of companies and financial institutions deemed insolvent. However, it has been perceived by many that these tight macroeconomic conditions set by the IMF were "highly controversial" and "dead wrong" because despite these policies the crisis-hit Asian economies continued to deteriorate including the failure of the high interest rates to attract capital inflows and prevent capital outflows, and the resultant rising level of debt service obligations.[12] Jeffrey Sachs, one of the well-known critics, argued that:

> The region does not need wanton budget cutting, credit tightening and emergency bank closures. It needs stable or even expansionary monetary and fiscal policies to counterbalance the decline in foreign loans.[13]

Even then World Bank's former chief economist Joseph Stiglitz critically stated that "[o]ne ought to focus on things that caused the crisis, not on things that make it more difficult to deal with."[14] The IMF's Policy Division Director Jack Boorman also admitted that "mistakes were probably made when it [the IMF] recommended the 16 bank closures without giving investors adequate guarantees" and "that the policy regarding depositor guarantees now appears to have been ill-advised."[15] In another occasion, Mr. Hubert Neiss, then IMF's top representative to Asia, added that "[h]ad we known the depth of the recession, we would not have recommended such a tightening of fiscal policy, instead of a loosening of policy."[16]

Expansionist, instead of restrictive, policies should have been implemented immediately to counteract the contractionary impact of the crisis. As Corden put it,

> The IMF is not straightforwardly right or wrong. It is probably now mostly right with its prescriptions and conditions for the countries affected by the Asian financial and currency crisis. But it went off the rails at the beginning in 1997, though it has gone gradually back on again, being flexible.[17]

However, there has been a chorus of disapproval as far as the role of the IMF is concerned, that is, whether the IMF had ameliorated or exacerbated the crisis situation. As a consequence, it has been suggested that there is a fundamental need to strengthen the international financial architecture including the need to reform the IMF. Among the proposals, the French suggested a need to boost the role of a 24-member IMF advisory group

---

[12] For more discussion, see James Dean, "Asia's Financial Crisis in Historical Perspective," *Journal of the Asia Pacific Economy,* Vol.3, No.3, 1998, pp.267-268.

[13] Jeffrey Sachs, "IMF Orthodoxy isn't what Southeast Asia needs," *International Herald Tribune,* November 4, 1997, p.8, as cited in Richard Robison and Andrew Rosser, "Contesting Reform: Indonesia's New Order and the IMF," *World Development,* Vol.26, No.8, 1998, pp.1594.

[14] *The International Herald Tribune,* January 16, 1998, p.11, as cited in James Dean, "Asia's Financial Crisis…," p.268.

[15] The Straits Times, "We badly misgauged Asian crisis," January 20, 1999, p.1.

[16] The Straits Times, "IMF to review bail-out conditions," January 29, 1999, p.93.

[17] Max Corden, "*The Asian Crisis: Is there a Way Out?*" Public lecture delivered in Singapore as a Distinguished Fellow in International Economics and Finance, ISEAS, Singapore, 1998, p.2.

that includes 10 representatives from emerging markets and give them a louder voice in IMF decisions. It has been perceived that the IMF policies reflect too much the views of the United States. However, the French proposal was opposed by the US.[18] The British proposed to merge parts of the Fund with the World Bank and the former US Secretary of State George Shultz proposed to scrap the IMF.

On the other hand, there are others who view that the IMF should continue to exist and what is needed is to inject additional resources to the IMF to provide temporary assistance to afflicted economies. As Corden further declared,

> The IMF is needed, desperately needed, in situations like the Asian crisis, that there is no need to establish a new organization, and that it would be foolish – as some US rightwingers propose - to abolish it. The IMF should be provided with adequate resources to cope with major crises and these resources should not be used primarily to rescue international banks and other financial institutions – nor the owners and managers of domestic institutions in crisis countries – but to provide temporary relief to allow for necessary adjustments without major recessions or adverse effects on the mass of the population, and especially the poorest.[19]

Second, was there immediate action on the part of the IMF, the United States and the European Union? The answer is NO. The lack of immediate financial support from the international community contributed to the worsening of the crisis. The IMF admitted on January 19, 1999 that it had "badly misgauged" the severity of the Asian economic crisis. A long delay in the US Congress' approval of the increased funding for the IMF certainly proved to be a very costly exercise for the crisis-hit economies. The European Union's assistance came indirectly – that is, through its contribution to the IMF. Moreover, the Southeast Asian region is considered to be a much lower priority for the EU as compared to the Central and Eastern European countries including Russia where an enormous amount of financial assistance was given by the EU.

Third, why were Asian-based initiatives not supported? During the early phase of the crisis, Japan proposed the establishment of an Asian Monetary Fund to be capitalized at US$100 billion in order to provide the immediate financial assistance to the crisis-hit economies. Japan had good reasons for putting its money on the table as its banks were heavily exposed in Thailand, South Korea and Indonesia and it is in their interests to stabilize the volatile currency markets.[20] Moreover the Japanese economy is deeply integrated with its neighbors so that any slowdown or collapse would affect Japan immediately. The United States simply dismissed Japan's proposal as it would diminish the effectiveness of the IMF and its policies. Moreover, the US and the IMF feared that they would lose their influence in the Asian region. On its own initiative, Singapore also proposed the establishment of a multilateral fund to provide financial guarantees that would assist Indonesian's traders, but it did not receive much support from developed countries.

Fourth, should there be a bailout mechanism by the IMF? Who actually benefits from this bailout? It is argued that no firm or company should be shielded from bankruptcy by the IMF nor should there be any official bailout nor should foreign lenders be bailed out, knowing that

---

[18] The Straits Times, "Camdessus supports plan," October 8, 1998, p.42.

[19] Max Corden, "The Asian Crisis ...," 1998, p.61.

[20] Nicola Bullard, Walden Bello and Kamal Mallhotra, "Taming the Tigers: the IMF and the Asian Crisis," *Third World Quarterly*, Vol.19, No.3, 1998, pp.505-555.

'it was misguided allocation of credit that got Asian countries into difficulty."[21] It is also viewed that this bailout mechanism has actually benefited, not the poor population, but a rather limited number of people including investors and lenders at the expense of the larger majority of the population. In the Mexican case, it was the bailout that punished 100 million people and in the Thai case, the rescue package, rather than benefiting the 60 million people, can end up in the hands of politically connected speculators who will bail out their money-losing ventures.[22] Johnson also stated that the IMF's money which went to Thailand, Indonesia and South Korea did not go the people of those countries as it went to the foreign banks that made too many shaky and imprudent loans to Thai, Indonesian and South Korean banks and businesses in the first place.[23] Thus, Corden proposed that in the restructuring of the financial architecture, both the creditors and investors should also be made accountable and share the consequences should a crisis occur.[24]

Demand-Management Policies

These are the orthodox policies aimed at affecting the various components of aggregate demand; namely, private consumption, private investment, government spending, exports and imports. These policies come in the form of (i) fiscal policy through changes in government spending and/or taxes, (ii) monetary policy through changes in money supply or interest rates, and (iii) exchange rate policy through intervention in the foreign exchange market to keep the exchange rate fixed or allowing the exchange rate to float but the Central Bank engages in some form of market intervention.

Fiscal and Monetary Policies

During the early phase of the crisis, Thailand and then Indonesia after some time, followed some expenditure-reducing policies through restrictive fiscal and monetary policies, following the IMF's prescribed policies. As Lane and Schulze-Ghattas stated:

> Macroeconomic policy adjustment was an essential element of the [IMF-supported] programs: monetary policy was aimed mainly at preventing a spiral of depreciation and inflation from emerging, while fiscal policy was initially intended mainly to provide some modest support for external adjustment and make room for the non-inflationary financing of the carrying costs of the needed bank restructuring.[25]

The Thai and Indonesian governments undertook austerity measures and reduced the expansion of domestic credit. With credit squeeze, private consumption, particularly of consumer durables, declined. Moreover, given the lack of animal spirits, a tight credit market and high interest rates, private investment also fell markedly. Singapore, Malaysia and the Philippines also adopted IMF-like austerity measures in some areas particularly on current

---

[21] See James Dean, "Asia's Financial Crisis...," p.268.

[22] Anna Schwartz, "International Financial Crises: Myths and Realities," *The Cato Journal*, Vol.17, No.3, 1998, p.4. as obtained from [http://www.cato.org/pubs/journal/cj17n3-3.html].

[23] Chalmers Johnson, "Economic Crisis in East Asia: The Clash of Capitalisms," *Cambridge Journal of Economics*, Vol.22, 1998, pp.653-661.

[24] Max Corden, "The Asian Crisis...," 1998, p.61.

[25] See Timothy Lane and Marianne Schulze-Ghattas, *IMF-Supported Programs..., p.1.*

government operations. Singapore, however, has continued to increase its expenditure on areas which could increase its productivity including investments on infrastructure and education.

The problem with the IMF's restrictive measures is that given an economic slowdown, any further tight fiscal and/or monetary policies would certainly aggravate the recessionary conditions faced by Southeast Asian economies. In the case of Singapore, it continued to implement infrastructure development projects to counteract the slowing down of its economy. With the turn of events in Malaysia, monetary policy had become expansionist with massive injection of domestic liquidity and the consequent lowering of interest rates. Benchmark interest rates fell from 11 percent to 8 percent on September 7, 1998. Moreover, statutory reserve requirements were reduced from 14.5 percent in March 1989 to 4 percent in September 1998. The lowering of interest rates was expected to boost domestic spending particularly private investment. Despite cuts in some sectors, overall government spending would be increased by 20 percent with increased spending in investments in physical and social infrastructure projects.

The effect of an expansionist fiscal and/or monetary policy is smaller in Singapore than in Malaysia given that the former is more highly open economy than the latter. Equivalently, the expenditure multiplier and hence the impact on GDP and employment will be much smaller in Singapore than in Malaysia.[26]

Exchange Rate Policies

As the Thai baht, Indonesian rupiah, Malaysian ringgit, Philippine pesos and Singapore dollar faced mounting attacks during the initial phase of the crisis, the respective central banks in Southeast Asia defended their currencies by intervening in the foreign exchange market, that is, selling US dollars in exchange for domestic currencies. Is it simply the Southeast Asian people doing the selling? Definitely not. It would certainly take an incredibly huge magnitude of currency sale to effect large fluctuations of the exchange rate and that substantial part of these transactions had taken place outside the Southeast Asian region.

It was argued that the hedge funds had contributed significantly to the massive exchange rate changes as they specialize in high risk financial instruments which involve currency and stock movements. Since 1992, the number of hedge funds had expanded more than three times to around 1500 funds. These hedge funds had managed assets worth more than US$200 billion including the large investments of some giant international banks.[27] However, some of these banks incurred huge losses from these investments in hedge funds. For example, Citigroup's Salomon Smith Barney unit lost US$1.33 billion in trading during the third quarter of 1998. Another example is UBS Warburg Dillon Read unit which lost money in 1998 and the near collapse of the hedge fund LTCM cost the bank 790 million francs. Bank America lost about US$573 million on loans to D.E. Shaw and Co., a hedge fund and securities firm.

Given the hefty depreciations of their respective currencies in the July-December 1997 period, could the central banks then continue to fight and defend their own currencies? The answer is NO as their holdings of foreign exchange reserves are limited. They would simply

---

[26] See Figure 10.1 in Appendix 1 for graphical analysis of demand-management and supply-side policy responses to the 1997/98 economic crsisis.

[27] The Straits Times, "Banking giants beat hasty retreat after hedge fund losses," January 27, 1999, p.47.

deplete their stocks should they continue to do so. Instead, they should allow their exchange rates to float. The Bank of Thailand had indeed wasted a large proportion of its foreign exchange reserves in order to defend the baht but to no avail. In an interview during the World Economic Forum at Davos in 1999, former Senior Minister Lee Kuan Yew (now Minister Mentor) noted that the Thai mistake was not that they did not know that hedge funds were attacking their currency, but that they tried to defend it – with the result that their reserves were depleted by US$23 billion.[28] This was indeed a very costly mistake which was further made serious by the Bank of Thailand's (through the Financial Institutional Development Fund) extension of financial support to the beleaguered financial institutions in the amount of 1.1 trillion bath (US$29 billion).

In the case of South Korea, its former central bank governor admitted that the Bank of Korea wasted up to US$26 billion between late 1996 and February 1997 in a futile attempt to defend the won.[29] In the Philippines, when speculation against the peso became heavy in July 1997, the authorities used almost one billion US dollars of reserves within few days without any positive results.[30] In Malaysia, Bank Negara Malaysia sold close to US$1.5 billion to prop up the ringgit when it came under heavy speculative attack in mid-May 1997.[31] The intervention in the foreign exchange markets became very costly as it resulted in the depletion of foreign exchange reserves at a time when regional economies were experiencing an export slowdown which adversely affected the inflow of foreign exchange earnings.[32]

Faced with tremendous attacks on their currencies and given the limited amount of international reserves, Thailand and Indonesia could no longer defend their currencies under the fixed exchange rate system. Consequently, the Thai baht and the Indonesian rupiah were floated on the July 2, 1997 and on August 13, 1997, respectively. The Thai bath/US$ rate moved immediately from 25 to 30 and rose drastically to 55 by January 1998.[33] It subsequently moderated to 45 by February 1998. The Indonesian exchange rate reached Rp15,000 per dollar in late January 1998 from Rp2,658 per dollar immediately before the August 1997 devaluation.[34] The Malaysian ringgit, the Philippine peso and the Singapore dollar also experienced significant weakening, but of different magnitudes. The devaluation of their respective currencies has the expenditure-switching effect away from imports (as imports become expensive) towards domestic goods. However, despite deep currency devaluations, the region's exports continued to be very weak. This indicates that devaluation by itself is no guarantee for an export-led recovery. The main problem faced by the Southeast Asian manufacturers was the lack of trade finance as most banks had restrained from extending loans due to fear of losing money.

---

[28] The Straits Times, "Europe can differentiate now, says SM," February 3, 1999, p.3.
[29] The Straits Times, "Seoul wasted forex reserves in bid to halt meltdown," January 26, 1999, p.15.
[30] Gerardo Sicat, "The Philippine Economy…," 1998, p.292.
[31] Prema-chandra Athukorala, "Swimming against the Tide…," 1998, p.282.
[32] Bank Negara Malaysia, *The East Asian Crisis – Causes, Policy responses, Lessons and Issues.* Group of 15 Working Paper No.4, Switzerland, June 1998, p.6.
[33] Peter Warr, "What Happened to Thailand?" *The World Economy,* Vol.22, No.5, 1999, p.645.
[34] George Fane, "Indonesian Economic Policies…," 1999, p.662

Supply-Side Policies

Supply-side policies include those which affect capital, labor, technology and other factors of production – policies which affect the costs of doing business. Short-run policies include those which the government can directly influence such as cuts in both labor and non-labor costs including office and industrial rents, utility charges, statutory charges and port tariffs.

As Singapore is a very open economy, reliance on expansionist demand-management policies would indeed generate a very limited expansion of GDP and employment. As such, Singapore has depended heavily on supply-side policies aimed at reducing the costs of doing business in Singapore. These policies consisted of a S$10.5 billion cost-cutting measures.[35] This package consisted of a 10-percent rebate in corporate taxes, property tax rebates, cuts in industrial land rentals of up to 40 percent, lower transport charges through cuts in customs and excise duties for cars and petrols, and lower utility and telecommunication rates. Even in the case of the 1985/86 recession, Singapore also implemented cost-cutting measures to restore competitiveness including a reduction in compulsory employers' contribution to the Central Provident Fund (CPF) from 25 percent of wages to 10 percent, a reduction in corporate taxes, and accelerated depreciation.[36]

A large component of the production costs is labor cost. Thus, the Singapore government has depended on wage guidelines including wage cuts, restraint in wage increases, and even cuts in the contribution rates to the CPF, a compulsory savings scheme in Singapore in which both employers and employees each contribute 20 percent of the employees' salary to this fund. As part of the cost-cutting package cited above, the government reduced the annual variable component for civil servants in 1998 to ¾ month, down from the two months given last year. High salary officers and civil servants also received wage cuts from 1 to 5 percent. Even ministerial pay was cut by 10 percent. A significant component of the package is a 10-percentage point CPF cut in the employer's contribution rate from January 1999 for up to two years.

However, in high-inflation countries (due to hefty devaluation of their currencies), like Indonesia and the Philippines, cuts in nominal wages will lead to reduction in real wages. Singapore had experienced falling consumer prices as a result of the crisis. Had Singapore allowed its currency to depreciate according to market forces, this would result in higher domestic prices. Consequently, a cut in (or even freezing of) nominal wages would lead to erosion of real wages. For example, in Indonesia, the minimum wages in 1998 were frozen at 1997's level, but given high rates of inflation to hit 50 percent in 1998, Indonesia's real incomes were halved.[37]

Long-run policies include training and re-training programs for workers and more research and development activities for innovations and improvement in technology aimed at improving productivity. In Singapore, there are more than 600,000 workers with less than secondary education. As such, it is extremely important that these workers upgrade their skills and learn new tasks to be more productive and to be more employable in the future. There are also other schemes such as the job re-design programs implemented by the Singapore

[35] The Straits Times, "Government decides on $10.5 billion cut," November 25, 1998, p.1.
[36] Max Corden, *Pragmatic Orthodoxy: Macroeconomic Policies in Seven East Asian Economies*. Occasional Papers No.61. New York: International Center for Economic Growth, 1996, p.36.
[37] The Straits Times, "Indonesia's urban poor: wage freeze set to halve real incomes," April 1, 1999, p.4.

Productivity and Standards Board which involves changing both job content and arrangement to encourage workers to become more productive.

Supply-side policies also include those policies which will stimulate an increase in capital formation. These include incentives to save and invest including cuts in corporate taxes and liberalization of some investment rules particularly on foreign direct investments as it contributes to capital formation. Given the crisis, it is indeed difficult to woo foreign investors without generous incentives including loosening the rules on foreign ownership. In Thailand, George Soros decided to invest in Thai steel mills and Thai companies dealing with electronics components. Singapore's DBS Bank bought Thai Sri Danu, Thailand's 12th largest bank, and ABN Amro of the Netherlands took a 75 percent stake in the Bank of Asia. Bangkok Bank and Thai Farmers Bank are among the many other banks seeking foreign capital.[38] Thus, the crisis had effectively forced the region's governments and firms to make deals with foreigners - with US and European investors rushing to acquire companies at bargain prices. The region's companies needed capital to recover. It is foreign capital which can provide the financing gap as domestic savings fall with erosion of per capita incomes in the region.

Capital Controls

Malaysia was also hit by the crisis as manifested in the loss of investors' confidence, significant capital outflows, depletion of foreign exchange reserves, severe impact on the stock markets, and marked depreciations of the ringgit. With Anwar Ibrahim as then finance minister, Malaysia followed IMF-like policies including tight monetary and fiscal policies (essentially, a combination of high-interest rate and reduced government spending policy) together with financial reforms. However, with the sacking of Anwar Ibrahim in August 1998, former PM Mahathir rejected the IMF-like policies. Instead, taking over from Anwar Ibrahim as finance manager, PM Mahathir tried to rescue the Malaysian economy through a combination of easier fiscal and monetary policies (i.e. higher government spending and lower interest rates, respectively) and imposition of capital controls.

Former PM Mahathir argued strongly that the speculators were mainly responsible for the crisis and suggested that international monetary authorities led by the IMF should be able to impose measures that would contain the flows of international financial capital particularly short term. While Malaysia continued to experience massive pressures on its ringgit and while no concrete measures were done to curtail short-term capital movements, Malaysia unilaterally imposed currency and capital controls on September 1, 1998. The controls which cover external accounts, authorized deposit institutions, trade settlement and currency held by travelers, were expected to contain the speculation on the ringgit and to minimize the impact of the short-term capital flows on the domestic economy.[39] The ringgit was also fixed to the US dollar at RM3.80. Malaysia was not the first, or only country in the world that imposed capital controls. As at 1997, the IMF reported that 128 countries have still regulated their international financial transactions in some ways.[40]

[38] The Washington Post, "US, European firms finding Asian companies willing to deal," May 24, 1998, p.H4.

[39] Zainal Aznam Yusof, "Malaysian Economic Outlook: Moving Towards a Slow Recovery," Paper presented at the 1999 Regional Outlook Forum, organized by ISEAS, Singapore, January 1999, p.5.

[40] The Straits Times, "Malaysia's real problem," October 7, 1998, p.37.

These controls were largely aimed at the substantial offshore ringgit market in Singapore which constrained the ability of Malaysia's authorities to lower domestic interest rates. Consequently, all offshore ringgit had to be brought on shore by the end of September 1999. Moreover, the government restricted capital outflows by imposing a one-year holding period for repatriation of portfolio capital inflows. As Singapore's economy has been too closely linked with that of Malaysia, the Singapore government decided to stop trading on its Central Limit Order Book (CLOB) over-the-counter market, which was dominated by Malaysian stocks. This act resulted in a temporary freezing of over US$10 billion worth of Malaysian assets held in Singapore.

Certainly, Malaysia's imposition of capital controls met with strong criticisms from many countries as such policy has been viewed to derail the on-going financial liberalization activities. The long-term effects would be harmful due to lack of investors' confidence as could be gauged from a ranking by Euromoney. Malaysia was ranked 51st with a score of 41.89, which was 21 places down from its ranking in 1997. Singapore ranked 21st with a score of 89.17, the top in the league of Asian nations. All 180 countries involved were assessed on nine criteria ranging from economic performance and political risk, to debt indicators and access to long- and short-term financing, and other criteria.[41]

The imposition of capital controls is indeed costly and ineffective arising from administrative problems and rampant evasion. However, it was argued that short-term effects would be favorable to Malaysia. In fact, Malaysia reported that its current account balance had improved and that its foreign exchange reserves had increased. With capital controls, the Malaysian government was able to inject domestic liquidity into the economy aimed at boosting domestic demand particularly domestic investment and has allowed the economy to pick up. In May 1999, the former IMF managing director Michel Camdessus noted Malaysia's ability to recover from the crisis through its adoption of "soft system of control" together with structural reforms.[42] Thus, as Tomoika stated, "Malaysia subsequently proved that the negative opinions *[about its capital controls]* were not necessarily prophetic, as the economy has shown a relatively health recovery."[43]

The question most people asked then was "How long would Malaysia keep its capital controls?" In an interview at the World Economic Forum in Davos in 1999, former PM Mahathir stated that the controls would not be permanent, but would remain in place "until the international community devises a new financial regime that curbs currency traders."[44] However, the Malaysian government looked into the possibility of adjusting the 12-month holding period for portfolio investors, considering two of the possible options – exit tax and a most-favored investor status which gives exemptions to long-standing investors from exit taxes under certain conditions. About a fifth of the total KLSE re-capitalization of RM300 billion (end-November 1998) is owned by foreign interests. It was expected that after September 1, 1999 around RM5 billion to RM20 billion of funds would be repatriated.[45] In February 1999, the one-year holding period was replaced with a system of graduated exit levies, and was further relaxed in September 1999. As Haggard stated, capital controls *[in*

[41] The Straits Times, "Singapore still least risky Asian nation," October 11, 1998, p.32.
[42] Business Times, May 18, 1999, p.9.
[43] Noriyuki Tomioka, "Causes of the Asian Crisis, Asian-style Capitalism and Transparency," *Asia-Pacific Review*, Vol.8, No.2, 2001, pp.47-65.
[44] The Straits Times, "Start of KL's exit tax 'weeks away," January 31, 1999, p.2.
[45] Zainal Aznam Yusof, "Malaysian Economic Outlook…," 1999, p.8.

Malaysia] were carefully crafted to assure foreign direct investors and by mid-2001, they had been dismantled.[46]

Bank Restructuring

The first set of policies involves comprehensive measures and restructuring in the banking sector including the closure of insolvent banks and finance companies, as well as recapitalization and mergers of weak but viable financial institutions. In Indonesia, sixteen banks were closed in November 1997 and four state banks were merged into a single institution. The government established the Indonesian Banking Restructuring Agency (IBRA) to supervise and manage the restructuring of banks in poor financial condition and to manage the assets acquired during the restructuring process. Immediately, IBRA acquired 54 banks which accounted for 40 percent of the banking assets. In August 1998, it further took over seven major banks and the activities of seven other banks were frozen. It was estimated that the restructuring of the banking system will require a huge amount of over 400 trillion rupiahs, which is equivalent to more than half of the country's GDP.[47]

In Thailand, the Financial Institution Development (FIDF) has been created to repair the banking system including the screening of the rehabilitation plans submitted by the 58 suspended financial companies in order to determine their status. This led to the closure of the 56 financial companies. In the first half of 1998, it was reported that borrowings by FIDP to finance its bail-out of weaker financial institutions has reached over 700 billion baht in May 1998. To lessen its dependence on the costly repurchase securities market, the Thai government passed a new law in May 1998 which enabled it to issue government bonds of up to 500 billion baht to pay for the debt of the FIDF.[48] Moreover, with seed money of 1 billion baht, the Thai government established the Asset Management Corporation to manage the disposal of the assets which belonged to the closed finance companies.

In Malaysia, the Asset Management Company (AMC) called Danaharta was created to repair the banking sector. It intended to acquire 18 banks under Phase I (weaker banks that require recapitalization by Danamodal). As at end-December 1998, Danaharta had signed agreements with 13 banks and expected to acquire the remaining banks by the first quarter of 1999.[49] A significant step undertaken by the Malaysian government was the merger of 58 financial institutions into six large banking groups which were expected to provide competition with foreign banks.[50]

The second set of policies involves restructuring of the external debt including rolling over and rescheduling the settlement of external debt particularly short-term debt. By the end of March 1998, Indonesia's private sector debt was estimated at about US$72.5 billion of which about half was to be repaid within one year. It was found that Indonesia's private

---

[46] Stephen Haggard, "Politics, Institutions and Globalization: The Aftermath of the Asian Financial Crisis," *American Asian Review*, Vol.19, No.2, 2001, pp.71-98.

[47] Hadi Soesastro, "The Indonesian Economy under Habibie," Paper presented at the 1999 Regional Outlook Forum, organized by ISEAS, Singapore, January 1999, p.14.

[48] Sussangkarn Chalongphob, "Thailand: Toward Economic Solvency," Paper presented at the 1999 Regional Economic Outlook, organized by the Institute of Southeast Asian Studies (ISEAS), Singapore, January 1999, p.3.

[49] Zainal Aznam Yusof, "Malaysian Economic Outlook…," 1999, p.10.

[50] M. Shanmugam, "Merger by Decree," *Malaysian Business*, October 16, 1999, p.11.

sector debt is very difficult to manage as it is spread among hundreds of corporations with issued paper of widely differing quality. Various activities have been undertaken to help manage Indonesia's private debt including the creation of the Indonesian Debt Restructuring Agency (INDRA) whose operation involves a conversion of the foreign exchange loans of participating domestic debtors into rupiah denomination and their repayment switched to INDRA, which will make the repayments in foreign exchange to international creditors. Another instrument, called the Jakarta Initiative, was created to help companies restructure their debt and facilitate out of court settlement. However, both INDRA and the Jakarta Initiative have no takers.[51] In the case of Thailand, it was reported that at the start of 1998, it had about US$35 billion in short-term debt. The risks were not over yet as there was still about US$25 billion of short-term debt remaining which needed to be restructured including debt-equity conversion.[52] In the case of Malaysia, a "club loan" was formed by a group of 12 foreign banks incorporated in Malaysia and extended a loan of RM5.13 billion (US$1.35 billion) to the Malaysian government to help restructure banks.[53]

Privatization

Southeast Asian economies have adopted privatization activities that have provided additional financial resources and more competition. Privatization aims to eliminate the weak and inefficient producers particularly those which have received massive government protection. In Indonesia, the government planned to sell 12 state-owned enterprises (SOEs) to raise revenues estimated at Rp15 trillion, as part of an agreement with the IMF. However, the first privatization exercise (the selling of PT Semen Gresik, a group of cement companies) was not successful due to the protests of the people in West Sumatra against privatization. In the end, the Cemex from Mexico was only a minority shareholder as it was allowed only to buy a 20 percent share.[54] An estimated target of Rp13.0 trillion was set for the fiscal year 1999-2000, but only half of it was realized due to some problems including its unpopularity among the Indonesian people because of their belief that some public enterprises should remain government-owned and because of the threat felt by them due to loss of privileges or due to unemployment arising from privatization.[55]

In the case of Malaysia, its privatization programme involves the sale, in full or part, of government companies; contracts for private companies to invest and run services such as hospital maintenance and concessions to invest and operate attractive projects such as the national sewerage system. Malaysia's privatization was, however, not directly in response to the crisis as it began as early as 1984. It was reported that privatization in Malaysia has helped the government save about RM7 billion (S$2.8 billion) annually in operating expenditure and RM73 billion in development spending. The sale of government-owned shares and assets had generated more than RM20 billion. Since the early 1990s, however, problems have cropped up as many investors saw privatization as a way to get rich and

---

[51] Hadi Soesastro, "The Indonesian Economy…," 1999, p.14.
[52] Sussangkarn Chalongphob, "Thailand …," 1999, p.2.
[53] Zainal Aznam Yusof, "Malaysian Economic Outlook…," 1999, p.9
[54] Hadi Soesastro, "The Indonesian Economy…," 1999, p.7.
[55] George Fane, "Survey of Recent Developments," *Bulletin of Indonesian Economic Studies,* Vol.36, No.1, April 2000, p.28.

nothing else. Government's contracts are given to those with a track record and not overnight wealth-seekers.[56]

In the case of Thailand, privatization includes government-owned enterprises in transport, utilities, energy and communications. It is expected that the privatization of a large number of government-owned enterprises including the Rathachaburi project, the Airport Authorities and the Thai Airways, would be completed before the end of the year 2000.[57]

IMPROVING THE GLOBAL FINANCIAL ARCHITECTURE

The globalization of financial markets has taken place at a much more rapid pace than the globalization of commodities and labor because of the tremendous developments in the information and communications technologies that have made financial transactions easier, faster and cheaper. However, the only constraints to financial transactions are national regulations which have been liberalized at a fast pace. As Tobin stated, "most observers, West and East, public and private, in governments and international institutions, in banks and businesses, in big countries and small, now agree that *financial globalization went too far too fast*."[58] He further stated that:

> As these *[national regulations]* have been liberalized in country after country, international financial flows have flooded national securities markets and inundated banking systems all over the world. These flows could be the vehicles by which savings in the advanced capitalist democracies are channelled into productive capital investments in the developing countries of Asia, Africa, and Latin America. Or they could be causes of currency crises, recessions and depressions, unemployment and deprivation in those countries. Or both.[59]

In East Asia, there have been 80-100 crises over the past quarter century.[60] Crises have become more frequent and more severe indicating a fundamental weakness in global economic arrangements. In the case of the 1997/98 economic crisis, the impact was so devastating that even the ADB characterized the economic hardship during the crisis as similar to that suffered during the Great Depression.[61] The severity of the crisis, the speed of its transmission, and the weak international response have all contributed to wide-ranging deliberations on the governance of international finance. The resultant issues discussed have focused on the need to improve the global financial architecture to prevent future crisis, and to manage it more effectively should it occur. The 1999 issue of the *Asian Development Outlook* published by the ADB provides an excellent analysis of the proposals aimed at strengthening the international financial architecture, namely, (a) controlling capital flows, (b) improving regulatory standards, (c) rethinking exchange rate regimes, (d) creating an

[56] The Straits Times, "KL's privatization policy draws flak," April 21, 1998, p.24.

[57] Dredner Kleinwort Benson, "Privatization in Thailand 2000," Asiamoney, May 2000, p.17-18.

[58] James Tobin, "Financial Globalization," World Development, Vol.28, No.6, 2000, p.1102.

[59] James Tobin, "Financial Globalization," ... p.1101.

[60] Carl-Johan Lindgren, Gillian Garcia, and Matthew I. Saal, *Banking Soundness and Macroeconomic Policy,* Washington D.C.: International Monetary Fund, 1996, p.20, as cited in Joseph Stiglitz, "Capital Market Liberalization, Economic Growth, and Instability," *World Development,* Vol.28, No.6, 2000, p.1075.

[61] See Asian Development Bank, *Asian Development Outlook 1999,* New York: Oxford University Press, p.21.

international lender of last resort, and (e) bailing in the private sector. Each of these proposals will be briefly discussed below.[62]

Capital Controls

The Asian crisis showed that ill-planned liberalization of capital flows could lead to financial instabilities. As Jeffrey Sachs has argued, "It was financial market reform that allowed the Thai and South Korean banks to tap into short-term international loans in the early 1990s, thereby bringing together these banks with excited young investors who were happy to be in Bangkok and Seoul for the first time."[63] When countries free up their capital accounts, they become more susceptible to crisis because of the weaknesses in the domestic financial system arising from the lack of adequate and stringent supervision and regulation of financial institutions. As pointed by Ha-Joon Chang, the Korean crisis is a crisis from under-regulation rather than from over-regulation.[64] In Thailand's case, Dr. Olarn Chaipravat, the president of Siam Commercial Bank, admitted that Thailand committed two mistakes involving its financial and foreign exchange market regulations:

> The first mistake lay in the Bank of Thailand's lax regulations, which allowed the inexperienced local commercial banks to directly conduct foreign exchange transactions with offshore banks. The Bank of Thailand also had no experience in dealing with direct US dollar/baht transactions with offshore banks, except with the International Monetary Fund.... *[The second mistake]* involves the lax finance and banking regulations in supervising the offshore baht denominated debt market. During the early 1990s, at the height of the financial bubble, Thai companies avoided high interest rates at home to fight inflation by floating commercial paper in the offshore market as a means to raise cheap money. [65]

Even Joseph Stiglitz used an analogy by comparing capital account liberalization to putting a race car engine into an old car and setting off without checking the tires or training the driver. He further stated that:

> Perhaps with appropriate tires and training, the car might perform better; but without such equipment and training, it is almost inevitable that an accident will occur. One might actually have done far better with the older, more reliable engine: performance would have been slower, but there would have been less potential for an accident. Similarly, the international economic architecture must be designed to "work" not just in the presence of perfect economic management, but with the kind of fallible governments and public officials that in fact occur in democratic societies.[66]

---

[62] For a complete discussion, see Asian Development Bank, *Asian Development Outlook 1999,* pp.38-45.

[63] Jeffrey Sachs, "Global Capitalism: Making it Work," *The Economist*, September 12, 1998, p.24, as cited in Kanishka Jayasuriya and Andrew Rosser, "Economic Orthodoxy ...," p.386.

[64] See Ha-Joon Chang, "Korea: The Misunderstood Crisis," *World Development,* Vol.26, No.8, 1998, pp.1555-1561.

[65] *The Nation,* "Learning from Thailand's Mistakes," November 17, 1998, p.B1.

[66] Joseph Stiglitz, "Capital Market Liberalization, Economic Growth, and Instability," *World Development,* Vol.28, No.6, 2000, p.1075.

There are two types of challenges that could result from private capital inflows.[67] First, massive inflows of capital have resulted in economic overheating and the problems associated with the appreciation of the real exchange rate. Second, sharp reversals in capital inflows have proved disruptive and costly. To minimize the risks associated with capital mobility, there are two sets of proposals: first, those measures aimed at slowing down capital inflows, and second, those measures aimed at controlling capital outflows.

To control *capital inflows*, particularly "hot money," James Tobin proposed the introduction of a "simple small tax on foreign exchange transactions, levied at an agreed common rate by all countries where such transactions originate in significant amount."[68] Another measure is to tax foreign borrowings. As in Chile's case, domestic companies borrowing abroad had to place 30 percent of the proceeds at the Chilean central bank for a period of one year. Also another way is to set limits on open foreign currency positions of *both* domestic banks and companies since a regulation that focuses only on local banks will shift the foreign borrowings to local companies.

The policy of controlling *capital outflows* will enable the central bank authorities to lower the domestic interest rates in order to stimulate the domestic economy. However, this policy is viewed to be risky as it can unsettle the domestic markets and possibly generate negative impacts for the market access of other developing economies. Moreover, the imposition of controls on capital outflows can create incentives for corruption and hence weakens the political support towards unpopular structural policy reforms.

Improving Regulatory Standards

There are several proposals which came from the Group of 22 (G22) working reports aimed at improving the international standards of financial regulation and supervision. One set of proposals is concerned with transparency and accountability like requiring private companies to follow national accounting standards and requiring financial institutions and companies to compile and publish data and other related information on their international transactions. Another set of proposals, which is concerned with strengthening the financial systems, identifies the weaknesses and problems of many domestic financial sectors like inadequate risk management, defective deposit insurance schemes, and the mismatched assets and liabilities. The proposal is to encourage both industrial and developing countries to adopt the international supervisory standards prescribed in the Basle Capital Accords including requiring banks to adhere to the minimum capital adequacy standards. To improve the existing regulatory standards, several proposals include the need to tighten the rules on foreign borrowing in developing countries and the need to update the Basle capital adequacy standards (as the risk weightings for short-term loans are much lower than for the long-term loans and hence induces banks to provide more short-term rather than long-term loans). A

[67] Pradumna Rana, "Private Capital Flows to Asian Developing Countries: Past Trends and Future Prospects," *Asian Economic Crisis: Causes, Consequences and Policy Lessons,* Development Papers No.20, Bangkok: United Nations Economic and Social Commission for Asia and the Pacific, 1999, p.91.

[68] According to Tobin, a tax of 0.1 or 0.2 percent means nothing for a round trip of a year or more from one currency to another and back. But for one-week round trips, it would be equivalent to a difference between interest rates in the two markets of 10 or 20 percent per year. See James Tobin, "Financial Globalization," ... p.1104.

more radical proposal to improve regulatory and supervisory standards is to create an international financial authority for financial institutions and a board of overseers of global financial markets. Although the creation of a global financial authority is viewed as unrealistic, the G7 has created a "Financial Stability Forum" which brings together central bank officials, finance ministers, financial regulators and representatives of multilateral organizations. The Forum aims to identify and evaluate the issues and uncertainties affecting the international financial system, and to determine the policy actions needed to respond to these uncertainties.

Rethinking Exchange Rate Regimes

The experiences of some Asian countries during the July 1997/98 crisis showed that fixed, but adjustable, exchange rate system could not be sustained given an increasingly mobile global capital. With speculative attacks on their currencies, the monetary authorities had to impose tight monetary and fiscal policies, that is, high interest rates and budget cuts. Moreover, the fixed exchange rate system had encouraged domestic financial institutions and companies to engage in heavy foreign borrowings without hedging.

The general consensus now is for countries to link their currencies to another by adopting a currency board system or by forging a currency union, or by allowing their currency to float. A flexible exchange rate system has several advantages. First, countries with fixed exchange rates have to defend their currencies in times of speculative attacks by depleting their limited foreign reserves and hence suffer crisis of investor confidence. With a flexible exchange rate system, countries are less likely to face this crisis of investor confidence. Second, countries with a fixed exchange rate system cannot inject domestic liquidity to the financial system given the limited stock of foreign reserves. In a flexible exchange rate system, the exchange rate adjusts and hence gives monetary authorities the freedom to provide domestic liquidity to the system.

Creating an International Lender of Last Resort

While central banks act as the lender of last resort in national economies, it has been proposed that an international body be created to perform the similar function in an international environment with highly integrated capital markets. It has been suggested that the International Monetary Fund should be given this role since it has generally been performing this function. It has injected liquidity in some countries with balance of payments crises.

Several conceptual and practical problems, however, exist regarding this lender of last resort role. For example, the lender of last resort should be able to provide indefinite amount of liquidity if a country suffers from liquidity crisis, and it should demand restructuring and adjustment if a country suffers from insolvency crisis. However, the experience of the 1997/98 Asian crisis showed that it is difficult to distinguish between illiquidity and insolvency. Another problem arises from the fact that while central banks have the power to close or merge insolvent banks and financial institutions, the same does not apply to an international lender of last resort, that is, it has no power to close down national central banks, much more an erring government. The third problem refers to the inability or the lack of capacity of the international lender of last resort to print more money in order to provide an unlimited amount of liquidity. This problem arises because of the limited amount of resources of this lender of last resort.

An interesting proposal put forward by Japan is the establishment of regional currency support mechanisms, for example, in Asia, Western Hemisphere and Eastern Europe, with the objective of complementing the role and function of the IMF. Countries that are economically interdependent through trade and investments could pool their financial resources together to provide for this regional currency support mechanism. An example of this mechanism is the proposal by Japan to form an Asian Monetary Fund (AMF) in September 1997. While the ADB complements the World Bank, the proposed AMF could also complement the IMF. The AMF could provide early warning signals of impending financial crisis most effectively at the regional level given its familiarity with the regional conditions (informational advantage) and regional location. The proposed initial funding was set at US$100 billion half of which would come from Japan and the balance from China, Hong Kong, Singapore and Taiwan. From these funds, the AMF could provide immediate financial support to the crisis-hit countries instead of waiting for a much delayed response from the IMF and other international agencies. The immediate injection of the much needed liquidity into the financial system could prevent the sharp weakening of the regional currencies as experienced in the 1997/98 crisis. Because of the resistance by the IMF and the US due to its potential conflict, the AMF proposal did not push through despite Malaysia's strong support. Alternatively, Japan came up with a US$30 billion Miyazawa initiative for the Asian region, half of which would be used to finance short-term trade, and the other half was to finance medium- and long-term projects for economic recovery of the region.

"Bailing in" the Private Sector

At the center of this proposal is the need to minimize moral hazard. "Bailing in" the private sector will enable some of the burden of the financial crisis to be borne by the private investors and banks. One of the proposals is to encourage the IMF to "lend into arrears" whereby the IMF would lend to countries that are in default to private creditors, as long as the countries involved pursue policy adjustments and the private creditors negotiate for debt restructuring. A more radical proposal is the creation of an international bankruptcy court that will be responsible for restructuring the countries' debt. However, this proposal is not feasible because it would involve nations to give up their sovereignty and because of the differences in the national bankruptcy codes that would make it impossible for countries to reach a single international bankruptcy code.

CONCLUSION

In this chapter, we analyzed the various policy responses which the crisis-hit countries have adopted. Southeast Asian governments responded differently to the crisis including financial assistance, demand-management policies, supply-side policies, capital controls and others. Those differences are reflective of the following circumstances. First is in terms of the willingness of the political leadership to subscribe to the IMF and its conditionalities including implementation of restrictive fiscal and monetary policies, in exchange for its financial rescue package. Thailand followed the IMF's prescription and was awarded its efforts with a US$17 billion package. Indonesia, on the other hand, brought up the idea of setting up a currency board system but was unsuccessful and had to succumb to IMF's loan package and its conditionalities. Malaysia, on the other hand, strongly resisted the IMF's rule and money as former PM Mahathir did not want to follow a high-interest rate and reduced spending strategy imposed by the IMF. As such Malaysia pursued an expansionary fiscal and monetary policy. Such a policy would help the Malaysian economy to recover. Second is in terms of the relative effectiveness of expansionary demand-management in the case of Malaysia and supply-side policies in the case of Singapore. In the case of a very open economy like Singapore, demand-management policies would be less effective. Thus, in addition to increased fiscal spending on infrastructures, Singapore has relied on supply-side measures. Short-run measures include wage cuts, cuts in CPF contribution and cuts in non-wage costs. Long-run measures include training and retraining programs. Third is in terms of the lack of concrete measures to control the outflows of short-term capital which prompted the Malaysian government to impose capital and currency controls.

APPENDIX 1

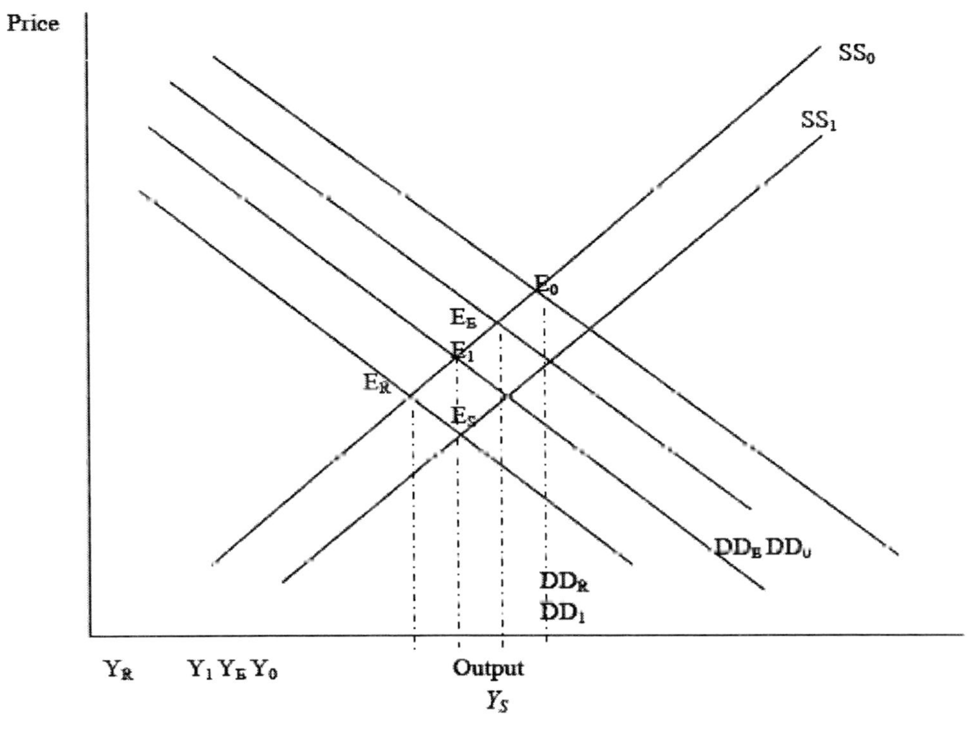

Figure 1. Demand-management and Supply-side Policy Responses to the Crisis

From an initial equilibrium position at E_0, the reduction in overall demand shifts the demand curve from DD_0 to DD_1. Income falls from Y_0 to Y_1 creating unemployment problem. A restrictive demand policy shifts the demand curve to DD_R. Income falls further to Y_R and unemployment worsens. During the initial phase of the crisis, the Malaysian government adopted a restrictive policy with the expected contractionary outcome on output and employment. However, it changed its stance to an expansionist one with increased government spending which shifts the demand curve to DD_E and income rises to Y_E. In the case of a very open economy like Singapore, the relative ineffectiveness of demand-management policy has prompted the government to rely heavily on supply-side policies which shifts the supply curve from SS_0 to SS_1. Output is expected to increase from Y_1 to Y_S.

Questions For Discussion

1. In response to the 1997/98 economic crisis, there were two sets of policy responses. First, each of the affected economies in Southeast Asia responded independently by adopting their own economic policies. Second, these economies joined together to pursue a regional approach to the crisis. Discuss how you would reconcile these two sets of policy responses.
2. Discuss what factors account for the differences in the policy responses by Southeast Asian governments.
3. Discuss clearly the lessons that can be derived from the 1997/98 economic crisis in Southeast Asia.

Suggested Materials for Case Studies

Fane, George, 1999, "Indonesian Economic Policies and Performance," *The World Economy*, Vol.22, No.5, pp. 651-668.

Haggard, Stephen, 2001, "Politics, Institutions and Globalization: The Aftermath of the Asian Financial Crisis," *American Asian Review,* Vol.19, No.2, pp.71-98.

References

Asian Development Bank, 1999, *Asian Development Outlook 1999,* New York: Oxford University Press.

Athukorala, Prema-chandra, 1998, "Swimming against the Tide: Crisis Management in Malaysia," *ASEAN Economic Bulletin,* Vol.15, No.3, pp.281-289.

Bank Negara Malaysia, 1998, *The East Asian Crisis – Causes, Policy responses, Lessons and Issues.* Group of 15 Working Paper No.4, Switzerland.

Benson, Dredner Kleinwort, 2000, "Privatization in Thailand 2000," *Asiamoney,* May.

Bloomberg News, "Banking giants beat hasty retreat after hedge fund losses," *The Straits Times,* January 27, 1999, p.47.

Bullard, Nicola, Walden Bello and Kamal Mallhotra, 1998, "Taming the Tigers: the IMF and the Asian Crisis," *Third World Quarterly*, Vol.19, No.3, pp.505-555.

Chalongphob, Sussangkarn, 1999, "Thailand: Toward Economic Solvency", paper presented at the 1999 Regional Economic Outlook, organized by the Institute of Southeast Asian Studies (ISEAS), Singapore.

Chang, Ha-Joon, 1998, "Korea: The Misunderstood Crisis," *World Development,* Vol.26, No.8, pp.1555-1561.

Corden, Max, 1998, "*The Asian Crisis: Is there a Way Out?*" Public lecture delivered in Singapore as a Distinguished Fellow in International Economics and Finance, ISEAS, Singapore.

Corden, Max, 1996, *Pragmatic Orthodoxy: Macroeconomic Policies in Seven East Asian Economies,* Occasional Papers No.61. New York: International Center for Economic Growth.

Dean, James, 1998, "Asia's Financial Crisis in Historical Perspective," *Journal of the Asia Pacific Economy,* Vol.3, No.3.

Djiwandono, Soedradjad, 2000, "Bank Indonesia and the Recent Crisis," *Bulletin of Indonesian Economic Studies,* Vol.36, No.1, pp.47-72.

Fane, George, 1999, "Indonesian Economic Policies and Performance," *The World Economy*, Vol.22, No.5, pp. 651-668.

Fane, George, 2000, "Survey of Recent Developments," *Bulletin of Indonesian Economic Studies,* Vol.36, No.1, pp.13-45.

Haggard, Stephen, 2001, "Politics, Institutions and Globalization: The Aftermath of the Asian Financial Crisis," *American Asian Review,* Vol.19, No.2, pp.71-98.

Johnson, Chalmers, 1998, "Economic Crisis in East Asia: The Clash of Capitalisms," *Cambridge Journal of Economics,* Vol.22, No.6, pp.653-661.

Lane, Timothy and Marianne Schulze-Ghattas, 1999, *IMF-Supported Programs in Indonesia, Korea and Thailand: A Preliminary Assessment,* Occasional Paper No.178, Washington D.C.: International Monetary Fund.

Lindgren, C., G. Garcia and M Saal, 1996, *Banking Soundness and Macroeconomic Policy,* Washington D.C.: International Monetary Fund, p.20, as cited in Joseph Stiglitz, 2000, "Capital Market Liberalization, Economic Growth, and Instability," *World Development,* Vol.28, No.6.

Rana, Pradumna, 1999, "Private Capital Flows to Asian Developing Countries: Past Trends and Future Prospects," *Asian Economic Crisis: Causes, Consequences and Policy Lessons,* Development Papers No.20, Bangkok: United Nations Economic and Social Commission for Asia and the Pacific.

Rosenberger, Leif Roderick, 1998, "Southeast Asia's Currency Crisis: A Diagnosis and Prescription," *Contemporary Southeast Asia,* Vol.19, No.3, pp.223-252.

Sachs, Jeffrey, 1997, "IMF Orthodoxy isn't what Southeast Asia needs," *International Herald Tribune,* November 4, p.8, as cited in Robison, Richard and Andrew Rosser, 1998, "Contesting Reform: Indonesia's New Order and the IMF," *World Development,* Vol.26, No.8, pp.1594.

Sachs, Jeffrey, 1998, "Global capitalism: making it work," *The Economist*, September 12, p.24, as cited in Kanishka Jayasuriya and Andrew Rosser, "Economic Orthodoxy and the Asian Economic Crisis," *Third World Quarterly,* Vol.22, No.3, pp.381-396.

Sadli, Mohammad, 1998, "The Indonesian Crisis," *ASEAN Economic Bulletin,* Vol.15, No.3, 1998, pp.272-289.

Schwartz, Anna, 1998, "International Financial Crises: Myths and Realities," *The Cato Journal*, Vol.17, No.3, 1998, p.4. [see http://www.cato.org/pubs/journal/cj17n3-3.html].

Shanmugam, M., 1999, "Merger by Decree," *Malaysian Business,* October 16, p.11.

Sicat, Gerardo, 1998, "The Philippine Economy in the Asian Crisis," *ASEAN Economic Bulletin,* Vol.15, No.3, pp.281-289.

Stiglitz, Joseph, 2000, "Capital Market Liberalization, Economic Growth, and Instability," *World Development,* Vol.28, No.6, pp. 1075-1086.

Soesastro, Hadi, 1999, "The Indonesian Economy under Habibie," Paper presented at the 1999 Regional Outlook Forum, organized by ISEAS, Singapore.

The International Herald Tribune, January 16, 1998, p.11, as cited in James Dean, 1998, "Asia's Financial Crisis in Historical Perspective," *Journal of the Asia Pacific Economy,* Vol.3, No.3, p.268.

The Nation, "Learning from Thailand's Mistakes," November 17, 1998, p.B1.

The Straits Times,

---, "Thailand gets reprieve with fresh financing plan from ADB," Feb 14, 1998, p.53.

---, "Jakarta agency wards off starvation," April 21, 1998, p.20.

---, "KL's privatization policy draws flak," April 21, 1998, p.24.

---, "Malaysia's real problem," October 7, 1998, p.37.

---, "Camdessus supports plan," October 8, 1998, p.42.

---, "Singapore still least risky Asian nation," October 11, 1998, p.32.

---, "Government decides on $10.5 billion cut," November 25, 1998, p.1.

---, "We badly misgauged Asian crisis," January 20, 1999, p.1.

---, "Seoul wasted forex reserves in bid to halt meltdown," January 26, 1999, p.15.

---, "IMF to review bail-out conditions," January 29, 1999, p.93.

---, "Start of KL's exit tax 'weeks away," Jan 31, 1999, p.2.

---, "Europe can differentiate now, says SM," February 3, 1999, p.3.

---, "Indonesia's urban poor: wage freeze set to halve real incomes," April 1, 1999, p.4.

The Washington Post, "US, European firms finding Asian companies willing to deal," May 24, 1998, p.H4.

Tobin, James, 2000, "Financial Globalization," *World Development,* Vol.28, No.6, pp. 1101-1104

Tomoika, Noriyuki, 2001, "Causes of the Asian Crisis, Asian-style Capitalism and Transparency," *Asia-Pacific Review,* Vol.8, No.2, pp.47-65.

Warr, Peter, 1999, "What Happened to Thailand?" *The World Economy,* Vol.22, No.5, pp.631-50.

Zainal Aznam Yusof, 1999, "Malaysian Economic Outlook: Moving Towards a Slow Recovery," Paper presented at the 1999 Regional Outlook Forum, organized by ISEAS, Singapore.

In: Asian Economic and Political Issues, Volume 11
Editor: Harvey E. Roth, pp. 47-71
ISBN: 1-60021-192-5

Chapter 3

CAUSES AND CONSEQUENCES OF THE CRISIS[1]

Teofilo C. Daquila

ABSTRACT

The 1997/98 economic crisis faced by the Southeast Asian economies was linked to the interactions between the households, corporate and government sectors in the pursuit of their three main activities such as production, demand and income. The first section of this chapter investigates the various conditions which existed before the crisis and which contributed to the crisis. These include rising income expectations, worsening current account deficits, rising external indebtedness, and rapid expansion of domestic credit. The second section analyzes the impacts of the crisis on the four sectors such as the external (trade and financial capital flows), production, labor and financial sectors.

INTRODUCTION

As discussed in the first chapter, the economies of Southeast Asia (such as Indonesia, Malaysia, the Philippines, Singapore and Thailand) had achieved a remarkable economic growth for an average of about 7.0 per cent during the 1960-96 period. However, the region was hit by the financial crisis in 1997 which began in Thailand and had spread to the rest of the region. The crisis came as a total shock. It was not predicted even by the IMF. As Vassily Mikheev, a Russian economist stated,

> As the IMF annual edition "*World Economic Outlook*" suggests, in May 1997, the Fund was still being pretty optimistic about the development prospects in Asian states that were shortly to find themselves neck-deep in crisis. The IMF forecast a 6.8% GDP

[1] Earlier versions of this chapter include guest lectures and seminar presentations at the following institutions: El Colegio de Mexico (1998), Nordic Institute of Asian Studies (Copenhagen, 1999), Ludwig-Maximilians Universitaet Muenchen (Munich, 1999), University of Sweden's Center for Pacific and Asian Studies and Stockholm School of Economics (1999), and the University of Paris Sciences-Po Asia-Europe Program (1999); and invited conference papers presented at Chulalongkorn University (1999) and the Center for the Study of International Institutions (Austria, 2003).

growth in Thailand in 1997, further increasing to 7% in 1998; Indonesia was supposed to hit the 8.5% growth rate within 1997-98; Malaysia, 6.4%; and the Philippines, 3.6%, likewise within a two-year period.[2]

There were others who argued that even the international credit rating agencies should be blamed because their ratings did not give the correct signals to the international lenders. Examples of these agencies are Standard and Poor's and Moody's whose ratings did not accurately reflect the true ability to repay debts as in the case of Korea whose credit ratings were AA- until October 24, 1997.[3] Even Radelet and Sachs also pointed out that the credit ratings for all the would-be crisis economies were actually improving from 1995 until the eve of the crisis.[4]

On July 2, 1997, the Bank of Thailand announced the floating of the baht after its intervention in the foreign exchange market to keep the exchange rate failed. What began as a currency crisis resulted in a banking crisis and eventually generated a contagion effect to other neighboring countries including Indonesia, Malaysia, the Philippines and Singapore.[5] However, it was not contagion from Thailand that made the countries vulnerable to a financial crisis but because of the home-grown economic problems which include a growing current account deficit, excessive short-term foreign borrowings, a banking sector weighed down by speculative property loans and, corrupt government and business practices.[6] The disturbances, however, were not limited to the Southeast Asian region, but the rest of the Asian region. As Krugman predicted:

> Almost every economy in Asia will feel the ripples from this summer's [1997] wave of devaluations: higher interest costs because the international markets fear further devaluations, lower export prices because the devaluations will intensify competition, reduced capital inflows because once ebullient foreign investors have become suddenly wary, and maybe a growth slowdown.[7]

Wade even extended the impact of the crisis to the rest of the world as follows:

> The devaluation of the Thai bath in July 1997 precipitated a wave of currency crises or financial instability from Thailand, to the rest of Southeast Asia, to Taiwan, to Hong

---

[2] Vassily Mikheev, "The Financial Crisis in Asia and Its Economic and Political Consequences," *Far Eastern Affairs,* No.2, 1998, p.53.

[3] See, for example, Youn-Suk Kim and Hyeng Keun Koo, "Asia's Contagious Financial Crisis and its Impact on Korea," *Journal of Asian Economics,* Vol.10, 1999, p.115.

[4] Steven Radelet and Jeffrey Sachs, "The East Asian Financial Crisis: Diagnosis, Remedies and Prospects," *Brookings Paper on Economic Activity,* 1998, Vol.1, pp.1-90, as cited in Ha-Joon Chang, "The Hazard of Moral Hazard: Untangling the Asian Crisis," *World Development,* Vol.28, No.4, 2000, p.784.

[5] The crisis even spread outside the region hitting Asia's third largest economy, South Korea in November 1997 with the won falling sharply by 10 percent per day, the limit of its trading band. Moreover, several major firms became insolvent, and by mid-December smaller companies collapsed at the rate of fifty per day. Korea's short-term interest rates increased to 30 percent and above. For more discussion, see James Dean, "Asia's Financial Crisis in Historical Perspective," *Journal of the Asia Pacific Economy,* Vol.3, No.3, 1998, pp.267-283. For excellent discussion on the nature of the Korean crisis, see Ha-Joon Chang, "Korea: The Misunderstood Crisis," *World Development,* Vol.26, No.8, 1998, pp.1555-1561.

[6] Anna Schwartz, "International Financial Crises: Myths and Realities," The Cato Journal, Vol.17, No.3. 1998. [http://www.cato.org/pubs/journal/cj17n3-3.html].

[7] Paul Krugman, "What Ever Happened to the Asian Miracle?" *Fortune,* August 18, 1997, p.12

Kong, to Korea, to the Philippines, to Russia, to Brazil, to Estonia, to Australia and New Zealand.[8]

Adelman and Yeldan also spoke about the global impact of the crisis:

> The Asian financial crisis has had a profound impact on the global economy. Global growth has been slower; risks have been higher; and the international flows of capital have been severely disrupted.[9]

Pre-Crisis Conditions

The economic crisis facing the Southeast Asian region can be linked to the interactions between the households, corporate and government sectors in the pursuit of their three main economic activities; namely, production, demand and income. There are various economic conditions which existed prior to the crisis and which contributed to the crisis. These include rising income expectations, worsening current account deficits, rising external indebtedness, and rapid expansion of domestic credit. An investigation of these conditions is necessary following the breakdown of the orthodox economists' explanation of the East Asian miracle in the context of a set of policies known as the "Washington consensus" which includes "financial sector liberalization, privatization of state-owned enterprises, fiscal discipline and trade, exchange rate and foreign investment deregulation."[10] The crisis has called for a reconsideration of the so-called "East Asian miracle." Even Jeffrey Sachs pointed out that "[o]f course, all is not well in Asia's economic management." He further stated that:

> East Asia's currencies remained peg to the U.S. dollar too long after the dollar strengthened sharply against the Japanese yen and the German mark. The result was that Asia's economies lost export competitiveness vis-à-vis Europe and Japan. They also lost competitiveness to China which devalued the yuan against the dollar in 1994, which helped spur sharply higher exports. Some of that increase in Chinese shipments marked a shift in business away from other countries of East Asia. If the East Asian currencies had been floating in the market place, they would have declined gradually against the dollar from 1995 onward. As it turned out, they came down with a thud this past summer.
>
> In addition to short-term currency mismanagement, the region also played with fire by encouraging large inflows of short-term capital from abroad. In many countries in the region, capital markets were liberalized in the 1990s, while supervision of banks and other financial institutions was lax. Many of the short-term loans from abroad found their way into real estate ventures and other speculative investments, in some cases controlled by cronies of government officials. Following the currency devaluations and tightening of credit, many of these projects will now go into default, and may even lead to bank closures in the region. Even as exports pick up in 1998, the construction sector is likely to remain depressed in parts of Southeast Asia.[11]

---

[8] Robert Wade, "The Asian Debt-and-Development Crisis of 1997-?: Causes and Consequences," *World Development,* Vol.26, No.8, 1998, p.1535.

[9] Irma Adelman. and Erinc Yeldan, "The Minimal Conditions for a Financial Crisis: a Multiregional Intertemporal CGE Model of the Asian Crisis," *World Development,* Vol.28, No.6, 2000, p.1087.

[10] Kanishka Jayasuriya and Andrew Rosser, "Economic Orthodoxy and the East Asian Crisis," *Third World Quarterly,* Vol.22, No.3, 2001, pp.381.

[11] Jeffrey Sachs, "Asia's Miracle is Alive and Well," *Time,* September 29, 1997.

Rising Income Expectations

Economic agents in Southeast Asia had been used to and had lived with high level of growth over the past 35 years. Consequently, they had expected that the "economic miracle" would continue and had made their economic decisions based on rising income expectations particularly on decisions affecting their consumption and investments including investments in property and capital markets. The so-called 'East Asian economic miracle' had dulled the willingness to take risks of people acting on capital markets, and that these people had been moved to "irrational exuberance," as Alan Greenspan put it, or what Garnaut referred to as the "psychology of a long boom."[12] Even Krugman pointed out that "... too many investors, domestic and foreign, took it as an excuse to believe that the good times could just keep on rolling – in particular that the overheated Southeast Asian boom of the mid-'90s ... could continue without limit."[13] The idea that high growth could go on forever seems to have become firmly implanted.[14]

As the Southeast Asian economies grow and continue to grow, incomes per capita and hence savings increase. With high growth and rising incomes, economic agents tend to increase their demand for goods and services. Demand tends to rise further if agents expect their economy to continue to grow. Prior to the crisis, evidence shows that broadly, all demand indicators expanded markedly. This is shown in Table 1. First, private consumption increased in all but Indonesia, with significant expansion in Malaysia and Thailand during the 1990-95 period relative to 1980-90. Second, general government consumption grew in all but Indonesia and Singapore, with marked expansion in Malaysia and the Philippines. Third, domestic investment demand by both private and public sectors rose markedly for all countries – growing by about twice in Singapore, more than double in Indonesia and in the Philippines, and about six-fold in Malaysia. Finally, merchandise imports also increased significantly in all countries. In particular, the import of machinery and transport equipment for ASEAN-5 rose from an average of 30 per cent in 1980 to 44 per cent in 1995.

On the production front, as the economy grows and continues to grow, it experiences a structural transformation away from the traditional agricultural sector towards modern non-agricultural (manufacturing and services) sector and hence indicates a change in the preferences of producers to accommodate the changing tastes and preferences of demanders. Consequently, resources are re-allocated away from agriculture towards manufacturing and services sectors. In 1995 relative to 1970, Indonesia, Thailand and Malaysia experienced a rapid structural transformation with the shares of their agricultural sectors declining from 46 to 17 per cent of GDP, from 32 to 13 per cent, and from 30 to 11 per cent, respectively. On the other hand, the share of the manufacturing sector increased significantly from 11 to 24 per cent of GDP, from 16 to 33 per cent, and from 18 to 29 per cent, respectively.

---

[12] Ross Garnaut, "Economic Lessons," in Ross McLeod and Ross Garnaut, eds., *East Asia in Crisis: From being a Miracle to Needing one?* London: Routledge, 1998, p.354.

[13] Paul Krugman, "Wrong, It Never Existed," *Time*, September 29, 1997, p.37.

[14] Helmut Hesse and Laura Auria, "The Financial Crisis in Southeast Asia: Causes and Effects on the Global Economy," *Economics*, Vol.57, 1998, p.58.

Table 1. Growth Rates of Demand Indicators in Southeast Asia, (in %)

	INDONESIA	MALAYSIA	PHILIPPINES	SINGAPORE	THAILAND
(1) Private Consumption					
1980-90	5.5	3.7	2.6	5.8	5.9
1990-95	4.7	7.2	3.2	6.6	8.1
(2) Private Consumption Per Capita					
1980-90	3.6	1.0	0.2	4.1	3.9
1990-95	3.0	4.7	1.0	4.5	7.1
(3) Central Government Consumption					
1980-90	4.6	2.7	0.6	6.7	4.2
1990-95	3.1	8.8	2.9	6.1	5.0
(4) Gross Domestic Investment					
1980-90	7.0	2.6	-2.1	3.7	9.4
1990-95	16.3	16.0	3.2	6.0	10.2
(5) Merchandise Exports					
1980-90	-0.3	8.6	3.9	9.9	14.0
1990-95	11.7	20.0	16.2	17.6	18.6
(6) Merchandise Imports					
1980-90	2.6	7.7	2.9	8.0	12.7
1990-95	11.5	20.3	18.0	15.5	15.3

Source: World Bank, *World Development Indicators*, Washington D.C.: World Bank, 1997, pp.179-180 for items (1) to (4) and pp.155-156 for items (5) and (6).

Moreover, as the economy expands, more institutions have been created and supplied to provide a wider variety of goods and services in response to changing demand conditions. In the manufacturing sector, about a third of the manufacturing value-added in Indonesia, Thailand and the Philippines was in food and beverages. In Malaysia and Singapore, the manufacture of machinery and transport equipment increased significantly during the 1980-1995 period from 20 to 36 per cent and from 44 to 58 per cent of the total manufacturing valued added, respectively (see Table 2).

In the financial sector, more financial institutions have been established including commercial banks, savings banks, merchant banks, insurance companies and others. Households have been provided with a wider variety of financial instruments ranging from simple deposits, stocks, bonds, unit trusts, foreign currency accounts, etc. Real estate and construction activities increase as households purchased houses, as firms built more factories, and as government built more infrastructure facilities. The prices of stocks and property rose markedly and generated a bubble economy in the Southeast Asian region prior to the crisis. There was an enormous increase in wealth arising from substantial capital gains. Gross domestic investment in Indonesia expanded by 16.3 per cent in 1990-95 period as compared to 7.0 per cent in the 1980-90 period as seen in Table 1. For Malaysia, Singapore and Thailand, investment grew by 16 per cent from 2.6 per cent, by 6.0 per cent from 3.7 per cent, and by 10.2 per cent from 9.4 per cent, respectively. In the case of the Philippines, while investment contracted by an average of 2.1 per cent in 1980-90 period, it expanded by 3.2 per cent in the 1990-95 period.

Table 2. Structure of Manufacturing in Southeast Asia, (% of value added in manufacturing)

	Value Added (US$ million)	Food and beverage Value Added	Textiles and Clothing Value Added	Machinery and Transport Equipment Value Added	Chemical Value Added	Other Manufac-turing Value Added
Indonesia						
1980	10133	32	14	13	11	30
1994	41186	26	15	12	10	36
Malaysia						
1980	5054	24	7	20	5	43
1994	22387	9	6	36	10	39
Philippines						
1980	8354	30	13	12	14	31
1994	14917	31	11	14	16	28
Singapore						
1980	3415	5	5	44	5	41
1994	18119	4	2	58	9	28
Thailand						
1980	6160	55	8	9	7	21
1994	40791	...	...	...	...	...

Source: World Bank, *World Development Indicators*, Washington D.C.: World Bank, 1997, pp.151-152.

Worsening Current Account Deficits

With higher growth rate and rising expectations that growth will continue, overall demand increases. When total spending (absorption) exceeds income, we have a current account deficit, or equivalently, a national deficit. Thus, a current account deficit arises when (i) both private and public sectors have deficits, (ii) private sector deficit is greater than public sector surplus, or (iii) public sector deficit is greater than private sector surplus. Singapore had the strongest net external financial position as it registered a current account surplus of about 14 per cent of GDP during the 1993-95 period as shown in Table 3. Singapore's public and private sectors were both in healthy surplus positions. The other Southeast Asian economies had high levels of current account deficits, with Thailand having the largest deficit at 6.3 per cent of GDP and Indonesia, the smallest deficit at 2.2 per cent of GDP. Since the public sectors in these countries were broadly in surplus positions during the 1993-95 period, the net external deficit were attributed mainly to the private sector deficits in these countries.

The issue is whether to allow the current account deficit to continue or not. If current account deficit continues, this can be financed by depleting foreign exchange reserves. However as reserves are limited, the current account deficits cannot be sustained. Assuming instead that the government intends to correct the deficit, it can undertake (i) expenditure-switching policies via a devaluation of the exchange rate making exports cheaper and imports expensive, and (ii) expenditure-reducing policies via a tight fiscal policy (e.g. reduce government spending or increase taxes) and/or a tight monetary policy (e.g. reduce money supply or increase interest rates) aimed at reducing domestic demand. However, in a model with financial capital mobility, it is possible for the current account to be sustained. The massive influx of foreign capital including foreign direct investments and foreign borrowings can be used to finance the current account deficits. In cases where foreign direct investments are insufficient to cover the deficit, the difference can be financed by foreign borrowings. Moreover, with capital mobility the need to devalue the exchange rate consistent with the market rate, given huge current account deficits, is not at all that urgent and hence results in an overvalued exchange rate.

Table 3. Indicators of Net External Financial Position: 1993-95 (% of GDP)

	INDONESIA	MALAYSIA	PHILIPPINES	SINGAPORE	THAILAND
(1) Current account balance	-2.2	-4.7	-4.3	13.9	-6.3
(2) Gross domestic savings	35.6	36.7	16.0	...	36.2
(3) Gross domestic investment	35.1	38.1	23.5	34.9	41.6
(4) Savings-investment gap	0.5	-1.4	-7.5	...	-5.4
(5) Overall fiscal deficit	...	2.1	...	5.3	2.3
(6) Private sector deficit	...	-3.5	...	...	-7.7
(7) Net FDI					
- 1980	0.2	3.8	-0.3	...	0.6
- 1995	2.2	6.8	2.2	...	1.2

Source: World Bank, World Development Indicators, Washington DC: World Bank, 1997, pp.187-188 for items (1), (2), (3) and (5) and pp.233-234 for item (7). Item (4) = (2) – (3) and item (6) = (4) – (5).

Rising External Indebtedness

Why have countries not learned from bad debt experiences? During the early 1980s, the Philippines faced a severe debt crisis arising from a substantial exposure in short-term loans accounted for mainly by the public sector. However, such an experience did not seem to provide meaningful lessons for other countries in the region as other Southeast Asian economies incurred rising levels of foreign debt. Indonesia had the highest level of foreign debt among Southeast Asian countries reaching US$108 billion in 1995, a five-fold increase relative to 1980 as shown in Table 4. About 80 per cent of it has long-term maturity. In 1997, about half of Indonesia's debt had a short-term maturity due to the increase in Indonesia's corporate debt. Malaysia's external debt also rose five times reaching US$34 billion in 1995, of which about a third was in short-term private non-guaranteed debt. Thailand's external debt increased sharply to about US$57 billion, a seven-fold increase relative to 1980. The proportion of private debt rose markedly from 20 percent to 37 percent. In 1997, this share reached 50 per cent. The punishingly high domestic interest rates in Thailand prompted increasing numbers of Thai borrowers to go overseas for cheap capital and this resulted in a flood of cheap foreign money that allowed banks to make foreign currency loans in U.S. dollars at interest rates lower than loans in bath.[15] For example, Thai corporate borrowers discovered that they could borrow at an interest rate of 5-8 percent instead of paying more than 13 percent when borrowing domestically and therefore could earn more money simply by borrowing abroad and depositing the baht in Thailand.[16] Consequently, Thailand's foreign debt in July 1998 stood at US$87 billion, 68 percent of which was private debt. The amount of foreign debt created by the banks and finance companies totalled US$33 billion.[17]

In the case of the Philippines, the proportion of long-term debt increased to 85 percent in 1995, with short-term debt being about 9 percent. This shows an improvement in the Philippine foreign borrowing behavior which presumably reflects that the Philippines has learned from its severe debt problem in the 1980s. The Brady debt deal of 1992 and the sustained growth in exports helped a lot.[18] From a high debt service burden at the height of the 1980s crisis of close to 25 per cent of export earnings, the external debt service ratio fell to 16 per cent of export earnings in 1994 to just below 10 per cent by 1997.

Table 4. External Debt in Southeast Asia (% of total debt)

	Total Debt, Mln US$	Long-term debt	Public and publicly guaranteed debt		Private debt	Use of IMF Credit
			Total	IBRD		
Indonesia						
1980	20938	86.7	71.7	7.7	15.0	0
1995	107831	79.3	60.6	12.3	18.7	0
Malaysia						
1980	6611	79.5	60.6	7.6	18.9	0
1995	34351	78.8	46.2	3.1	32.7	0
Philippines						
1980	17417	50.6	36.5	5.5	14.1	6.0
1995	39445	84.8	75.8	13.1	9.0	1.8
Thailand						
1980	8297	68.0	47.5	8.5	20.5	4.2
1995	56789	67.8	30.3	3.4	37.4	0

Source: World Bank, World Development Indicators, Washington D.C.: World Bank, 1997, pp.219-220.

[15] Leif Roderick Rosenberger, "Southeast Asia's Currency Crisis: A Diagnosis and Prescription," *Contemporary Southeast Asia,* Vol.19, No.3, 1997, p.229.

[16] Laurids Lauridsen, "The Financial Crisis in Thailand: Causes, Conduct and Consequences," *World Development,* Vol.26, No.8, 1998, p.1576.

[17] Nidhiprabha Bhanupong, "Economic Crises and the Debt-Deflation Episode in Thailand", *Asean Economic Bulletin,* Vol.15, No.3, 1998, p.309.

[18] Gerardo Sicat, "The Philippine Economy in the Asian Crisis," *ASEAN Economic Bulletin,* 1998, Vol.15, No.3, p.291.

Rising external indebtedness, however, does not necessarily become a burden. This depends on how the proceeds of the foreign borrowings are used. An increase in external debt can be attributed to current account deficits, to increases in foreign exchange reserves, to private capital outflows, minus net outflow of portfolio investments and direct investments or a combination of these proximate sources. In the first case, we may look at a rising gross external debt to finance capital flight, not current account deficits. The government or the central bank borrows abroad or runs down existing foreign exchange reserves and sells foreign exchange to domestic residents so that they can acquire foreign assets. In this first case, there is no change in aggregate net foreign assets. If there is a current account deficit, then it is almost entirely financed by direct investment and portfolio capital inflows or by falling foreign exchange reserves under a fixed exchange rate regime.

In the second case, we may look at an increased external debt reflecting current account deficits and not capital flight. We can probably assume here that direct investments and portfolio investments finance only a part of the current account deficits so that external debt rises by the difference. In practice, the cumulative current account deficits are the more common counterpart of increased external indebtedness, which results in a decline in aggregate net foreign assets (or an increase in aggregate net foreign liabilities). If the increase in external debt is used to finance current account deficits, then net foreign liabilities rise. Moreover, we have to distinguish between the two cases of an increase in external debt: (a) whether to finance consumption, or (b) whether to finance investments. If the increase in foreign debt is used to finance consumption, then we are simply mortgaging our future. If it used to finance investment, we have to distinguish between productive and unproductive investments. With productive and profitable investments, future repayments can be generated and simply we have liquidity problems. But if the proceeds of the loans are invested in non-performing assets and speculative activities, then there will be serious repayment problems. The quality and profitability of investments is what counts.

A common problem of many Asian banks is the weakness in the process of capital allocation as there were too many investments that failed to yield positive rates of return on a risk-adjusted basis.[19] The recent crisis has indeed given us a cause for alarm due to over-investment in unproductive, unprofitable and risky activities in some countries including real estate and construction activities which were financed mostly by short-term foreign capital. Property lending accounted for a quarter of total bank lending in Malaysia and the Philippines, and 20 per cent in Thailand. Thus, an investment bubble of careless lending was created since a substantial part of the loan money was channelled into already inflated assets in the real estate sector.[20]

Based on the incremental-capital-output ratio (ICOR) as a measure of the overall investment efficiency, the ICOR estimates in the Asian region had increased sharply in the 1993-96 period relative to the 1987-1992 period, suggesting that the efficiency of investments was already falling in the four years prior to the 1997 crisis.[21] For example, ICOR estimates for Thailand rose from 3.4 in the period 1987-1992 to 5.1 in the period 1993-1996, and for Malaysia, from 3.7 to 4.8 during the same comparative period. The risk increased as the

---

[19] Gunter Dufey, " Asian Financial Markets: A Pedagogic Note," *Journal of Asian Business,* Vol.15, No.1, p.66.

[20] Laurids Lauridsen, "The Financial Crisis in Thailand …," 1998, p.1576.

[21] Giancarlo Corsetti, Paolo Pesenti and Nouriel Roubini, "What Caused the Asian Currency and Financial Crisis?" *Japan and the World Economy*, Vol.11, 1999, p.317.

number of central business district offices in Bangkok rose, where vacancy rates were estimated to reach 15 per cent in 1997 and 20 per cent in 1998-99. In Indonesia, the vacancy rates were estimated to double in 1998-99 from 10 per cent in 1997. Moreover, during the 1992-1996 period, a total of 755,000 housing units were built in Bangkok, which was double the estimate in the national development plan, and this led to an excessive supply of housing units sending the vacancy rates to as high as 14 percent.[22]

The imprudent lending and borrowing by various economic agents were attributed to what is known as the moral hazard factor in which agents believe that they will be bailed out in the event of a crisis. Both international lenders and borrowers believed that a lender of last resort such as the IMF or the host government would bail them out. In this regard, the IMF has been criticized for encouraging moral hazard.[23] However, most accounts argue that the national institutions of the Asian countries to be the main sources of moral hazard that was behind the crisis.[24] The most popular variety of the moral hazard argument is that of crony capitalism where personal connections and political patronage, rather than entrepreneurial abilities, determine who gets access to credit and other resources. Moreover, Indonesia and Malaysia have experienced institutional weaknesses and financial systems that allocate funds based on political connection and government favors rather than the standard credit analysis found in Western countries.[25] The relatives and friends of the former president were in charge of concerns trying to make aircrafts, automobiles and banks. These people could gain access to banks and other financial institutions in order to finance their business enterprises regardless of viability.[26] One example was a US$236 million loan from Peregrine Hong Kong (which went bust in Jan 1998) to a taxi company in Jakarta, which was virtually unsecured but for the fact that one of the daughters of former President Suharto was a partner.[27]

The moral hazard problem in Asia magnified the financial vulnerability of the region during the process of financial markets liberalization in the 1990s, exposing its fragility vis-à-vis the macroeconomic and financial shocks that occurred in the period 1995-1997.[28] In Southeast Asia, domestic banks and financial institutions found it easier to obtain foreign loans.[29] Moreover, the moral hazard problem is compounded by the inefficiency of the central banks as in the case of the Bank of Thailand which made a mistake when it permitted local financial banks to conduct foreign exchange transactions with offshore banks.[30] In addition, before the floating of the baht, the Bank of Thailand had poured out an enormous amount of 430 billion baht to help shore up the failing financial institutions.[31]

---

[22] Laurids Lauridsen, "The Financial Crisis in Thailand ...," 1998, p.1576.

[23] Ronald McKinnon and H. Pill, "International Overborrowing – A Decomposition of Credit and Currency Risk", *World Development.* Vol.26, No.7, 1998, pp.1267-1282; Jeffrey Frankel, "The Asian Model, the Miracle, the Crisis and the Fund," A speech delivered at the US International Trade Commission, April 16, 1998.

[24] Ha-Joon Chang, "The Hazard of Moral Hazard: Untangling the Asian Crisis," *World Development,* Vol.28, No.4, p.775.

[25] Werner Baer, William Miles and Allen Moran, "The End of the Asian Myth: Why were the Experts Fooled?" *World Development.* Vol.27, No.10, 1999, p.1735.

[26] Graham Bird and A. Milne, "Miracle to Meltdown: A Pathology of the East Asian Crisis," *Third World Quarterly,* Vol.20, No.2, 1999, p. 425.

[27] Mohammad Sadli, "The Indonesian Crisis," *ASEAN Economic Bulletin,* Vol.15, No.3, p.273.

[28] Giancarlo Corsetti, Paolo Pesenti and Nouriel Roubini, "What Caused the Asian ..." 1999, pp.306-307

[29] Helmut Hesse and Laura Auria, "The Financial Crisis in Southeast Asia...," 1998, p.59.

[30] The Nation, "Learning from Thailand's Mistakes," *The Nation,* November 17, 1998, p.B1-B2.

[31] Ivory Tower, "Mexico 1994 versus Thailand 1997," *TDRI Quarterly Review,* Vol.12, No.3, 1997, p.12.

Rapid Expansion of Domestic Credit

Overall domestic credit provided by the banking sector as a proportion of GDP rose significantly in the Southeast Asian countries except Singapore (see Table 5). In Malaysia, it expanded by about two times to 132 percent of GDP in 1995 relative to 1990. In Thailand, it grew significantly to 137 percent of GDP. In the Philippines, it rose more than twice to about 63 percent of GDP. In Singapore, domestic credit expansion remained at 76 percent of GDP in 1990 and 1995 which indicates the ability of the Monetary Authority of Singapore to control credit expansion. Credit to the private sector was at extremely high levels in Malaysia and Thailand at 130 per cent and 140 per cent of GDP in 1995 as compared to 50 percent and 42 percent in 1980, respectively. In Singapore, credit to the private sector grew to about 107 percent of GDP in 1995 from 81 percent in 1980. The Philippines registered the lowest level of credit granted to the private sector at 45 percent of GDP in 1995 from 42 percent.

The rapid growth in overall domestic credit granted by the banking sector came from two sources: (i) an increase in domestic savings due to higher economic growth and rising per capita income as well as from massive capital gains due to higher asset prices, and (ii) massive inflows of foreign capital as foreign confidence built up with the expectations that the economy would continue to boom. Domestic credit expands rapidly when there are inadequate supervision and controls and particularly on the inflows of foreign capital. Table 6 shows that the net private capital flows and its three components (foreign direct investments, portfolio investments and bank and trade related-financing) expanded significantly in 1995 relative to 1980. The massive influx of foreign capital to the process of financial liberalization of interest rates, foreign exchange controls, portfolio management, and new facilities and institutions during the period from 1988 to 1996.[32]

Table 5. Domestic Credit Expansion in Southeast Asia (% of GDP)

	Domestic credit provided by the banking sector (1)		Liquid Deposits (2)		Quasi-liquid Deposits (3)		Credit to the private sector (4)	
	1990	1995	1990	1995	1990	1995	1980	1995
Indonesia	45.5	...	40.4	...	29.1	...	8.8	...
Malaysia	77.9	131.9	66.3	121.7	44.3	91.9	49.9	129.5
Philippines	26.9	62.9	36.8	55.1	28.1	44.9	42.2	45.0
Singapore	76.0	76.2	123.9	115.5	100.9	94.1	81.0	106.7
Thailand	90.7	136.5	74.8	79.5	65.9	70.2	41.7	139.9

Source: World Bank, *World Development Indicators*, Washington D.C.: World Bank, 1997, pp.269-270 for columns (1), (2) and (3), and pp.233-234 for column (4).

The problem, however, was that financial market liberalization in Asia occurred before there were appropriate state or collective institutions to monitor and regulate financial institutions or local expertise to manage them and which led to the establishment of a horde of

[32] Vichyanond Pakorn, "Thailand's Financial Evolution and the 1997 Crisis," Paper presented for the conference, The Miracle Undone: Asia's Financial Crisis, C.I.D.E. Mexico City, 20 February 1998.

new banks and finance companies, including the more than 200 banks in Indonesia, within a short span of time and with inadequate experience in money management.[33]

The maturity structure of the capital inflows changed from long-term foreign direct investment to short-term portfolio funds and loans and the build up of such investments in the domestic economy can make a country vulnerable to a sudden reversal of flows. The vulnerability and the excessive growth of the domestic credit has certainly contributed to instability in the banking and financial sector "as the allocation of credit was increasingly skewed towards the non-tradable and risky sectors, namely the property and stock markets.[34] And indeed when firms and banks in the Asian region failed to meet their foreign loan obligations, a financial panic took place which resulted in a huge withdrawal of capital from the Asian region. By the end of 1997, the net outflow of foreign bank loans reached US$34 billion.[35]

Table 6. Private Capital Flows in Southeast Asia (in US$ million)

	Net Private Capital Flows		Foreign Direct Investment		Portfolio Investments				Bank and trade-Related financing	
					Bonds		Equities			
	1980	1995	1980	1995	1980	1995	1980	1995	1980	1995
INDO	3325	11648	1093	4348	26	2248	312	4873	1804	180
MSIA	1799	11924	2333	5800	-212	2240	293	2299	-614	1585
PHIL	639	4605	530	1478	395	1060	0	1961	-286	449
SPORE	...	...	...	...	...	...	...	...	...	...
THAI	4498	9143	2444	2068	-87	2023	449	2154	1692	2898

Source: World Bank, *World Development Indicators*, Washington D.C.: World Bank, 1997, pp.237-238.

IMPACT OF THE CRISIS

The economic crisis which hit the Asian region had severely affected the Southeast Asian economies, particularly Thailand, Indonesia and Malaysia, and even Singapore and the Philippines.

External Sector

The external sector refers to the balance of payments which is the sum of the current account balance and the capital account balance. The current account balance is defined as the exports of goods and services less imports of goods and services plus net transfers. The

[33] Linda Y.C. Lim, "Whose Model Failed? Implications of the Asian Economic Crisis," *The Washington Quarterly*, Vol.21, No.3, 1998, p.28-29.

[34] Bank Negara Malaysia, *The East Asian Crisis – Causes, Policy Responses, Lessons and Issues.* Group of 15 Working Paper No.4, Switzerland, June 1998, p.6

[35] Steven Radelet and Jeffrey Sachs, *The Onset of the East Asian Financial Crisis,* Cambridge: National Bureau of Economic Research, 1998, p.10; see also Steven Radelet and Jeffrey Sachs, *The East Asian Financial Crisis: Diagnosis, Remedies and Prospects,* Cambridge: Harvard Institute for International Development, 1998.

capital account balance consists of short-term, medium-term and long-term capital flows. It is broken down into portfolio investments, direct investments and other investments including foreign loans.

Effect on the Exchange Rates

The most important variable that was attacked furiously is the exchange rate as it affects production, trade and capital flows. The speculative attacks on the regional currencies triggered the currency crisis and the eventual devaluation which led to severe weakening of the ASEAN currencies against the US dollar particularly the Thai baht, the Indonesian rupiah, the Malaysian ringgit and the Philippine peso. The Singapore dollar was also impacted but not as severely as the other currencies. Table 7 shows the average exchange rates of ASEAN currencies vis-à-vis the US dollar.

The fall in the rupiah was much more than the Thai bath for a number of reasons. First, the economic fundamentals of Indonesia were, in retrospect, much less stronger than they seemed.[36] In terms of the macroeconomic fundamentals such as the size and the rate of growth of the current account deficits, the level and decline of foreign exchange reserves, the slowing down of exports, the rate of inflation, and large private capital inflows, one could say that Indonesia would hardly be considered inferior to Thailand or that Indonesia's macroeconomy were in much better shape than that of Thailand.[37] Later, it became clear that the fundamental weakness in the Indonesian economy lay within the private sector, which went on an investment spending spree, abetted by an ever increasing volume of foreign loans made available at minimum security and prudence. Second, the negative market response to the ambiguity in the policy stance of former President Soeharto sent mixed signals of the sincerity of his commitment in the early stage of IMF intervention.

Table 7. Average Exchange Rates of ASEAN Currencies vis-à-vis the US dollar

	1997Q2	1997Q3	1997Q4	1998Q1	1998Q2	1998Q3
Indonesia	2437.2	2791.3	4005.7	9433.4	10460.8	12252.1
Malaysia	2.5081	2.7771	3.4818	3.9960	3.8451	4.0570
Philippines	26.371	29.798	35.384	40.639	39.379	42.865
Singapore	1.4348	1.4880	1.5960	1.6761	1.6449	1.7293
Thailand	25.90	33.034	40.662	47.094	40.331	41.059

Source: IMF, *International Financial Statistics*, Washington D.C.: International Monetary Fund, 1998.

Not only did the currencies weaken but also did the regional domestic interest rates rise as seen in Table 8. Indonesia had the largest increase in interest rates from the pre-crisis rate of 18.72 per cent to 34.9 per cent during the third quarter of 1998. The hefty devaluations and increases in interest rates generated severe impact on various sectors of the respective economics; namely, the external, production, labor and financial sectors. This section provides an analysis of the impact of the economic crisis on these sectors.

[36] Mohamed Sadli, "The Indonesian Crisis...," 1998, p.273.

[37] See Andrew MacIntyre, "Political Institutions and the Economic Crisis in Thailand and Indonesia," *ASEAN Economic Bulletin,* Vol.15, No.3, p.366; Hal Hill, *Southeast Asia's Economic Crisis: Origins, Lessons and the Way Forward,* Singapore: Institute of Southeast Asian Studies, 1998, p.8.

Table 8. Interest Rates in Southeast Asia (in %)

	1997Q2	1997Q3	1997Q4	1998Q1	1998Q2	1998Q3
Indonesia	18.72	23.38	26.19	26.33	32.16	34.93
Malaysia	9.34	9.60	9.98	11.16	12.21	n.a.
Philippines	13.21	17.42	20.70	20.43	17.06	.n.a.
Singapore	6.26	6.26	6.51	7.77	7.77	7.72
Thailand	12.75	13.92	14.92	15.25	15.25	14.83

Source: IMF, *International Financial Statistics*, Washington D.C.: International Monetary Fund, 1998.

Effect Onexports of Goods and Services

As exchange rate depreciates, exports become cheaper. But exports from the Southeast Asian region had remained stagnant due to weak demand from importing countries and the emergence of more competitive new markets. Table 9 shows that Southeast Asian global exports dropped significantly during the period from 1997Q3 to 1998Q3. The lack of international trade finance hindered the import-production-export capabilities of manufacturing firms particularly in Indonesia whose exports have collapsed as banks rejected letters of credit due to the concern about the viability and risks of Indonesian banks.

Table 9 Southeast Asia's Global Exports, (Quarterly Changes, %)

	1997Q3	1997Q4	1998Q1	1998Q2	1998Q3	1998Q4
Indonesia	0.4	-12.1	-42.4	-8.6	2.5	13.1
Malaysia	-5.7	-4.8	-24.0	-0.1	-3.1	4.1
Philippines	3.3	-4.4	-13.9	-8.4	6.4	1.4
Singapore	1.4	-5.3	-17.5	-4.6	-0.2	3.6
Thailand	-7.2	-13.9	-19.4	-2.1	-1.0	10.3

Source: IMF, *International Financial Statistics*, Washington D.C.: International Monetary Fund, 2000.

However, the type of commodity being produced and exported matters as far as the impact of the crisis is concerned. If a country produces a large proportion of its exports in the form of intermediate goods, then the impact of the crisis is much less severe as these goods are essential in the manufacture of other goods. For example, about 81 percent of Singapore's exports to the region are intermediate goods which are needed to manufacture products for exports to developed markets outside the region. However, the all important non-oil exports and even re-exports were affected by the crisis due to the weak import demand. Not only that exports of goods have been affected, even the exports of services from labor-abundant countries of Indonesia, Thailand and the Philippines to labor-scarce countries of Singapore and Malaysia.

Effect on Imports of Goods and Services

As exchange rate depreciates, imports become more expensive. This, combined with falling incomes, reduced the demand for imported goods by Southeast Asian countries as shown in Table 10 particularly during the first two quarters of 1998. The US trade data showed the substantial state-by-state picture of the value of the Asian marketplace to American exports in which thirty-percent of US exports went to Asia. Among eight states,

California, Washington and Oregon exported more than 50 per cent to Asia. US export sales to the hard-hit region fell by 11.5 per cent in the first quarter of 1998.[38] In Europe, Asia's financial crisis started to affect Europe's exports from heavy machinery to telephones inducing further unemployment.[39]

Table 10 Southeast Asia's Global Imports, (Quarterly Changes, %)

	1997Q3	1997Q4	1998Q1	1998Q2	1998Q3	1998Q4
Indonesia	4.9	-0.7	-10.0	-1.0	7.1	-1.4
Malaysia	0.9	-1.4	-12.0	-0.9	3.3	5.2
Philippines	12.8	2.6	-4.5	-0.4	11.5	3.2
Singapore	-0.1	-0.7	-8.9	0.2	-2.1	1.7
Thailand	4.0	1.9	-9.7	-1.7	4.4	2.5

Source: IMF, *Direction of Trade Statistics*, Washington D.C.: International Monetary Fund, 2000.

Even the imports of services including educational expenditures overseas of students from the region have dropped. In the case of Malaysia, prior to the crisis, there were about 50,000 Malaysians who were studying in Britain, the US, Australia and the Middle East. In response to the crisis, many universities in Britain had offered assistance to students through reduced tuition fees, reduced accommodation costs, and arranging flexible repayment schemes. Asian students studying abroad were asked to either return home, where educational fees are lower or cut their expenses and look for jobs to supplement their pocket and tuition money. This is particularly so for those Southeast Asian students in Japan where costs are extremely high.

Effect on Trade Balance and Current Account

Despite a lower export growth, some countries in the Southeast Asian region had in fact generated substantial trade surpluses due to cuts in import spending. A trade surplus of US$150 billion was generated jointly by Malaysia, Thailand, Indonesia, the Philippines and South Korea. Thailand's current account went into a substantial surplus throughout 1998, with a cumulated surplus of US$11.7 for the first 10 months. However, it was achieved at a very high cost particularly in terms of a severe economic recession and serious unemployment problems.[40] Malaysia was able to turn around from a current account deficit of RM14 billion in 1997 to about RM20 billion in 1998 as its trade surplus increased from RM11 billion to about RM43 billion.[41] Table 11 shows the improvement in the current account balance of Southeast Asian countries during the 1997-98 period.

[38] The Straits Times, "Billions of $ clients of US States," April 3, 1998, p.8.

[39] The Straits Times, January 21, 1999, p.52.

[40] Sussangkarn Chalongphob, "Thailand: Toward Economic Solvency," Paper presented at the 1999 Regional Outlook Forum, organized by the Institute of Southeast Asian Studies (ISEAS), Singapore, January, 1999.

[41] Zainal Aznam Yusof, "Malaysian Economic Outlook: Moving Towards a Slow Recovery," Paper presented at the 1999 Regional Outlook Forum, organized by ISEAS, Singapore, January, 1999, p.15.

Effect on Capital Account

The volatility and weakening of the regional currencies affected foreign investors' confidence. As such, there was massive short-term capital outflows and reduced foreign investments in the region including direct investments. This is shown by a sharp and largest reversal of capital flows from a net private capital inflow of US$97 billion in 1996 to a net private capital outflow of US$12 billion in 1997 for Indonesia, Malaysia, the Philippines, Thailand and South Korea. In East Asia, an aggregate of US$100 billion had flown out in the past 18 months since July 1997. This could be explained by what is known as the "reverse free-rider" behavior, which states that "if an individual investor sees other investors pulling out, that alone is an incentive for him to pull out, irrespective of the merits of the investment process itself."[42]

Table 11. Current Account Balance (% of GDP)

	1996	1997	1998
Indonesia	-3.3	-3.0	3.4
Malaysia	-4.9	-5.1	15.7
Philippines	-4.7	-5.2	2.0
Singapore	15.9	15.8	20.9
Thailand	-7.9	-1.9	12.2

Source: UNCTAD, *Trade and Development Report*, Switzerland: United Nations Conference on Trade and Development, 1999, p.31.

In the case of Southeast Asia, it was estimated that total FDI inflows during the January-June 1998 period was only half of that during the July-December 1997 period. The Singapore government targeted an FDI level of S$7.8 billion in 1998 which was lower than the S$8.5 billion in 1997. Thus far, about $5.7 billion was approved during the January-September 1998 period, with $1.8 billion in the third quarter. Thailand's FDI was expected to hit around US$10 billion in 1998 arising mainly from mergers and acquisitions of Thai firms and from investments in insurance and services. So far, Thailand had around US$7 billion in direct investment inflow during the first ten months of 1998. In the case of Indonesia, the value of foreign investments approved by the government from Jan-March 1998 fell by 22 per cent to US$5.1 billion amid concerns about rising inflation and a contracting economy.

While most of the Asian countries have been experiencing slowdown in FDI inflows, China has certainly benefited. As the second highest recipient of FDI in the world in the last four years, China generated an aggregate of US$27 billion from January-August 1998 and expected to hit US$40 billion by the end of 1998. Investments from Europe had increased by 87 percent and from the United States and Canada, by 19 percent. Taiwan's investments also had increased by a hefty 42 percent at US$695 million during the first six months of 1998. Investments from Southeast Asia had dropped: from Singapore, by 42 percent; from Thailand, by 30 percent; and from Indonesia, by 42 percent. Japanese investments also had fallen by 31 percent during the January-June 1998.

---

[42] See James Dean, "Asia's Financial Crisis...," p.275.

Production Sector

Various components of the aggregate demand were influenced severely by the crisis; namely, private consumption, private investment, government spending, exports and imports. Due to the inflationary pressures brought about by the weakening of the regional currencies and because of the shortage of basic commodities, prices increased significantly during the initial phase of the crisis particularly in response to panic-buying activities in some parts of the region. Thailand did not experience as much severe inflationary pressures as other countries as it has been blessed with abundant agricultural produce. With higher prices and declining incomes, private consumption fell. With massive losses combined with the on-going credit crunch and pessimistic business expectations, private investment was also affected severely. Even the government sector implemented some expenditure-cutting measures which include (i) budget cuts in the Malaysian government expenditure programs for the youth from M$1.2 million in 1997 to M$300,000 in 1998[43] and (ii) cancellation by the Thai government of the agreement for its purchase of F-18 from the United States.

With reduced export and import demand, total demand declined. Production and hence output also fell. Consequently, the rates of growth of real GDP contracted and economic projections were revised a number of times. This was true not only in the case of economies in Southeast Asia but also in other parts of the world as shown in Table 12. Among ASEAN, Indonesia was the worst hit with a growth contraction of real GDP by 13.7 per cent in 1998. This was followed by Thailand (-7.8 per cent) and Malaysia (-6.7 per cent). Singapore's growth estimate was between 0.5 per cent to 1.0 per cent, but actually grew by a modest 1.5 per cent. Other Asian economies also contracted in 1998; namely, South Korea (-5.6 per cent), Hong Kong (-5.1 per cent) and Japan (-2.8 per cent).

Table 12. Real GDP Growth Rates, in %

	1997	1998 Final Forecast	1998 Actual	1999 Forecast*
Indonesia	4.9	- 13.0	- 13.7	- 1.0 to +1.0
Malaysia	7.7	– 5.0	- 6.7	1.0
Philippines	5.2	- 1.0	- 0.5	2.5
Singapore	7.8	0.5 to 1.0	1.5	-1.0 to +1.0
Thailand	- 0.4	- 8.2	- 7.8	1.0
Japan	2.5	- 2.5	- 2.8	0.5
China	8.8	8.0	7.8	7.0
Hongkong	5.3	- 5.0	- 5.1	0.5
South Korea	5.5	- 7.8	- 5.6	2.0
Taiwan	6.8	5.0	4.8	4.8

Note. * National government forecasts, Source: Straits Times (Various issues), Sussangkarn Chalongphob, "Thailand: Toward Economic Solvency"; Zainal Aznam Yusof, "Malaysian Economic Outlook: Moving Towards a Slow Recovery"; Hadi Soesastro, "The Indonesian Economy under Habibie," Regional Outlook Forum, organized by ISEAS, Singapore, January 1999; and ADB Asian Development Outlook, Manila: Asian Development Bank, 1999.

[43] The Straits Times, January 20, 1998, p.27.

The Philippine economy posted a much lower contraction of 0.5 per cent and hence was not as severely affected as other Asian economies due to the following factors. First, the Philippine monetary authorities had implemented banking and financial reforms following the severe economic crisis in the early 1980s. Financial reforms commenced in the early 1980s and continued in the 1990s. These reforms include strengthening prudential regulations in relation to minimum capitalization requirements, increasing compliance with with the minimum capital to risk asset ratio, the single borrower limit, the limit on DOSRI loans, stipulations regarding interlocking directorships and management, making provisions for loan losses or doubtful accounts and reviewing the bailout policy for problematic banks, rehabilitation of the Central Bank, increasing bank's capitalization, and unification of the Manila and Makati exchanges and liberalization of foreign investment and foreign exchange transactions[44] Because of these reforms, authorities were in a better position to handle the crisis by lowering interest rates and a moderate rebound of the peso.

Second, the Philippine economy, with a low base growth, did not experience the high-growth phenomenon experienced by other Southeast Asian economies. It expanded only by 2.1 percent during the 1980s and by 2.8 percent during the 1991-96 period while the other economies grew by some 6 to 8 percent during the same period. Third, exports and private consumption remained high and helped offset the fall in private investment Philippine merchandise exports rose by 15-20 percent since much of these exports go to the United States which has had a strong economy.[45] Moreover, in terms of non-merchandise exports, a substantial source of foreign exchange revenues is a record US$6 billion remittance of overseas Filipino workers which have helped the affected families to cope up better with the crisis. Fourth, the Philippine foreign debt exposure has improved by significantly reducing the proportion of short-term private debt as analyzed earlier. Thus, the Philippine economy has proved to be more robust and resilient than Thailand, Indonesia, and South Korea particularly.

Labor Sector

Many workers were retrenched and some contracts were not been renewed. Unemployment increased. Indonesia has had the largest and fastest growing number of unemployed workers due to bankruptcies, closures, mergers and credit crunch. A case in point was highlighted in a *Far Eastern Economic Review* article depicting the sad plight of Sugiyanto:

> In mid-October (1997), 21 year old Sugiyanto was still swinging a shovel at a Jakarta construction site. Six months earlier he had made a personal pilgrimage by overnight bus to the capital from the village of Banjarjo in central Java. "On TV, it looked so easy to

[44] See Ponciano Intal, Jr., Melanie Milo, Celia Reyes and Leilani Basilio, "The Philippines," in *East Asia in Crisis: From Being a Miracle to Needing One*? Ross McLeod and Ross Garnaut (eds), London: Routledge, 1998, p.145-161; Gerardo Sicat, 1998, p.292; Stanley Fischer, "The Asian Crisis: The Beginning of the End?", Speech delivered at the Asia Society, Manila, February 26, 1999, at http://www.asiasociety.org/speeches/fischer.html

[45] R. McKee, 'Philippines could be worse," 2000. http://www.megastories.com/seasia/philippi/philippi2.html

> make money in Jakarta." The money, however, has since dried up. Indonesia's financial crisis has brought many construction projects to a halt. With new jobs scarce, Sugiyanto slunk home to Banjarjo in early November – only to find that his father's rice paddies had dried up too. Months of dry weather have turned the fields in to a parched brown expanse. No work, no monsoon, no escape. For Sugiyanto, there's nothing to do all day but slump over a motorcycle, hoping to cadge a few faded bills in return for offering lifts. There are few takers. Villagers would rather spend their money on water.[46]

In Malaysia, a total of 29,188 workers across the country were retrenched between May 1997 and the middle of March 1998. Most of those affected were in the construction and industrial sectors. There were about 1.3 million registered foreign workers and some 300,000 illegal workers in Malaysia. From 2.6 percent in 1997, Malaysia's unemployment rate was forecast by the Ministry of Finance to rise to about 5 percent in 1998.

In Thailand, about 44,753 workers were dismissed in 1997, with about 70 percent being laid off in the second half of 1997. Total unemployment was forecast to reach 2.2 million in 1998 according to the Thai Farmer Bank Research Center as Thailand shifts from a tight labor market to a surplus of low- and medium-skilled workers.[47] The national labor force survey estimated that Thai's unemployment rate would reach about 5 percent in 1998.[48] The social impacts in Thailand while widespread were not as noticeably severe as in some of the other crisis countries partly due to the agricultural sector which has been able to provide some form of safety net. Many migrants in the urban areas have families back on the farm whom they can turn to. As most Thai farmers own their land, they could reap most of the benefits from the increase in the prices of primary commodities, and could help to cushion the effects on relatives who had lost jobs in the cities and who eventually provided additional assistance in terms of manpower and a redundancy payment of six months wages.

The economy-wide unemployment rate in the Philippines reached some 13.3 per cent in the first quarter of 1998, higher than the 10.7 per cent rate in the same period a year ago. The unemployment rate in the Manila region alone jumped to around 19 per cent. In the whole Philippines, it was estimated that an additional 1 million jobs would be lost as more than 1,000 companies, mostly manufacturing, were closed and as the nation experienced a 9-month drought. From January 1, 1998 to September 30, 1998, some 2,402 enterprises resorted to closure and retrenchment of workers with the bulk of those affected coming from the National Capital Region of Metro Manila.[49]

Even Singapore workers were not spared. While Singapore experienced full employment of around 2 per cent from 1989 to 1997, the unemployment rate rose to 2.3 per cent in October 1998 and was estimated to reach 4-5 per cent in 1998. It was projected that retrenchment in 1998 would reach about 25,000, but it actually hit the 27,000 mark. The issue of cyclical versus structural unemployment was also discussed. Weak demand results in a cyclical unemployment. But with the intended shift towards a knowledge-based economy, structural unemployment arises as some 600,000 workers, mostly aged above 40, have lower

[46] See Margot Cohen, *Far Eastern Economic Review,* December 25, 1997, as cited in World Bank, *East Asia: The Road to Recovery,* Washington D.C.: World Bank, p.1.

[47] Chalamwong Yongyuth, "Economic Crisis, International Migration and the Labor Market in Thailand," *TDRI Quarterly Review.* Vol.13, No.1, 1998, p.14.

[48] Sussangkarn Chalongphob, "Thailand: Toward Economic Solvency…," 1999.

[49] Mario Lamberte and Josef Yaf, *Scenarios for Economic Recovery: The Philippines,* Discussion Paper No.99-05, Manila: Philippine Institute for Development Studies, 1999.

education. The difference between Singapore and other Southeast Asian economies is that the Singaporean government has resources to implement a training and re-training manpower program to ensure that workers' skills be upgraded and continued to be employable. There are much less opportunities for other ASEAN governments to follow Singapore's policy as they have less resources to work with.

What about the plight of foreign workers in Southeast Asia? Thailand, for example, reported that it would deport 300,000 foreign factory workers as part of a plan to repatriate one million illegal migrants (mostly from Myanmar) to make the jobs available for the Thais. Under the plan, employers of illegal workers would be given 45 days to prepare their repatriation, otherwise legal action would be taken against the employers [50] At least 2 million jobs were expected to be lost. In some other countries, a number of workers and expatriates had to return home as their contracts were not renewed or as a result of the restructuring and downsizing activities taking place in many companies. Some decided to look for other jobs or remained in their jobs but at less favorable terms including reduced wages and benefits. In some countries, while prices increased markedly due to hefty devaluation, lowering of nominal wages would lead to a reduction in the purchasing power of workers.

Financial Sector

The crisis has exposed the weaknesses of banking and financial sector as most banks and finance companies had massive amounts of non-performing loans. In Malaysia, the net non-performing loans (NPLs) of the banking system, on the basis of the 6-month criteria, decreased from 8.9 percent as at end-June 1998 to 8.1 percent as at end-September 1998. Based on a 3-month criterion, NPL increased to 12.8 percent. Standard and Poor estimated that it would reach 32 per cent of total loans in 1999. For Thai banks, the ratio of NPLs to total lending rose from 29.4 percent in 1998Q1 to 46 percent in October 1998 while the corresponding ratios for finance companies were 43.8 percent and 63.6 percent, respectively.

In Singapore, the Deputy Prime Minister announced to the Parliament in February 1998 that the regional exposure of domestic banks "was not alarmingly high" and that local banks had made provisions for their regional loans.[51] It was also reported that the six local banking groups exposure to the five worst hit economies reached some 17 per cent or S$5.9 billion of their loans as at August 1998, but was only 2.7 per cent of total loans. While housing loans in Singapore was valued at S$10.4 billion in 1985, it expanded to S$64 billion in March 1998. The total exposure of financial institutions such as the Housing Development Board and the Central Provident Fund reached some S$140 billion, out of which some S$25 billion was granted by the banks to building and construction industry.

As analyzed in the first section, the massive expansion of domestic credit prior to the crisis enabled both individuals and firms to borrow heavily and invest the proceeds of their loans in non-productive and speculative projects including real estate and construction business. The consequent massive losses of banks and finance companies resulted in their closures and mergers. For example, in Thailand, 56 finance companies were closed towards the end of 1997. This was reminiscent of the closure of 24 finance and security companies in

[50] The Straits Times, January 20, 1998, p.23.
[51] Business Times, February 20, 1998.

1983 arising from the financial crisis experienced by the Thai economy in the early 1980s due to poor managerial practices accompanied by inadequate regulations and supervision of financial institutions.[52] In 1998, four commercial banks were taken over by the state due to bad loan portfolios. The commercial banks need to raise 200 billion baht (S$8.3 billion). However, because of poor credit ratings, it had become difficult for the Thai banks to raise new capital. Thailand's five biggest banks had their credit ratings cut by Moody's Investors. These banks were Bangkok Bank, Krung Thai Bank, Thai Farmers Bank, Siam Commercial Bank, and Bank Ayudhya. The downgrading affected US$4.4 billion of outstanding debt.[53]

The stock markets also bore the brunt of the crisis because of the drastic decline in the stock prices which in turn led to the shrinking of people's wealth. For example, in Malaysia, between July 1997 and mid-January 1998, the all-ordinaries index of the Kuala Lumpur Stock Exchange fell by over 65 percent, whipping off almost US$225 billion of share values, the biggest stock market plunge among the crisis countries.[54] In the case of Singapore, the stock market price index, which rose by some 145 percent during 1990-96, had fallen by more than 60 percent off its peak by the third quarter of 1998, reflecting a serious erosion of investor confidence.[55]

Moreover, the massive losses of international banks with large exposure in the region have contributed to the shortage of foreign loans in the region. For example, Japanese banks were the biggest losers in the Asia-Oceania region for a combined net loss of US$36.8 billion from US$2.56 billion a year ago.[56] Bad loans of Japanese banks reached an aggregate of US$600 billion since the 1980s. The substantial exposure of Japanese banks in non-performing loans or bad loans is indeed worrisome and would certainly lead to credit squeeze in the region. The social unrest and political instability in some parts of the region had added to the lack of financial capital.

CONCLUSION

In this chapter, we identified the conditions which existed before the crisis and which contributed to the crisis. These include rising income expectations which had stimulated consumption and investment spending, huge current account deficits largely due to private sector deficits; serious external debt problems arising from higher proportion of short-term commercial loans; and rapid domestic credit creation which was due to massive capital inflows; and higher per capita savings. We also analyzed the severe consequences of the economic crisis including weaker domestic currencies, rising current account surpluses (due to reduced import spending combined with weaker exports), massive short-term capital outflows, reduced foreign direct investments, output contraction, massive unemployment as

[52] Barry Johnston, "Distressed Financial Institutions in Thailand: Structural Weaknesses, Support Operations and Economic Consequences," in Sundararajan V and Tomas Balino (eds), *Banking and Crisis: Cases and Issues*, Washington DC: IMF, p.234.

[53] The Straits Times, April 1, 1998, p.6.

[54] Prema-chandra Athukorala, "Swimming against the Tide: Crisis Management in Malaysia," *ASEAN Economic Bulletin,* Vol.15, No.3, 1998, p.282.

[55] Siow Yue Chia, "The Asian Financial Crisis: Singapore's Experience and Response," *ASEAN Economic Bulletin,* Vol.15, No.3, 1998, p.302.

[56] Asiaweek, September 11, 1998, p.83.

well as closures and mergers of banks and finance companies. The severity of the impact, however, varies across the crisis-hit countries with Indonesia and Thailand being the most severely affected, and Singapore, the least.

QUESTIONS FOR DISCUSSION

1. What has caused the 1997/98 economic crisis in Southeast Asia?
2. The 1997/98 crisis had devastating consequences on the different sectors of the economy. Some sectors were hit more than others. Discuss.
3. On the one hand, the rapid economic growth experienced by the Southeast Asian economies, particularly during the past three decades and a half prior to the 1997/98 crisis, could have not taken place had they not depended on developed countries particularly Japan, the United States and the EU for trade, investments, loans, technology and aid. On the other hand, it is this dependence on developed countries that contributed significantly to the crisis. Do you agree or disagree with these statements? Explain.

Suggested Materials for Case Studies

Asia

Lim, Linda Y.C., 1998, "Whose 'Model' Failed? Implications of the Asian Economic Crisis," *Washington Quarterly,* Vol.21, No.3, pp.25-36.

Malaysia

Jomo K.S., 1998, "Financial Liberalization, Crises and Malaysian Policy Responses," *World Development,* Vol.26, No.8, pp.1563-1574.

Philippines

Lim, Joseph, 2000, "The Effects of the East Asian Crisis on the Employment of Women and Men: The Philippine Case," *World Development,* Vol.28, No.7, pp.1285-1306.

REFERENCES

Adelman, Irma and Yeldan, Erinc, 2000, "The Minimal Conditions for a Financial Crisis: a Multiregional Intertemporal CGE model of the Asian Crisis," *World Development,* Vol.28, No.6, pp.1087-1100.

Asian Development Bank, 1999, *Asian Development Outlook*, New York: Oxford University Press for ADB.

Asian Development Bank, Various Issues, *Key Indicators for Asian and Pacific Developing Countries,* New York: Oxford University Press.

Asiaweek, September 11, 1998, p.3.

Athukorala, Prema-Chandra, 1998, "Swimming against the Tide: Crisis Management in Malaysia," *ASEAN Economic Bulletin,* Vol.15, No.3, pp.281-289.

Baer, Werner; Miles, William and Moran, Allen, 1999, "The End of the Asian Myth: Why were the Experts Fooled?" *World Development,* Vol.27, No.10, pp.1735-1747.

Bank Negara Malaysia, 1998, *The East Asian Crisis – Causes, Policy responses, Lessons and Issues.* Group of 15 Working Paper No.4, Switzerland.

Bhanupong, Nidhiprabha, 1998, "Economic Crises and the Debt-Deflation Episode in Thailand," *Asean Economic Bulletin,* Vol.15, No.3, pp.309-318.

Bird, Graham and A. Milne, 1999, "Miracle to Meltdown: a Pathology of the East Asian Crisis," *Third World Quarterly,* Vol.20, No.2, pp. 421-437.

Chalongphob, Sussangkarn, 1999, "Thailand: Toward Economic Solvency," paper presented at the 1999 Regional Outlook Forum, organized by the Institute of Southeast Asian Studies (ISEAS), Singapore, January.

Chang, Ha-Joon, 2000, "The Hazard of Moral Hazard: Untangling the Asian Crisis," *World Development,* Vol.28, No.4, pp.775-788.

Chia, Siow Yue, 1998, "The Asian Financial Crisis: Singapore's Experience and Response," *ASEAN Economic Bulletin,* Vol.15, No.3, pp.297-308.

Cohen, Margot Cohen, *Far Eastern Economic Review,* December 25, 1997, as cited in World Bank, *East Asia: The Road to Recovery,* Washington D.C.: World Bank, p.1.

Corsetti, Giancarlo, Paolo Pesenti, and Nouriel Roubini, 1999, "What Caused the Asian Currency and Financial Crisis?" *Japan and the World Economy*, Vol.11, No.3, pp.303-373.

Dean, James, 1998, "Asia's Financial Crisis in Historical Perspective," *Journal of the Asia Pacific Economy,* Vol.3, No.3, pp.267-283.

Dufey, Gunter, 1999, " Asian Financial Markets: A Pedagogic Note," *Journal of Asian Business.* Vol.15, No.1, pp.65-71.

Frankel, Jeffrey, 1998, "The Asian Model, the Miracle, the Crisis and the Fund," A speech delivered at the US International Trade Commission, April 16.

Hadi, Soesastro, 1999, "The Indonesian Economy under Habibie," paper presented at the 1999 Regional Outlook Forum, organized by ISEAS, Singapore, January.

Hesse, Helmut and Auria, Laura, 1998, "The Financial Crisis in Southeast Asia: Causes and Effects on the Global Economy," *Economics,* Vol.57.

Hesse, Helmut and Laura Auria, 1998, "The Financial Crisis in Southeast Asia: Causes and Effects on the Global Economy," *Economics.* A Biannual Collection of Recent German Studies, Tübingen: Institut für Wissenschaftliche Zusammearbeit, Vol. 57, pp. 45-70.

Hill, Hal, 1998, "Southeast Asia's Economic Crisis: Origins, Lessons and the Way Forward", Paper presented at the ISEAS 30th anniversary conference: Southeast Asia in the 21st Century, Singapore, July 30- August 1.

Intal, Ponciano Jr, Melanie Milo, Celia Reyes and Leilani Basilio, 1998, "The Philippines," in *East Asia in Crisis: From Being a Miracle to Needing One*? in Ross. H. McLeod and R Garnaut (eds.), London: Routledge, pp.145-161.

International Monetary Fund, Various Issues, *International Financial Statistics,* Washington DC.: IMF.

Johnston, Barry, 1991, "Distressed Financial Institutions in Thailand: Structural Weaknesses, Support Operations and Economic Consequences," in Sundararajan V. and Balino, T. (eds), *Banking and Crisis: Cases and Issues,* Washington DC: IMF.

Kim, Youn-Suk and Hyeng Keun Koo, 1999, "Asia's Contagious Financial Crisis and its Impact on Korea," *Journal of Asian Economics,* Vol.10, No.1, pp.111-121.

Krugman, Paul, 1994, "The Myth of Asia's Miracle," *Foreign Affairs*, Vol.73, No.6, pp. 62-78.

Krugman, Paul, 1997, "What Ever Happened to the Asian Miracle?" *Fortune,* August 18, p.12

Lamberte, Mario and Josef Yaf, 1999, *Scenarios for Economic Recovery: The Philippines.* Discussion Paper No.99-05. Manila: Philippine Institute for Development Studies.

Lim, Linda Y.C., 1998, "Whose Model Failed? Implications of the Asian Economic Crisis," *The Washington Quarterly,* Vol.21, No.3, pp.25-36.

MacIntryre, Andrew, 1998, "Political Institutions and the Economic Crisis in Thailand and Indonesia," *ASEAN Economic Bulletin,* Vol.15, No.3, pp.362-372.

McKinnon, Ronald and H. Pill, 1998, "International Overborrowing – A Decomposition of Credit and Currency Risk", *World Development.* Vol.26, No.7, pp.1267-1282.

Pakorn, Vichyanond., 1998, "Thailand's Financial Evolution and the 1997 Crisis," Paper presented for the conference, The Miracle Undone: Asia's Financial Crisis, C.I.D.E. Mexico City, February 20.

Radelet, Steven and Jeffrey Sachs, 1998, *The Onset of the East Asian Financial Crisis,* Cambridge: National Bureau of Economic Research.

Radelet, Steven and Jeffrey Sachs, 1998, *The East Asian Financial Crisis: Diagnosis, Remedies and Prospects,* Cambridge: Harvard Institute for International Development.

Rosenberger, Leif Roderick, 1997, "Southeast Asia's Currency Crisis: A Diagnosis and Prescription," *Contemporary Southeast Asia,* Vol.19, No.3, pp.223-251.

Sadli, Mohammad, 1998, "The Indonesian Crisis," *ASEAN Economic Bulletin,* Vol.15, No.3, pp.272-289.

Sicat, Gerardo, 1998, "The Philippine Economy in the Asian Crisis," *ASEAN Economic Bulletin,* Vol.15, No.3, pp.290-296.

The Nation, "Learning from Thailand's Mistakes," November, 17, 1998, p.B1-B2.

The Straits Times, January 20, 1998, p.27 and p.23.

The Straits Times, April 1, 1998, p.6

The Straits Times, "Billions of $ clients of US States," April 3, 1998, p.8.

The Straits Times, January 21, 1999, p.52.

Tower, Ivory, 1997, "Mexico 1994 versus Thailand 1997," *TDRI Quarterly Review,* Vol.12, No.3, pp.9-14.

UNCTAD, 1999, *Trade and Development Report*, Geneva: UNCTAD.

Wade, Robert, 1998, "The Asian Debt-and-Development Crisis of 1997-?: Causes and Consequences," *World Development,* Vol.26, No.8, pp.1535-1553.

World Bank, 1997, *World Development Indicators*, Washington DC: The World Bank.

Yongyuth, Chalamwong, "Economic Crisis, International Migration and the Labor Market in Thailand," *TDRI Quarterly Review.* Vol.13, No.1, pp.12-21.

Zainal A.Y., 1999, "Malaysian Economic Outlook: Moving Towards a Slow Recovery," paper presented at the 1999 Regional Outlook Forum, organized by ISEAS, Singapore, January.

INTERNET SOURCES

Fischer, Stanley, 1999, "The Asian Crisis: the Beginning of the End?", speech delivered at the Asia Society, Manila, February 26, at http://www.asiasociety.org/speeches/fischer.html

McKee, R. 'Philippines could be worse," 2000. http://www.megastories.com/seasia/philippi/philippi2.html

Schwartz, Anna, 1998, "International Financial Crises: Myths and Realities," *The Cato Journal*, Vol.17, No.3. as obtained from [http://www.cato.org/pubs/journal/cj17n3-3.html].

In: Asian Economic and Political Issues, Volume 11
Editor: Harvey E. Roth, pp. 73-95
ISBN: 1-60021-192-5

Chapter 4

CONTEMPORARY MONETARY POLICY AND FINANCIAL SYSTEM ISSUES OF JAPAN

Nobuyoshi Yamori[*]

ABSTRACT

It is well-known internationally that Japan has been experiencing serious economic and financial difficulties since the 1990s. This chapter aims to explain the current important issues regarding the Japanese monetary policy and financial system. Struggling with unprecedented deflation, the Bank of Japan has employed unusual policy tools, such as reducing target interest rates to zero and buying stocks. The financial system of Japan is having trouble with financial intermediation, risk sharing and liquidity services. It is notable that the Japanese financial system is quite different from that of a decade ago. In recent years, the Japanese household and business enterprise sectors as a whole are lenders, and the government and foreign sectors are borrowers. As a result, the business model of Japanese banks during the high growth period when banks collected money from households as deposits and lent it to large enterprises is no longer sustainable. In terms of households' portfolio investments, safe assets such as bank deposits and traditional insurance make up substantial shares and risky assets such as stocks are marginal. A bank-centered financial system like Japan's faces financial difficulties when the risk taking ability of financial institutions decreases, which actually occurred due to the huge non-performing loans of the 1990's. The government initiated the Japanese Big Bang to vitalize the financial market in Japan, but a satisfactory outcome has yet to be seen.

1. INTRODUCTION

This chapter discusses the current features of the Japanese monetary policy and financial system. The author believes that understanding the contemporary Japanese financial situation

[*] Nobuyoshi Yamori, Professor, Graduate School of Economics; Nagoya University; Furocho Chikusa-Ku Nagoya Aichi 464-8601 Japan; e-mail: yamori@soec.nagoya-u.ac.jp

is of interest to international readers for the following reasons. First, although Japanese economy had experienced serious economic difficulties in the 1990s, it is still the second largest economy in the world, preceded only by the United States[1]. Therefore, the performance of the Japanese economy significantly affects the world economy, particularly Asian countries. Second, Japan is said to be the first country to struggle with prolonged deflation. With the end of Cold War, many countries are facing deflationary pressures nowadays. Therefore, how the Bank of Japan has conducted its monetary policy in the deflationary economy is an example for all central bankers and those interested in monetary policy. Third, Japan, as well as many countries, experienced financial crises in the 1990s. Unfortunately, Japan's non-performing loans were exceptionally large. For example, Posen (2000) pointed out that the costs assumed by U.S. taxpayers in the SandL crises were about 3% of the U.S. GDP, while the expenses incurred in connection with non-performing loans in Japanese banks are 15% of the Japanese GDP. Therefore, understanding what caused the disastrous financial situation in Japan and how Japan has tried to solve the financial crises is instructive for countries wishing to avoid these problems and those who suffer from similar problems[2].

This chapter is organized as follows. Section 2 explains the Japanese macro economic performance since the burst of the bubble (i.e., in the 1990s). Section 3 provides an explanation on how the Bank of Japan conducted its monetary policy to combat deflation. Section 4 gives an overview of the Japanese financial system and Section 5 explains the deregulation of Japanese financial markets, namely the "Japanese Big Bang". Section 6 discusses banking issues in detail. Finally, Section 7 concludes this chapter.

2. The Lost Decade

After the collapse of the economic bubble, the Japanese economy remained in a prolonged recession and the term "the lost decade" took root. Here, I would like to examine the macroeconomic condition in Japan during the 1990s, focusing on the slowdown in GDP growth, developments in deflation, and the decline in asset values.

2.1. Stagnation of the Economy

GDP (gross domestic product) is the most basic indicator of economic activity. Figure 1 shows the real GDP growth over the last 20 years or so. The growth rate, which was approx. 3% in the early 1980s, reached a record high of 6.8% in 1988 during the economic bubble. But since 1990, the economic growth rate declined significantly, dwindling to almost nil in 1993. Though the economy showed a limited recovery tendency in 1995 and 1996, it lost momentum in 1997 and grew at a negative rate in 1998 (-1.1%). The fiscal tightening program implemented by the Hashimoto Cabinet that included raising of the consumption tax

[1] According to OECD (February 2005), Gross Domestic Product at current prices and exchange rates for 2004 of the United States is 11.7 trillion dollars. Japan's GDP for 2004 is 4.7 trillion dollars, followed by Germany (2.7 trillion dollars), United Kingdom (2.1 trillion dollars), France (2.0 trillion dollars), and Italy (1.7 trillion dollars).

[2] Actually, the Japanese financial crisis has been examined by many authors, such as Hoshi and Kashyap (2000).

rate and increasing medical costs placed on the people is generally cited as a major factor of the economic slowdown in 1997.

Since then, although the growth rate perked up due to the "IT boom" in 2000, it fell into the negative territory again in 2002 with its rebound. As a result of such low-rate growth, when the real GDP in 1983, 1993 and 2003, is compared, it can be noted that it increased 1.43 times from 1983 to 1993, but increased only 1.13 times from 1993 to 2003.

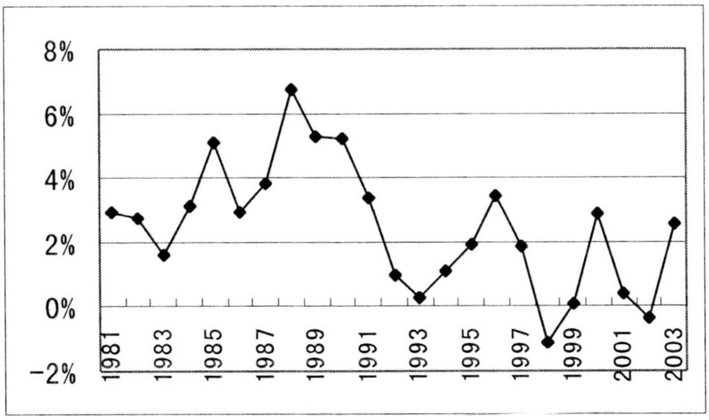

Note: Real GDP based on the 1995 standards.
Source: Economic and Social Research Institute, Cabinet Office, Government of Japan

Figure 1. Real GDP Growth Rate

2.2. Trends in Price Levels

Standard price indices currently used in Japan include the Consumer Price Index (CPI), the Corporate Goods Price Index (CGPI; formerly known as "Wholesale Price Index"), and the GDP Deflator. Figure 2 shows recent trends in the CPI and CGPI. A considerable difference between the movements of these two figures can be seen. However, by the beginning of the 1990s, a deflationary trend (in this figure, results with negative values) is evident by any indicator. For example, if we compare CGPI in 1990 and in 2003, we can see prices fell approx. 13%. Prices appear to have increased in 1989 and 1997 as the price of goods and services were increased to include the introduction of the consumption tax and the increase in the tax rate (from 3% to 5%).

2.3. Depressed Asset Prices

Representative examples of asset prices are the price of land and the price of stocks. The price of these assets experienced a substantial decline in the 1990s.

Major stock price indices in Japan include the Tokyo Stock Exchange Stock Price Index (TOPIX) and the Nikkei Stock Average. TOPIX is calculated from all stocks listed on Section 1 of the Tokyo Stock Exchange weighted against the number of listed stocks. On the other hand, Nikkei Stock Average is the arithmetical stock price average of 225 stocks chosen and calculated by Nihon Keizai Shimbun Inc., from companies listed in the TSE Section 1 regardless of company size.

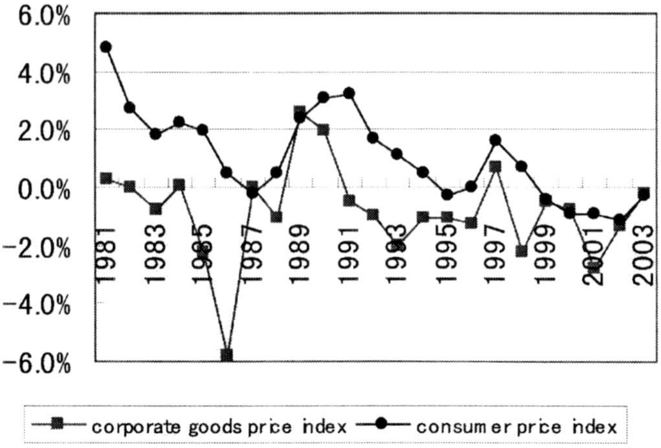

Source: CGPI from Bank of Japan; CPI from Ministry of Internal Affairs and Communications

Figure 2. The Rate of Price Fluctuation

Figure 3 shows the historical movements of the Nikkei Stock Average. The stock prices started to rise steeply in or around 1986, and, at the end of 1989, almost reached JPY40,000. Such ballooning in the price of stocks was a symbolic phenomenon of the bubble economy. By the start of the 1990s, the Nikkei Stock Average started to decline considerably, and in March 2003, it fell below JPY8000. This means the value of stocks bought at the end of 1989 dropped down to approx. one-fifth of the original value (on average).

Now, let us examine the land prices. Land transactions are not so frequently conducted as stock transactions, and no two pieces of land are under identical conditions, so it is difficult to demand an average land price. In Japan, major land price statistics include the official announcement of land prices (the Land, Infrastructure and Transportation Ministry announces the land price of surveyed areas on January 1st, each year), the prefectural land price survey (prefectures announce the land price of surveyed areas July 1st, each year) and the Japan Real Estate Institute's Urban Land Price Index.

Figure 4 shows fluctuations in the Urban Land Price Index. From 1987 to 1990, across the country, the commercial land price increased by more than 10% each year. However, in 1992, it began to recede and has remained stagnant. For example, the average commercial land price decreased approx. one-third nationwide from FY1990 to FY2003, and in FY2003, land price reached approx. the same level as 30 years ago (i.e., FY1972).

In Japan, prior to the 1990s, land prices never declined except for during the economic chaos caused by the first Oil Crisis (1974). Thus, many people acted on the premise that land prices would increase ("the myth of ever-higher land prices") and the decline of land prices during the 1990s had a greater-than-expected negative impact on the economy. In particular, financial institutions which were overly dependent on land-collateral loans could not fully recover funds from the sale of land pledged as security, and suffered losses due to the disposal of bad debts[3].

Note: Nikkei Stock Average 225's Performance.

Figure 3. Stock Price Performance

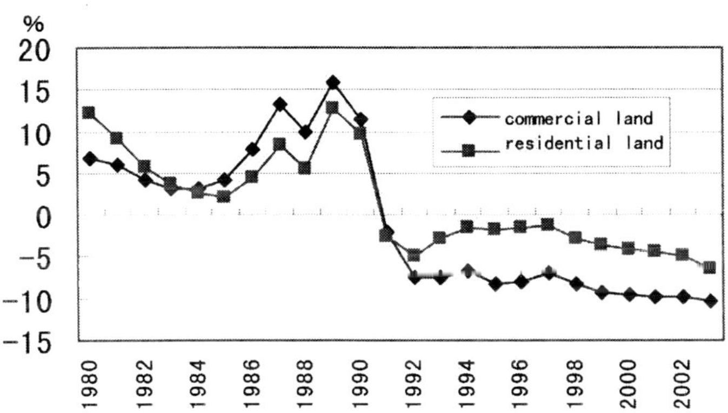

Source: Japan Real Estate Institute.

Figure 4. Fluctuation in Land Prices

The price of these assets went largely unnoticed in the monetary policy until the 1990s. In particular, as seen in Figure 2, commodity prices were quite stable during the "economic bubble" in late 1980s, and monetary tightening was not considered necessary. However, since the prices of stocks and land rose steeply during this period, as shown in Figures 3 and 4, the dominant opinion today is that if the Bank of Japan paid sufficient attention to the escalating asset prices and implemented a monetary policy in late 1980s, the economic bubble would not

[3] Krainer et al.(2004) examining Japanese land prices.

have become so inflated, and damage from the burst of the economic bubble in the 1990s could have been reduced[4].

3. Japanese Monetary Policy Since the 1990's: How Did It Respond to Deflation?

3.1. Official Rate Policy

Table 1 shows changes in the official discount rate since 1987[5]. 1987 marked the then-current historical low of 2.5%. Then, in response to overheated asset prices, the official discount rate was raised from 2.5% to 6%, in the span of one year and three months, from May 1989 to August 1990. Since 1991, the official discount rate was reduced again in response to the slowing of the economy and dropped to 0.5% in 1995 without achieving economic recovery.

In February 2001, the official discount rate was reduced to 0.35% and the "supplementary lending scheme (commonly known as Lombard-type lending)" was created and implemented in March 2001. In Lombard-type lending, any financial institution which can provide security (e.g., governmental bonds and quality corporate debentures) can borrow funds from the Bank of Japan at the official rate. Therefore, if the call rate is likely to exceed the official discount rate, it will be more favorable for banks to borrow funds from the Bank of Japan. In other words, as the official discount rate sets the upper limit of the call rate, banks are no longer concerned about a spike in interest rates.

Table 1. Changes in the Official Discount Rate by Date

2/23/1987	2.5%	7/27/1992	3.25
5/31/1989	3.25	2/4/1993	2.5
10/11/1989	3.75	9/21/1993	1.75
12/25/1989	4.25	4/14/1995	1
3/20/1990	5.25	9/8/1995	0.5
8/30/1990	6	1/4/2001	0.5
7/1/1991	5.5	2/13/2001	0.35
11/14/1991	5	3/1/2001	0.25
12/30/1991	4.5	9/19/2001	0.1
4/1/1992	3.75		

Note: Prior to January 2001, the rate for discount of commercial bills and the lending rate of the loans secured by government bonds or similar instruments; After January 2001, the basic discount rate and the basic lending rate.

In 1996, the Bank of Japan announced its decision not to use BOJ lending that applies the official discount rate as a monetary tool. Since the Lombard-type lending was introduced,

4 For example, Bernanke (2000) and Krugman (1999) criticized the Bank of Japan.

5 See Cargil et al. (1997) regarding the Japanese monetary policy before the mid 1990s.

traditional BOJ lending, where the timing and the amount of the loan is determined by the Bank of Japan, became unavailable.

Then in September 2001, in order to deter the negative impact of the terrorist attacks that occurred in the US, the official discount rate was reduced to 0.1%.

3.2. Zero Interest-Rate Policy

As with other developed countries, the main instrument for monetary policy in present Japan is the open market operation. To achieve policy objectives, the Bank of Japan conducts daily monetary control, keeping a close watch on the short-term money rate shaped by the short-term financial market (specifically, the overnight call rate of the unsecured call market).

In September 1998, the Policy Board / Monetary Policy Meeting, the supreme decision-making body of the Bank of Japan, decided to "encourage the unsecured call rate to shift to an average of approx. 0.25%". However, since goals for economic recovery had not been established, in February 1999, an "unsecured call rate around 0.15% was initially targeted and then, in line with market conditions, further decline would be steadily promoted". This is called the zero interest-rate policy as a massive amount of funds were supplied (buying operation) and the call rate was reduced to virtually zero percent. At the same time, they also announced a plan to continue the zero interest-rate policy until "the situation allows for the prospect of the elimination of deflationary concern".

A major turning point was reached in August 2000. Most of the Policy Board members thought "the prospect of the elimination of deflationary concern can be expected" and decided to "increase the unsecured call rate to an approx. average of 0.25%". But then, the participants from the Ministry of Finance and the Economic Planning Agency insisted that "it is still too early to lift the zero interest-rate policy at this time", and requested a postponement of the vote at the Policy Board until the next meeting under Article 19 of the Bank of Japan Law. However, the Policy Board turned down the government's request to postpone the vote by a majority (1 vote in favor versus 8 against) and approved lifting of the zero interest-rate policy by a majority (7 votes in favor versus 2 against) .

However, after lifting of the zero interest-rate policy, the economy started to wane again. So, after only six months from the time of raising the rate (i.e., in February 2001), a plan was developed to "promote the unsecured call rate to shift to an approx. average of 0.15%" to return to the zero interest-rate policy.

Reflecting on such policy, the actual changes in the call rates are shown in Figure 5. As seen in the Figure, changes in the call rates were almost in line with the actions of Bank of Japan.

3.3. Quantitative Relaxation

Though the zero interest-rate policy was re-launched, there was a growing awareness that it lacked the strength to hold back deteriorating economic conditions, so the Bank of Japan decided to take further measures to boost the economy at the Policy Board's Monetary Policy Meeting in March 2001. More specifically, the main target of the money market control was changed from the conventional unsecured call rate (overnight) to the balance of current accounts held at the Bank of Japan, and it was decided to "increase the balance of the current accounts held at the Bank of Japan to approx. JPY 5 trillion for the time being (an increase from the previous balance of slightly over JPY 4 trillion by approx. JPY 1 trillion)". This is called quantitative relaxation, as the quantity of money is targeted instead of the interest rate. As deposits in BOJ current accounts carry no interest, it will be more profitable for banks to apply funds to other instruments (i.e., loans and investment in securities) and earn interest. If a large amount of "excess" funds is available, the banks' approach to lending is expected to be more aggressive. In addition, a plan to continue this new approach to control the money markets until CPI's year-on-year rate of increase stabilizes above zero percent was announced.

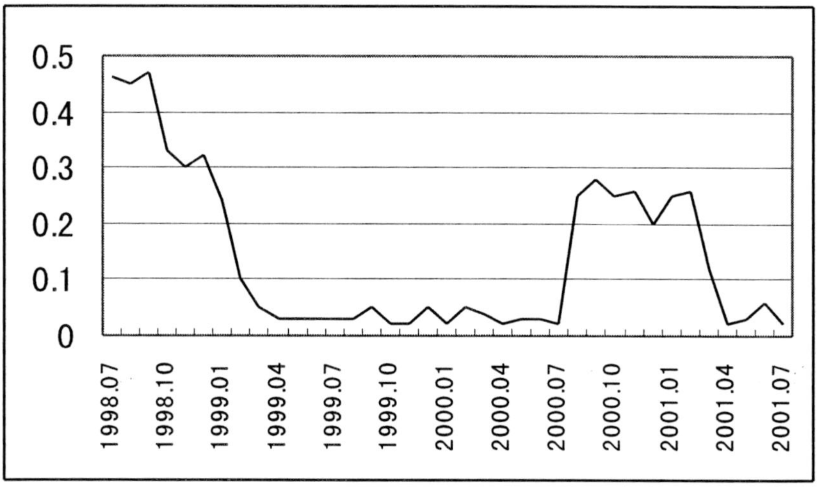

Note: Unsecured overnight rate, which is the policy target rate, is shown above (figures as of the end of the month).

Figure 5. Zero Interest-Rate Policy and Changes in Call Rates

Well, if money is supplied in high volume through quantitative relaxation, the interest rate - the price of money - should decline rapidly. In fact, as a result of this quantitative relaxation, the unsecured call rate started to shift virtually to zero percent. When the interest rate reached zero, the zero interest-rate policy cannot provide further relaxation. So, at that point, it was no longer possible to adopt a policy which targeted the interest rate (to be exact, the nominal interest rate). However, quantitative relaxation could still continue even when the interest rate became zero.

Figure 6 shows changes in the actual balance of BOJ current deposits and the policy objective levels over time. As shown in the Figure, the objective levels were increased many times and reached JPY 30-35 trillion in January 2004. The actual balance of BOJ current deposits increased almost in line with the increase in the target figures. Furthermore, as the legal reserve required for the deposit requirement system was approx. JPY 4 trillion during this period, approx. JPY 20 trillion was held by banks on a voluntary basis (free reserves) in January 2004.

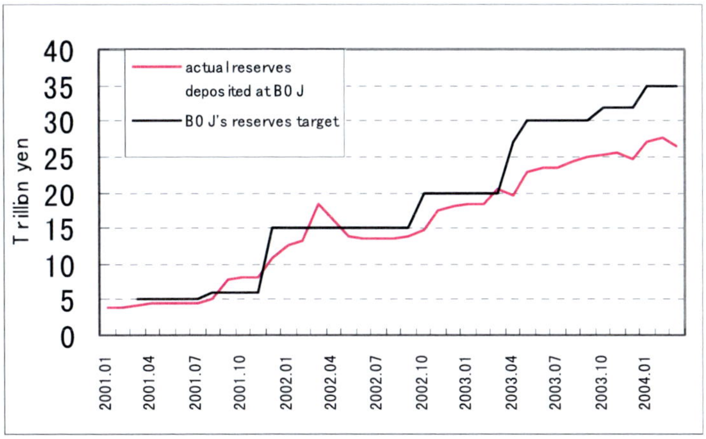

Note: Monthly average balance of BOJ current deposits. When the target level is within a certain range, the maximum value is shown in the graph. For example, the target in January 2004 was JPY30-35 trillion, so is shown as JPY35 trillion in the Figure. Prepared by the author based on the Bank of Japan's materials.

Figure 6. Quantitative Relaxation and BOJ Current Deposits

3.4. Expanding the Range of Assets for Buying Operations

Open-market operations are conducted by trading government bonds and other securities. In this regard, the meaning of supply and absorption of funds varies depending on the type of asset chosen for purchase.

According to the traditional monetary policy standpoint, central banks should provide liquidity in the market without taking credit risk. Therefore, assets for operation were restricted to government bonds and best-rated corporate bonds (and bills). However, as it was not possible to fully address the economic conditions by only buying these types of assets, so buying operations that included financial assets with credit risk (e.g., CPs and asset-backed securities) were launched.

It is worth noting that purchasing asset-backed securities started in July 2003. Asset-backed securities are securities that are backed by one or more assets such as loan receivables. Even if one of those receivables becomes irrevocable, as it is not the only asset which backs the securities, its impact on the asset-backed securities is lessened. The Bank of Japan mainly bought asset-backed securities backed by credited loans from small and medium companies. This scheme is as follows; (1) a bank makes loans to a number of small and medium sized companies, (2) the bank combines these credited loans to issue asset-backed securities, and (3) the Bank of Japan purchases these securities. It is essentially the same as the Bank of Japan making loans to small and medium companies. The Bank of Japan itself admitted that "it is exceptional for a central bank to directly accept credit risk from the private sector"; however, as it was necessary to supplement the financial intermediary function to the dysfunctional financial institution, and this scheme was implemented as a temporary measure, effective until March 2006 . As of the end February 2005, the Bank of Japan holds JPY 241 billion in asset-backed securities.

Furthermore, in September 2002, the Bank of Japan decided to create a stock purchase program exclusively for stocks held by banks, implemented as of November. Specifically, the Bank of Japan purchased the stocks of quality companies with a certain level of credit rating (at least BBB-) at the market price from banks whose stockholding value exceeded core equity capital (Tier 1 of the Basel Accord). The stock purchase program ended in September 2004 and JPY 2,018 billion of stocks were purchased. The Bank of Japan will dispose of the purchased stocks over 10 years from October 2007 to avoid a negative impact on stock prices.

4. Overviews of Japanese Financial System

4.1. Japanese Financial System from the Corporate Financing Structure Standpoint

Before exploring characteristics of the Japanese financial system, I would like to discuss the situation of corporate financing. Table 2 shows the status of Japanese company funding in 5 years increments. First, a significant decrease can be noted in the amount of funds raised. During the "bubble economy" period (1987-1991), the corporate sector raised approx. JPY 120 trillion per year; but recently, it has dropped to approx. one-third. This reflects the weak state of corporate investments.

Second, funds for investment are fully financed through internal funds (i.e., retained earnings and depreciation allowances) and the remaining portion is applied to the repayment of loans and the redemption of corporate bonds. As a result, as seen from Figure 1, under the Japanese financial structure, funds flow from the household and corporate sectors to the government and overseas sectors.

Table 2. Status of the Financing Activities of Business Corporations (JPY in trillions)

Financing		1987-1991	1992-1996	1997-2001
		570	278	198
	Capital Increase	32	11	11
	Corporate Debentures	25	-1	-3
	Long-term Borrowings	129	22	-14
	Short-term Borrowings	80	16	-11
	Earned Surplus	146	29	10
	Depreciation	158	201	205

Note: Figures for all businesses are from the "Financial Statement Statistics of Corporations by Industry", Ministry of Finance.

4.2. Characteristics of the Japanese Financial System from the Households' Invested Assets Standpoint

Next, to examine the characteristics of the financial system from the fund management perspective, the composition of the financial assets held by the household sectors in Japan, the

US and Germany is outlined in Figure 8. The first characteristic of Japanese households is that the percentage of cash and deposits is quite high, and half of the household financial assets are deposited with banks (including the Post Office). In Germany, the percentage of cash and deposits was also relatively high, but the percentage dropped significantly during the 1990s. In contrast, the percentage increased in Japan.

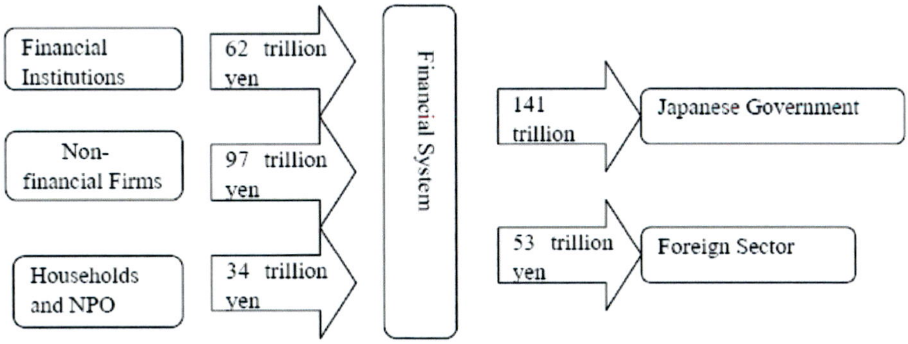

Note: Prepared by the Author based on the Bank of Japan "Flow-of-Funds Accounts". Figures in arrows represent the total financial surplus or deficit during 4 years from FY2000 to FY2003.

Figure 7. Recent Flow of Funds in Japan

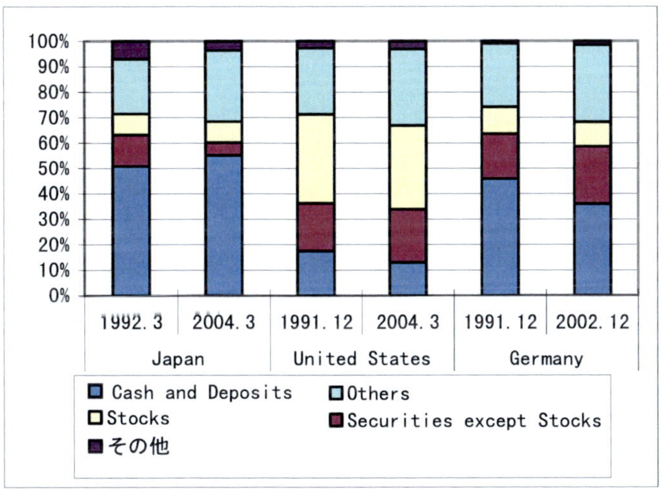

Note: Based on the flow of funds account of each country.

Figure 8. Household Financial Assets in Japan, the US and Germany

Second, capital-safe financial instruments are dominant in Japan. In addition to deposits, since fixed-benefit type products are the core of insurance policies and pension plans, more than 80% of the household assets are defined-capital type financial instruments. In other words, the Japanese household sector bears almost no financial risk. On the contrary, in the US, not only is the percentage of cash and deposits low, but most of insurance policies and pension plans are products without defined benefits or capital safety, including variable policies and 401k plans (defined-contribution pension plans), and the household sector bears significant financial risk.

In Japan, instead of the household sector, financial institutions bear financial risk. Though such exposure to risk worked effectively during the years of steep economic growth in Japan, when financial institutions lose strength and are unable to take risk, the risk-taking capacity of the society as a whole significantly declines. Japan's weakness in this regard was exposed during the 1990s.

4.3. Overview of the Financial Market

The fact that banks are dominant in the Japanese financial system means the securities market is relatively small and weak. However, as evident from the fact NASDAQ and other securities markets supported IT companies, playing a central role in the growth of the US economy during the 1990s, it is necessary to enhance the capabilities of the securities market during times of rapid change (Allen and Gale, 1999; Royama, 2002). In fact, as discussed in Section 5, deregulation (the financial Big Bang) in Japan was promoted to activate the securities market. As a result, on the institutional front, Japanese markets are said to have reached a level comparable to the US and European markets; however, the function of the securities market has yet to be fully realized.

Table 3 outlines the major financial markets in Japan and their sizes. Short-term money markets are markets where funds for a year or less are traded, and are generally classified into interbank markets, which are limited to banks and other financial institutions and the open markets where non-financial companies can participate.

The interbank market, where financial institutions manage their temporary financial surplus or deficit, is the main ground for the Bank of Japan to perform credit control. Among open markets, public and corporate bonds and the TB/FB market are relatively large. The bond loan market is the market where bonds (mainly government bonds) are loaned against cash collateral, and from the bond lender's view, he is a borrower of cash. It is also covered by the Bank of Japan's open market operations and has grown to become a key market for monetary adjustment. Both TBs and FBs, which mean "treasury bills" and "financing bills" respectively, are issued for up to one year for fund management by the government. In the US, the TB and FB markets constitute the core of the short-term financial market and these markets have begun to play a greater role in Japan as well.

In the long-term financial market, funds that mature after one year are traded and generally classified into the bond or stock market. For bonds, the government's budget deficit continues and the amount of outstanding government bonds is ballooning. The stock market includes traditional stock exchanges (e.g., Tokyo Stock Exchange, Osaka Stock Exchange, Nagoya Stock Exchange, etc) and the JASDAQ market operated by the Japan Securities Dealers' Association. Among traditional markets, the Tokyo Stock Exchange Section I maintains the dominant share. The JASDAQ market is a market where stocks of middle-standing companies are traded and had been placed as an OTC market in the past, but became a securities exchange market in 2004. As a result, the companies now can list their shares both on the traditional securities market and the JASDAQ market, and participants can place discretionary orders for trading.

In addition, as part of the financial Big-Bang, in order to provide stock markets for emerging companies, Tokyo Stock Exchange and Osaka Stock Exchange opened new markets called Mothers and NASDAQ Japan (the name was changed to Hercules due to

NASDAQ's withdrawal from Japan), respectively. As the listing criteria of these securities markets for emerging companies are relatively flexible in comparison to those of traditional securities markets, these markets broadened the base for company listings. Furthermore, through the financial Big Bang, securities companies are now allowed to create private securities markets on the Internet.

Table 3. Major Financial Markets in Japan and Their Size

		Balance (Market Capitalization)	(JPY in hundred millions)
Long-Term Financial Markets	Bond Market	Straight Corporate Bonds	624,434
		Straight Government Bonds	5,488,230
	Stock Market	TSE (all companies listed)	3,630,393
		JASDAQ	113,922
Short-Term Financial Markets	Interbank Market	Call	186,529
		Bill	297,900
	Open Market	Public and Corporate Bonds Repurchase Market	178,806
		Public and Corporate Bonds Loan Market	575,097
		CD	302,333
		CP	155,753
		TB/FB	1,267,672
		Tokyo Offshore	398,461

Note: Balance as of the end March 2004. Figures of the balance of the public and corporate bond loan market are figures of bonds loaned.

Source: the Bank of Japan's website, except figures of the interbank market from Tokyo Tanshi's website.

5. Financial System Reforms

5.1. Too Many Regulations in the Financial System

In Japan, strict financial regulations have been implemented, and is sometimes described as including "even how to use chopsticks". Basic pricing rates within the financial system, including banks' deposit rates, securities companies' stock trading commissions, and insurers' premiums, were all controlled. The creation of a new bank, or a new insurance or securities company was rarely approved, except for foreign companies' entering Japan. Also, mutual entry among these 3 financial industries was prohibited. Furthermore, within the banking and insurance industries, the lines of business were regulated in detail. For banks, the regulations allowed long-term credit banks and trust banks to issue bank debentures and conduct the trust businesses exclusively. For insurance companies, mutual enrollment in life and non life insurance companies was prohibited.

These regulations decreased competition among financial institutions and proved quite effective in preventing financial institutions from failing due to competition and filing for bankruptcy. In other words, the result of these policies is that no financial institutions failed for approx. 50 years after the war.

5.2. Background of the Japanese Financial Big Bang

In or around 1980, side effects of overregulation became evident, and due to domestic and international pressures, financial deregulation made gradual progress. However, even in the mid-1990s, the following issues regarding the Japanese financial system remained.

First, the financial and capital markets were hollowing out. "Hollowing out" is where financial activities that should be carried out in Japan are diverted to other countries due to regulation or other factors. For example, the trading of Japanese equity derivatives flourish in the overseas markets, and a large number of foreign companies suspended listing on the Tokyo Stock Exchange. Second, institutional stress of the financial system became evident. Examples to illustrate this include the huge amount of nonperforming loans and the failure of many financial institutions. Third, the country is rapidly aging. For life-after-retirement security, attractive investments for personal financial assets were needed.

Prime Minister Ryutaro Hashimoto felt that gradual deregulation of finances could not solve these problems and that sweeping changes needed to be quickly made, and in November 1996, he directed "financial system reforms" to be made by the ministers concerned. The series of reforms implemented based on his directions are called the Japanese financial Big Bang. "Big Bang" is a scientific term used to describe the huge expansion when the universe began, and in the financial world, it refers to the essential reforms to the securities market conducted in the UK. Hashimoto wanted to carry out a "Japanese version" of these reforms.

5.3. Japanese Financial Big Bang

The Japanese financial Big Bang was aimed at establishing a new, free, fair and global financial system that would be competitive with the New York and London markets. For that purpose, the Financial System Reform Law was enacted in May 1998 and became effective in December of the same year.

Key revisions are summarized as follows: (1) Enhance asset management instruments (the introduction of new investment trust products including company-type mutual funds and privately placed investment trusts, the sale of over-the-counter investment trusts by banks, and the complete liberalization of securities derivatives) ; (2) deregulate price control (complete liberalization of commissions and fees in stock brokerage and, for fire and automobile insurances premiums, the abolishment of the obligation to use premium rates established by insurance rating associations); (3) promote new entries (shifting from a licensing system to a registration system in principle for securities companies; promoting mutual entry among banking, securities and insurance businesses); (4) develop diversified markets (eliminating the obligation to concentrate transactions on securities exchanges, and introducing a private trading system); (5) enhance user protections (improving disclosure; enhancing user protection during failure).

By 2001, most of the planned reforms were completed (see Table 4). However, they do not go far enough to achieve the original goals of reform (i.e., the establishment of a financial system with international competitiveness).

Table 4. Deregulation in the Financial Markets

1993	April	The Financial Institution Reform Act came into effect (establishment of securities and trust banking subsidiaries, regional financial institutions' entry into the trust business, etc)
	June	Complete liberalization of term deposit rates
1994	October	Liberalization of demand deposit rates
1996	November	Prime Minister Hashimoto directed financial system reforms (the financial Big-Bang)
1997	October	Introduction of multiple purpose securities accounts
	December	Banks were allowed to sell investment trusts (initially a shop lending method)
1998	April	Revisions to the foreign exchange law became effective (currency exchange at convenience stores became possible)
	April	Partial liberalization of commissions and fees in stock brokerage
	June	The Financial System Reform Law enacted
	July	Obligatory use of insurance rating organizations was abolished (insurance companies were allowed to individually establish premium rates.)
	December	The Financial System Reform Law comes into effect (core of the financial Big Bang)
1999	May	The nonblank bond issuance law becomes effective (financial service providers can issue bonds for the loan business)
	October	Complete liberalization of commission and fees in stock brokerage
2000	October	Banks' subsidiaries were allowed to enter into the insurance business
2001	January	Complete liberalization for mutual entry between life and nonlife insurers into the third sector
	April	Banks were allowed to sell life insurance products over the counter

Note: Prepared by the author based on FSA's materials

6. Current Banking Issues in Japan

6.1. A Series of Bank Failures

Following the burst of the economic bubble in Japan, a number of banks and corporative financial institutions failed. Beginning with the Hyogo Bank in August 1995 until Chubu Bank in March 2002, 16 banks went bankrupt. To dispose of the failed banks, large sums of money are required. For example, pecuniary donations of more than JPY 3 trillion were provided for the Long-Term Credit Bank of Japan and Nippon Credit Bank. Table 5 shows the list of failed banks and the amount of pecuniary donations from the Deposit Insurance Corporation; by the end of March 2003, pecuniary donations of JPY 17.9 trillion were provided to dispose of failed financial institutions. Essentially, such costs should be covered by the deposit insurance premiums; however, as deposit insurance premiums were far too short to cover the costs, JPY 9.9 trillion of government funds were contributed.

Table 5. Failed Banks and Disposal Costs

Date of Failure	Failed Financial Institution	Pecuniary Donation from Deposit Insurance (JPY in hundred millions)	Date of Failure	Failed Financial Institution	Pecuniary Donation from Deposit Insurance (JPY in hundred millions)
8-30-95	Hyogo Bank	4,730	12-14-98	Nippon Credit Bank	31,414
4-1-96	Taiheiyo Bank	1,170	4-12-99	Kokumin Bank	1,837
11-21-96	Hanwa Bank	806	5-24-99	Kofuku Bank	4,941
10-14-97	Kyoto Kyoei Bank	438	6-14-99	Tokyo Sowa Bank	7,626
11-17-97	Hokkaido Takushoku Bank	17,732	8-9-99	Namihaya Bank	6,526
11-25-97	Tokuyo City Bank	1,238	10-4-99	Niigata Chuo Bank	3,817
5-15-98	Midori Bank	7,711	12-28-2001	Ishikawa Bank	1,809
10-23-98	Long-Term Credit Bank of Japan	32,350	3-8-2002	Chubu Bank	944

Source: Deposit Insurance Corporation.

6.2. Management Integration in Progress

Reorganization among banks that have not gone bankrupt is now underway. In particular, reorganization has been accelerated among city banks that play a central role in the Japanese banking system. City banks are banks based in Tokyo, Osaka and other major cities with nationwide branch networks which mainly trade with large companies. In March 1990, there were 13 city banks, but in March 2003, they were integrated into 5 banking groups. These are called banking groups because they adopted a bank holding company system and have multiple banks as subsidiaries. Mitsubishi Tokyo Financial Group, Mizuho Financial Group, Sumitomo Mitsui Financial Group and UFJ Holdings are called four major banking groups (megabanks). Furthermore, in February 2005, the merger between Mitsubishi Tokyo Financial Group and UFJ Holdings was officially agreed and a banking group with a market capital exceeding JPY 10 trillion will be created (see Figure 9). This new group aspires to become one of the global top 5 by market capitalization by FY2008.

On the other hand, regional financial institutions which are said to have fallen behind major banks in reorganization, have become actively engaged in business consolidation in recent years. Table 6 shows changes in the number of Japanese private-sector financial institutions including major banks, over time. In 10 years, from 1980 to 1990, the number of credit cooperatives decreased considerably, but the number of other financial institutions remained almost unchanged. In the following 10 years from 1990 to 2000, the decrease was most significant for city banks, showing a decline from 13 to 9 (31%). Credit cooperatives decreased by 123 or 30%. Credit associations (or Shinkin Banks), though the reduction rate was not as high, also decreased by 15%. In contrast, the number of regional banks remained unchanged.

Even during the approx. 5 years from March 2000 to January 2005, financial institutions have continued to decrease. The number of city banks further decreased by 2, to almost half of the original number. The second-tier regional banks also decreased by 6 to less than 50. However, a notable feature since 2000 is the significant decrease in the number of credit associations/credit cooperatives. Credit associations decreased by 85 in just 5 years.

The decrease in the number of Japanese financial institutions has been considerable within such a brief period. Furthermore, unlike the US, except for foreign banks and subsidiary banks of financial institutions, there were less than 10 new entrants such as online banks during this period[6].

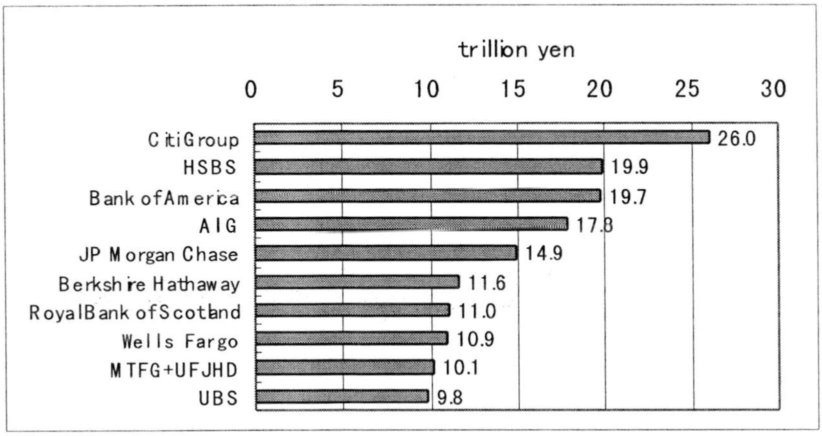

Source: Nihon Keizai Shinbun, February 19, 2005.

Figure 9. Market Capitalization of Major Financial Institutions Worldwide

Table 6. Changes in the Number of Private-Sector Financial Institutions by Business Type over Time

	3/1980	3/1990	3/2000	1/2005
City Banks	13	13	9	7
Regional Banks	63	64	64	64
Second Regional Banks	71	68	54	48
Credit Associations	462	454	386	301
Credit Cooperatives	483	414	291	179

Note: source: Inoue (2003) and materials on Nikkin's website

6 See Yamori et al. (2005) for a detailed analysis of the current situation of new types of banks such as online banks.

6.3. Problems with Non-Performing Loans

The biggest problem faced by Japanese banks is non-performing loans. Non-performing loans are monetary loans and valuable securities for which interest or the principal is not paid as promised. Japanese banks usually take land as a collateral when processing loans, but as the land prices dropped significantly, they cannot recover credited loans by selling the land in lieu.

Figure 10 shows the amount of non-performing loans held by Japanese banks in the Figure, non-performing loans are called Risk Management Loans according to the definition under the Banking Law and the amount of loss incurred to dispose of non-performing loans (loss from the disposal of bad debts). During the peak year, a loss of approx. JPY 15 trillion was incurred, causing continued account deficits (in FY2001, 58 out of 133 banks were in red). Moreover, even though such a huge amount of non-performing loans were written off, it was still hard to decrease the amount of bad debts.

Fortunately, since 2002, supported by the government's financial revitalization program which encouraged major banks to quickly dispose of nonperforming loans, and economic conditions and stock prices heading towards recovery, the balance of non-performing loans decreased significantly. However, the level is still much higher than that of the 1990s, and if economic slowdown occurs again, non-performing loans may increase, so it is still too early to say that the problem of non-performing loans has been solved.

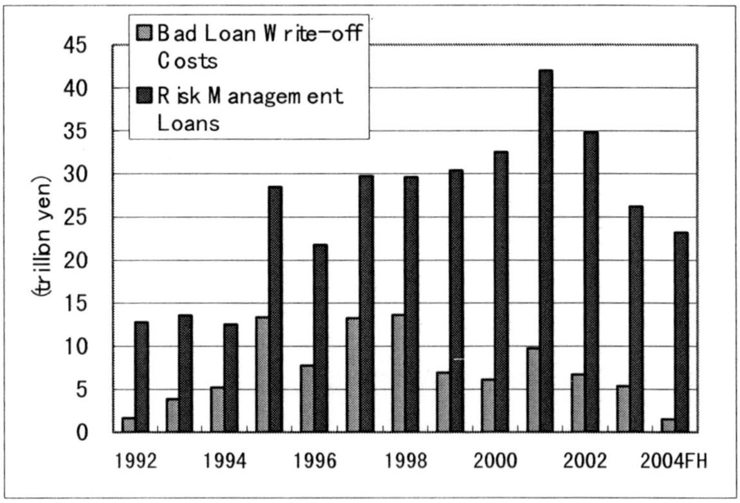

Figure 10. Non-performing Loans and Write-off Costs by Japanese Banks

Note: Figures from FY 1992 to FY1994 cover only major banks (i.e., city bank, long-term credit banks, and trust banks). Figures since FY 1995 cover all banks (i.e., major banks and primary and secondary regional banks). Figures for FY 2004 are until the end of the first half of FY2004.

Source: Financial Services Agency.

6.4. Changes in Main Bank Relationships

One characteristic of the Japanese banking system is the stable long-term relationship between banks and companies (the main bank system). A "main bank" is a bank that fulfills the following conditions: (1) the bank has the largest loan share, (2) the bank is a major shareholder, and (3) directors are dispatched from the bank. Main banks are said to have the following functions (e.g., Horiuchi et al. 1988; Sheard 1990; Hoshi et al. 1990). First, it provides other lenders with information as a key monitor. As corporate financial activities are carried out through the bank account held at the main bank, the main bank can monitor the company on a daily basis. Therefore, other financial institutions can rely on the main bank for monitoring the company. In this way, monitoring costs of the society as a whole can be reduced. Second, it can provide rescue and reorganization assistance. For example, at the outset of a crisis, the main bank develops measures to avoid bankruptcy as the representative of the creditors. From the viewpoint of companies, it serves as a kind of insurance.

However, as the needs of corporate funding changed (in particular, major companies are increasingly less dependent on bank loans for financing) and the soundness of banks deteriorated, so too the relationship with the main bank changed. This is succinctly expressed in the ongoing dissolution of cross stockholdings which served as the symbol of the main bank relationship. Figure 11 shows the changes in the percentage of equity held by stable shareholders over time, and it can be seen that the percentage started to decline rapidly from around 2000. Main factors include the downturn in stocks in the 1990s causing huge losses from equity holdings, and banks and companies developing a strong awareness of stockholding risks, and the enactment of the law limiting bank stockholdings[7].

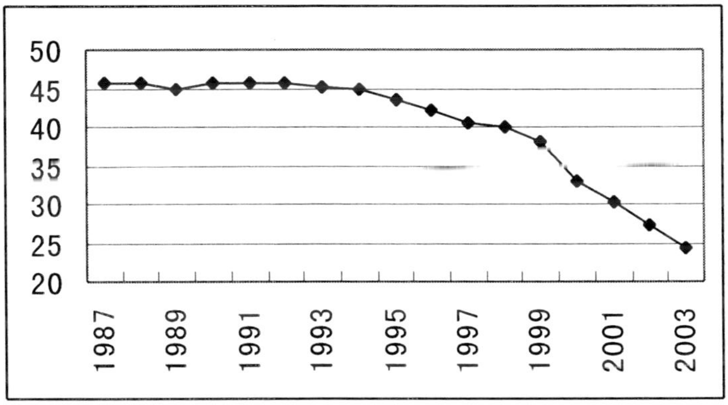

Note: "stable stockholding" means cross stockholdings, stocks held by financial institutions, stocks of financial institutions held by business corporations, and stocks held by affiliate companies.
Source: "Survey on the Status of Cross Stockholding" NLI Research Institute

Figure 11 Changes in the Stable Stockholding Ratio over time.

[7] The law limiting bank stockholdings enacted in 2001, limited the bank stockholdings to up to the amount of their equity capital from the term ending September 2004. As of the end March 2001, the stockholdings of major banks (14 banks) were JPY 32.6 trillion (book value), exceeding their equity capital (JPY 21.8 trillion) by approx. JPY 11 trillion. So, major banks had to sell JPY 10 trillion or more of stocks if equity capital was not increased. For reference, the law was revised in August 2003 and the date of compliance to the regulation was extended from September 2004 to September 2006.

Some positive aspects are expected from the dissolution of cross stockholding, such as more effective investment of assets held and the stabilization of bank and corporate management; however, if there are no buyers of the stocks sold through the dissolution of cross stockholding, a depression in stock prices is a concern. Therefore, the government established the Bank Equity Purchasing Corporation in January 2002 to take over stocks held by banks, and the Bank of Japan started to purchase stocks held by banks in November 2002.

6.5. Need for a New Business Model

Many critics think that the low profitability of Japanese banks is a problem. The major source of profit-making for Japanese banks is the difference between the loan and the deposit rates (deposit-loan interest rate spread). However, the spread is very thin. For example, as shown in Figure 12, the deposit-loan interest rate spread of Japanese banks is slightly less than 2%. In contrast, the US bank spread is nearly 4%. Moreover, since loss incurred by nonperforming loans should be regarded as costs for lending, if the amount is taken into consideration, the deposit-loan interest rate spread remains negative for some years.

In addition, Japanese banks do not earn much income from commissions other than interest rate spreads. Thus, they are not apt to earn profits if they do not increase the amount of loans. However, as seen in Table 2, companies do not only borrow money but also make repayments, so bank profits will dwindle if they rely too heavily on these companies (especially large companies). A new banking business model must be developed.

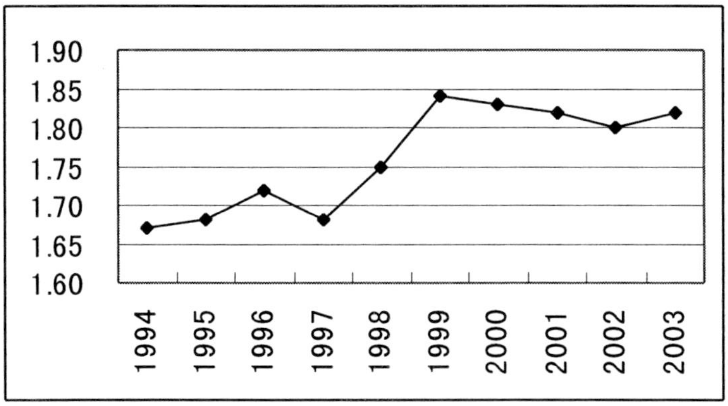

Source: Japanese Bankers Association, *Analysis of Financial Statements of All Banks*, various issues.

Figure 12. Deposit-Loan Interest Rate Spread for Japanese Banks

In this regard, the March-2003 report of the Council on Financial Services, the advisory council at the Financial Services Agency, is suggestive. In this report, titled as "In preparation of the reinforcement of relationship banking", the council recommended that financial institutions, particularly *regional* institutions such as regional banks, Shinkin banks, and credit unions, develop the capability to create loans for regional customers. In other words, the report suggests that regional financial institutions have no choice but to engage in relationship banking; a banking business model that banks provide financial services such as loans to customers using soft information accumulated through its long-term, close relationship with its customers. Of course, the importance of relationships in regional banking services has been well-recognized even before the council's report was published, but the Council on Financial Services emphasized the weak ability of many regional institutions and that financial institutions need to take immediate action to develop their ability for relationship banking.

7. CONCLUSION

This chapter aims to explain the current characteristics and important issues regarding the monetary policy and financial system of Japan. Struggling with the unprecedented deflation, the Bank of Japan has employed unusual policy tools, such as reducing target interest rates to zero and buying stocks.

The financial system of Japan is having trouble with financial intermediation, risk sharing and liquidity services. Regarding the financial system issues, it is notable that the Japanese financial system is quite different from that a decade ago. In recent years, the Japanese household and business enterprise sectors have become lenders, and the government and foreign sectors have become borrowers. As a result, the business model of Japanese banks during the high growth period when banks collected money from households as deposits and lent it to large enterprises is no longer sustainable. In terms of households' portfolio investments, safe assets such as bank deposits and traditional insurance make up substantial shares and risky assets such as stocks are marginal, in spite that the deregulation of financial markets has been well advanced. A bank-centered financial system like Japan's faces financial difficulties when the risk taking ability of financial institutions decreases, which actually occurred due to the huge non-performing loans of the 1990's. The government initiated the Japanese Big Bang to vitalize the financial market in Japan, but a satisfactory outcome has yet to be seen. Japanese banks must change their business model. The author believes that relationship banking is a key concept for most regional financial institutions.

ACKOWLEDGEMENT

This paper was presented at the 21st Freiburg and Nagoya Joint Seminar 2005, which was held at Nagoya University in March 2005. The author appreciates all participants in the seminar for their valuable comments. The author also appreciates Ishii Memorial Foundation For Securities Research for its financial supports.

REFERENCES

Allen, F., and Gale, D. (1999). *Comparing Financial Systems*, Boston, MA: MIT Press.

Bernanke, B. (2000). Japanese Monetary Policy: A Case of Self-Induced Paralysis? In R. Mikitani and A. Posen (Eds.), *Japan's Financial Crisis and Its Parallels to U.S. Experience*, Special Report 13 (pp.149-166). Washington D.C.: Institute for International Economics.

Cargil, T., Hutchison, M., and Ito, T. (1997). *The Political Economy of Japanese Monetary Policy*. Cambridge, MA: MIT Press.

Horiuchi, A., Packer, F., and Fukuda, S. (1988). What Role Has the "Main Bank" Played in Japan? Journal of the Japanese and International Economy, 2, 159-80.

Hoshi, T., Kashyap, A., and Scharfstein, D. (1990). The Role of Banks in Reducing the Costs of Financial Distress in Japan. Journal of Financial Economics, 27, 67-88.

Hoshi, T., and Kashyap, A., (2000). The Japanese Banking Crisis; Where Did It Come from and How Will It End? In B. S. Bernanke and J. J. Rotemberg (eds.) NBER Macroeconomics Annual 1999 (pp.129-201). Cambridge, MA: National Bureau of Economic Research.

Krainer, J., Spiegel, M.M., and Yamori, N. (2004). Asset price declines and real estate market illiquidity: evidence from Japanese land values. Working Papers in Applied Economic Theory 2004-16, Federal Reserve Bank of San Francisco.

Krugman, P. (1999). It's baaack: Japan's Slump and the Return of the Liquidity Trap. Brookings Papers on Economic Activity 2, 137-205.

Posen, A. (2000). Introduction: Financial Similarities and Monetary Differences. In R. Mikitani and A. Posen (Eds.), *Japan's Financial Crisis and Its Parallels to U.S. Experience*, Special Report 13, (pp.1-25). Washington D.C.: Institute for International Economics.

Royama, S. (2002) *A Future Vision about Financial System and Administration.* Tokyo Japan: Zaikei-Shoho-Sha. (in Japanese).

Sheard, P. (1989). The Main Bank System and Corporate Monitoring and Control in Japan. Journal of Economic Behavior and Organization 11, 399-422.

Yamori, N., Harimaya, K., and Asai, Y. (2005). Recent Development of Information Technology in Japanese Banks. Economic Research Center Discussion Paper E-Series No.E05-3, Nagoya University.

In: Asian Economic and Political Issues, Volume 11
Editor: Harvey E. Roth, pp. 95-111
ISBN: 1-60021-192-5

Chapter 5

THE INDUSTRIAL SECTOR IN SOUTHEAST ASIA: DEVELOPMENT EXPERIENCES AND POLICIES

Teofilo C. Daquila

ABSTRACT

This chapter analyzes the industrial sector and its significance in the transformation process of Southeast Asian economies. These economies have different industrial patterns and development experiences. They have different modes of industrial development including import-substitution, export-promotion and export-substitution policies. The Philippines had the longest import-substitution policy while Singapore, the shortest. Malaysia, Thailand and Indonesia are in between. Country experiences, problems and policies are discussed.

INTRODUCTION

Industrialization is a process which involves the promotion and expansion of the industrial sector which broadly consists of manufacturing, mining and quarrying, and other secondary industries. This process has the following essential characteristics. First, the share of the industrial sector to gross domestic product increases except for cyclical fluctuations. Second, the share of industrial employment to total employment also broadly shows an increasing trend. However as Bagchi (1989) pointed out:

> While these two ratios are increasing, the income per head of the population goes up, except for temporary interruptions ...There are cases in which the per capita income goes up, income derived from secondary industry per head of the population also goes up, but there may be little growth either in the proportion of income derived from the secondary sector or in the ratio of the working force engaged in that sector. Such cases, except when they are observed for a highly developed country, not only make the unambiguous

labelling of the process of development as industrialization difficult; they also pose questions regarding the sustainability of the process that has been observed.[1]

Developing countries, including Southeast Asia, have relied on industrial development in order to solve its major problems which include poverty, overpopulation and economic backwardness. It is hoped that by promoting and expanding the industrial sector, people will find employment particularly in labor-intensive manufacturing industries, receive their wages, and increase their income. Moreover, consumption demand and investment demand will be stimulated, and hence increase production. It is assumed that as the industrial sector grows and develops, the economy and the society becomes wealthier. Industrialization and the growth of that part of the working population that is engaged in industry, is therefore a means of raising national income per capita.[2]

However, rather than discuss the entire industrial sector, this chapter focuses on the manufacturing sector as it is the most dominant sub-sector in Southeast Asia. Indonesia, Malaysia, the Philippines, Singapore and Thailand are at different stages of industrialization with Singapore being the most industrially advanced, Indonesia being relatively a new comer, and Malaysia, Thailand and the Philippines lying in between. This chapter discusses the various modes of industrial development in Southeast Asia, and individual country experiences.

Modes of Industrial Development

In Southeast Asia, there were three various modes of industrial development; namely, import substitution, export promotion, and export substitution.[3] Some of the salient characteristics of these approaches are discussed below.

Import-Substitution Approach

The import-substitution industrialization (ISI) approach is one in which the output of the industrial sector is geared towards the domestic market. Domestic industries are created to produce simple and inexpensive consumer goods. The objective is to protect the domestic industries by way of prohibiting imports of the traditional consumer goods. The government imposes a host of protectionist measures like higher tariffs, exchange controls, subsidies and direct government intervention. Thus, ISI approach is very costly as it is implemented by the government without regard for cost or efficiency. Its economic viability and sustainability depends to a large extent on the size of the consumer market – the bigger the market, the more viable and sustainable this approach becomes.

---

[1] Amiya Kumar Bagchi, "Industrialization," in John Eatwell, Murray Milgate and Peter Newman (eds), *Economic Development*, London and Basingstoke, UK: The Macmillan Press, 1989, pp.160-173.

[2] Gunnar Myrdal, *An International Economy*, Harper & Bros., New York, 1956.

[3] *For a detailed discussion of these approaches, see Hank Lim, "Pattern of ASEAN Industrialization," in Swee Hock Saw (ed.),* ASEAN Economies in Transition, *Singapore: Singapore University Press, 1980, pp.169-242.*

The ISI policy can be illustrated with experiences of the Philippines and Indonesia. The ISI approach evolved because of economic nationalism which was expected to create a local entrepreneurial class with the government's significant support and protection. In order to do this, the government utilized the agricultural profits from the exports of primary products to subsidize the local industrialists who were expected to replace the foreign industrialists who controlled the economy during the colonial period. The ISI approach was followed in the Philippines as government heavily favored industrial interests. In Indonesia, ISI signified an act of economic nationalism to break away from the Dutch colonial industrialists.

Export-Promotion Approach

The industrial sector is also geared towards the domestic market. However, the industrial output consists of goods and services which are necessary to stimulate the expansion of primary exports. Its economic viability and sustainability depends on the continued availability of the country's natural resources to produce primary exports.

This approach can be illustrated by the industrialization experiences of Malaysia and Thailand in the early 1960s. Their industrial development relied heavily on the promotion and expansion of primary product exports. Both these countries operated under a relatively free market system in contrast to the Philippines and Indonesia's ISI policy which involved heavy government intervention. However, Malaysia's experiences differed from those in Thailand in terms of the extent of local and foreign participation. In Malaysia, the utilization of natural resources was based upon foreign technology and capital to produce those primary products like rubber, tin and palm oil. However, Thailand's production of rice has not involved foreign participation, and hence described as an indigenous export product.

In Malaysia and Thailand, the production of primary exports was supported by commercial and processing activities supplied by the industrial sector. In Malaysia, there was a flow of modern inputs from industry to export agriculture. In Thailand, the servicing function contributed a smaller role given the slow expansion of supply of domestic raw materials from primary sector to domestic industries.

Export-Substitution Approach

This approach is applicable to an economy which does not export primary products because it simply does not have them. What it has is abundant supply of labor. As such, it can manufacture labor-intensive consumer goods. Given the limited size of the internal consumer market, the viability and sustainability of this approach depends on the economy's ability to direct its output to the external market, that is, to find overseas buyers for its industrial goods. This approach is commonly referred to as export-oriented industrialization (EOI) policy.

Among Southeast Asian economies, Singapore has adopted this approach following a short implementation of ISI policy. During the early 1960s, Singapore had a very bleak future given the diminishing importance of entrepot trade, massive unemployment, rising population, lack of natural resources, and most importantly, its separation from Malaysia in 1965. Singapore recognized the limitation of ISI policy as it could not reap economies of scale. Thus, the Singapore government shifted its industrial policy away from ISI and towards EOI policy.

INDUSTRIAL POLICY EXPERIENCES IN SOUTHEAST ASIA

The Philippines

Several studies have analyzed the industrialization process in the Philippines.[4] The Philippines has the longest history of import substitution among the five Southeast Asian countries. The adoption of this inward-looking industrialization policy during the 1950s to the mid-1960s was based on what Antonio (1997) termed as biases, namely, the resentment of foreign domination as the country started its break from its colonial past, and a belief in the effectiveness of government intervention which was drawn from the prevailing economic model of Keynesianism. First, to replace imports by domestically-produced goods was an indication of economic liberation from the Philippine's former colonial masters. Second, the Philippine government intervened heavily by maintaining an overvalued currency and through its liberal use of tariff walls in order to protect the domestic infant industries from foreign competition.

The adoption of ISI approach has generated both benefits and costs to the Philippine economy. On the positive front, an import-dependent import-substituting policy provided a less demanding entry point for stabilization, reduced significantly the risks of failure for local entrepreneurs, and did not require high levels of technology. On the negative front, the ISI policy led to the following effects. First, it created an industrial structure which was dominated by import-dependent, import-substituting industries directed mainly to the domestic market and which was made profitable by government protection from foreign competition. Second, the import-dependent nature of industries resulted in an economy susceptible to foreign exchange crises including the existence of a black market for foreign exchange. Third, it brought about corruption and smuggling activities. Fourth, it led to heavy concentration of industries around the Metro Manila area as international shipping ports and airports were located in Manila, which in addition, provided a large domestic market for manufactured products. Fifth, it penalized exporters as they had to pay more for their inputs because of the overvalued exchange rate and because highly protectionist policies raised the costs of both imports and local production.[5]

In the late 1960s, the Philippine government adopted policies aimed at encouraging exports and foreign investment. For example, the Investment Incentives Act of 1967, the Foreign Business Regulations Act of 1968, and the Export Incentives Act of 1970 were adopted to streamline and rationalize foreign investment policy in the Philippines. The Board

---

[4] Some of these studies include World Bank, *The Philippines: Priorities and Prospects for Development.* Washington DC: The World Bank, 1976; Romeo Bautista, John Power and Associates, *Industrial Promotion Policies in the Philippines*, Manila: Philippine Institute for Development Studies, 1979; Erlinda Medalla, Gwendolyn Tecson, Romeo Bautista and John Power, *Catching Up with Asia's Tigers,* Vol.1, Main Report, Manila: Philippine Institute for Development Studies, 1995; and Emilio Antonio Jr., "Industrial Policies in the Philippines: Growing Reliance on Market Mechanisms," in Seiichi Masuyama, Donna Vandenbrink, and Siow Yue Chia (eds), *Industrial Policies in East Asia*, Japan: Nomura Research Institute and Singapore: Institute of Southeast Asian Studies, 1997, pp.233-252.

[5] World Bank, The Philippines: Priorities and Prospects for Development, 1976.

of Investment was created in 1970 to set up an investment priorities plan in order to identify the industries which would be given government incentives. With the declaration of martial law in 1972, Presidential Decree 66 was promulgated for the creation of export processing zones. Moreover, the government had taken over or had strong presence in several industries including electricity generation and distribution, petroleum refining industry, coconut and sugar industries, the development of the energy sector and the selection of eleven strategic industries. Thus, the period from the late 1960s to the 1970s was characterized mainly as the rise of crony capitalism since economic incentives were given to businessmen who were friends or close to the seat of political power. Heavy protection of domestic consumer goods industries by the government reflected the continuation of the old import-substitution bias, with effective rates of protection on industrial consumer goods being four times higher than those on capital goods in both 1965 and 1974, and with the number of quantitative restrictions on imports doubling from 1970 to 1980.

During the 1980s, the Philippine economy experienced severe political and economic crises including the external debt crisis in the early 1980s, the Aquino assassination in 1983, the overthrow of the Marcos government in 1986, and the military uprisings during Corazon Aquino's regime (1986-1992) - all these contributed to the economic and political instabilities in the Philippines during this period.

Ironically, however, the 1980s also witnessed significant market-oriented policy reforms. First, tariffs were gradually reduced and quantitative restrictions on imports were relaxed. The average tariff rate was reduced from 43 percent in 1980 to 28 percent in 1985. Moreover, from 1981 to 1988, the share of import items that were restricted decreased from 47 percent to 10 percent in terms of number and from 33 percent to 14.5 percent in terms of value. Second, investment incentives were also reformed with the promulgation of the Omnibus Investment Code of 1981 which consolidated government incentives for investment and exports. Further simplification and consolidation were implemented through Executive Order 225 of Feb 1987.

During the 1990s, more market-oriented reforms were implemented. First, the second tariff reform was implemented in July 1991 under Executive Order 470 which provided for the reduction in the number of commodity lines with high tariffs, the increase in the number of commodity lines with low tariffs over a five-year period, and for the reduction of the average tariff rate from 28 percent to 18 percent. Second, the Foreign Investment Act of 1991 liberalized investment regulations by allowing foreign equity participation up to 100 percent in all areas not specified in the Foreign Investment Negative List, by identifying in advance the areas or sectors where foreign investment was allowed or restricted, and by reducing government bureaucratic procedures involved in cases where foreign equity participation exceeded 40 percent. Third, more market-oriented reforms were implemented which include further liberalization of: laws on foreign investment, on entry of foreign banks, on foreign ownership of property, on opening of infrastructure building to foreign participation; of key sectors like telecommunications, power, insurance, shipping, and the capital market; interest rates and eliminating preferential and credit targeting. Thus, the industrial policies since the 1980s indicate the considerable diminishing role of the government and the rising importance of market-oriented policies.

Malaysia

Several studies have analyzed the industrialization process in Malaysia.[6] The Malaysian economy has undergone tremendous structural changes away from being a primary commodity producer into an increasingly diversified economy with an expanding industrial base. To a significant extent, this transformation is attributed to the accelerated industrialization drive of the Malaysian economy.

Since its independence in 1957, the Malaysian economy has adopted two phases of industrialization, an ISI phase followed by an EOI phase. Like many developing countries initiating the first phase of their industrialization program, Malaysia adopted an ISI strategy, which involved the introduction of various industrial policies in order to encourage the development of domestic industries, particularly, the manufacture of simple consumer goods like canned food and beverages for the domestic market. The policy instruments include tariff protection, fiscal incentives and the establishment of industrial estates. The Pioneer Industries Ordinance was introduced in 1958 which provided generous tax relief and tariff protection to selected local industries.

In the 1960s, several government institutions were created to provide conducive environment for industrialization. In order to provide or generate industrial finance, the government established the Malaysian Stock Exchange and the Malaysian Industrial Development Finance Berhad. In addition, the Tariff Advisory Board was established to formalize the system of tariff protection. It should be noted, however, that Malaysia's experience, in terms of tariff protection, was different from other developing countries as import substitution in Malaysia did not result in excessively high tariffs. The average rate of tariff protection in Peninsular Malaysia rose from 15 percent in 1962 to 45 percent in 1969 which was relatively low compared with those in other countries where the rate was as high as 250 percent.[7] In 1968, Malaysia's industrialization took a different route when the government shifted towards EOI strategy because of the limited size of its domestic market and the need to generate jobs in order to absorb the rapidly rising the labor force. In order to create a more conducive investment environment for industrial development, the Investment Incentives Act was broadened in 1968. With the adoption of an EOI policy, the import-substitution gradually lost its significance in terms of output and employment generation, although it continued to co-exist with the former[8]

In 1971, the New Economic Policy (NEP) was introduced giving emphasis on industrialization as the main vehicle to achieve its objectives particularly in terms of employment generation and equity restructuring. Under the First Outline Perspectives Plan

---

[6] These studies include Sundaram Jomo, *Growth and Structural Change in the Malaysian Economy*, London: Macmillan Press, 1990; Imran Lim and Helen Nesadurai, "Managing the Malaysian Industrial Economy" in Seiichi Masuyama, Donna Vandenbrink, and Siow Yue Chia (eds.), *Industrial Policies in East Asia*, Japan: Nomura Research Institute and Singapore: Institute of Southeast Asian Studies, 1997, pp.185-215; Sundaram Jomo, Rajah Rasiah, Rokiah Alavi and Jaya Gopal. "Industrial Policy and the Emergence of Internationally Competitive Manufacturing Firms in Malaysia," in Kazuo Takahashi (ed.) *Asia's Development Experiences – How Internationally Competitive National Manufacturing Firms Have Developed in Asia*, Tokyo, Japan: Foundation for Advanced Studies on International Development, 1998, pp.178-261; Vijayakumari Kanapathy, "Industrial Restructuring in Malaysia: Policy Shifts and the Promotion of New Sources of Growth," in Seiichi Masuyama, Donna Vandenbrink, and Siow Yue Chia (eds.), *Industrial Restructuring in East Asia,* Japan: Nomura Research Institute and Singapore: Institute of Southeast Asian Studies, 2001, pp.139-165.

[7] Bank Negara, "The Accelerated Industrialization Drive," *Bank Negara Annual Report*, 1991,pp.53-63.

[8] Sundaram Jomo, Rajah Rasiah, Rokiah Alavi and Jaya Gopal, "Industrial Policy…," 1998.

(OPP1) for the period 1971-1990, the manufacturing sector would act as the main engine of economic growth. The NEP and the OPP1 were implemented aimed at promoting growth to restructure the Malaysian society and to foster national unity.

During the 1970s, the Malaysian government participated heavily in the industrialization process through the following activities. These include the establishment of Non-financial Public Enterprises (NFPEs), the regulation of commercial and industrial activities, and the promotion of private investment in the manufacturing industry. In addition, with the passage of the Free Trade Zone Act in 1971, the government set up export-processing or free-trade zones (FTZs) where companies were given fiscal incentives including tax holidays, exemptions from import and export duties, and unrestricted and tax-free remittances of profits and dividends. This Act attracted mainly export-oriented labor-intensive industries like electric/electronic, textile/garment, and rubber industries. In the subsequent years, the FTZs were occupied mainly by highly organized multinational subsidiaries dealing with the assembly of electrical machinery, appliances, parts and components. In 1975, the controversial Industrial Co-ordination Act (ICA) was adopted aimed at ensuring the orderly development and growth of the manufacturing sector with the end-in-view of inducing Bumiputra participation towards Malaysian industrial development.

In the early 1980s, the government began its second phase of ISI policy with its launching of the "big push" on heavy industry projects led by the Heavy Industries Corporation of Malaysia (HICOM). Because of large capital outlays and long gestation periods, both the government and the private sector jointly participated in a number of heavy industrial projects which included iron and steel, cement, the national car, and small engine plants. However, bulk of these projects was financed by heavy foreign borrowings. In 1982, the Malaysian economy experienced a twin-deficit problem so that a structural adjustment was implemented which involved the reduction of government spending and encouraging the private sector to act as the main engine of growth. Thus, in 1984, the government began its move towards deregulating the economy, reducing the role of its public sector and, more importantly, adopting an EOI-strategy.

From 1985 to 1987, the government implemented some reforms towards greater economic liberalization. First, amendments were made to the guidelines on the issuance of licenses as provided for in the Industrial Coordination Act of 1975. Second, the Promotion of Investments Act was introduced in 1986 which replaced the Investment Incentives Act of 1968. This Act broadened the scope of incentives to include small- and medium-scale industries, tourist and hotel projects.

Those reforms resulted in a comprehensive review of industrial policies and led to the launching of the Industrial Master Plan (IMP) to chart the industrialization strategy for the period 1986-95. It aimed to promote outward-oriented industries with particular emphasis on three things, namely, (a) the continued promotion of resource-based industries like processed palm oil, cut logs and timber, rubber products, and petroleum and liquefied natural gas industries, as these industries were expected to help improve Malaysia's trade balance and promote inter-sectoral linkages, (b) the diversification of non-resource based industries (like electronics and electrical products, machinery, metal products, transport equipment, plastics and basic metals) in order to serve as important sources of growth, and (c) the promotion of several heavy industries (like automobiles, cement, and iron and steel products) which were seen as vital in industrializing Malaysia.

In 1991, Malaysia embarked on a renewed economic development path with the formulation of new development plans called the Second Outline Perspective Plan (OPP2) and the Sixth Malaysia Plan (6MP). These plans would be implemented within the overall framework of the National Development Policy (NDP, the successor to NEP). With the NDP, the government eliminated all limits on minimum percentage of Bumiputra participation in approved projects. In order to provide a favorable investment climate, the government has also supported the development of facilities like infrastructure projects in super-highways, well-equipped industrial estates, industrial parks, and airport and port upgrading.

The development plans adopted since the 1990s aimed to set the pace for Malaysia to become a developed nation by 2020. The manufacturing sector would become the main driving force of the Malaysian economy, following its 'Look East' policy – that is, based on the successful development experiences of the dynamic East Asian economies which includes South Korea, Taiwan, Hong Kong and Singapore which centered on the development of human resources. Thus, in order to achieve its 'Vision 2020' target which projects sustained rapid growth over the next 30 years, Malaysia would need to strengthen its drive towards the development of its human resources. This would enable Malaysia to make the transition towards a more sophisticated industrial base.

Singapore

Singapore's industrial development, policies, and experiences have been extensively chronicled.[9] Since 1960, the industrialization program in Singapore has followed several phases. In the first phase from 1960 to 1965, ISI policy was pursued because of the anticipated merger of Singapore into a larger Malaysian common market. The first protective tariffs were implemented in 1960 and tariff protection was extended and accelerated during Singapore's tenure in Malaysia between 1963-65. In 1961, the government created the Economic Development Board in order to lead the industrialization drive through industrial investment promotion, development of industrial infrastructure and facilities, participation in industrial financing, and administering tax incentives.

Following its separation from Malaysia in August 1965, the ISI phase was clearly not sufficient to sustain manufacturing growth in Singapore given its small domestic market. Thus, the second phase of Singapore's industrialization strategy began in 1965 when the government dismantled its ISI policy and switched towards export-oriented and labor-

[9] These studies include Siow Yue Chia, "Direct Foreign Investment and Industrialization in Singapore," in Chong-Yah Lim and Peter Lloyd (eds.), *Singapore Resources and Growth,* Singapore: Oxford University Press, 1986, pp.79-117; Linda Lim, "Foreign Investment, the State and Industrial Policy in Singapore," in Howard Stein (ed.), *Asian Industrialization and Africa,* St. Martin's Press, New York, 1995, pp.205-238; Poh Kam Wong and Chee Yuen Ng, "Singapore's Industrial Policy to the year 2000," in Seiichi Masuyama, Donna Vandenbrink and Siow Yue Chia (eds.), *Industrial Policies in East Asia*, Japan: Nomura Research Institute and Singapore: Institute of Southeast Asian Studies, 1997, pp. 121-141; Poh-Kam Wong, Sock-Yong Phang, Jong-Say Yong and Meng-Kng Chng, "Development of Internationally Competitive Indigenous Manufacturing Firms in Singapore," in Kazuo Takahashi (ed.), *Asia's Development Experiences – How Internationally Competitive National Manufacturing Firms Have Developed in Asia,* Tokyo, Japan: Foundation for Advanced Studies on International Development, 1998, pp. 372-447; and Siow Yue Chia, "Singapore: Towards a Knowledge-based Economy," in Seiichi Masuyama, Donna Vandenbrink and Siow Yue Chia (eds.), *Industrial Restructuring in East Asia*, Japan: Nomura Research Institute and Singapore: Institute of Southeast Asian Studies, 2001, pp.170-208.

intensive industrialization. The labor-intensive export-manufacturing strategy was chosen taking into account Singapore's scarcity of land and natural resources for extraction, small domestic market, and the need for mass employment creation. The unemployment rate reached a record high of 10 percent in 1965, with population and labor force growing by 3.3 percent and 5.0 percent, respectively.[10] Moreover, given Singapore's lack of domestic entrepreneurial class and lack of foreign capital and technology, the government assigned a strong role to foreign corporations through foreign direct investment. Thus, the three leading export-oriented industries were petroleum refining, transport equipment and oil rigs, and electronic products and components, which by 1971 accounted for a combined share of 43.6 per cent of total manufacturing value added.

During the second phase, government intervention in the domestic economy was pervasive and extensive and took two forms: first, involving infrastructural activities, and second, direct establishment of wholly-owned or partly-owned industrial and commercial ventures including the national shipping line, the airlines, the Development Bank of Singapore, the Singapore Petroleum Company, the National Iron and Steel Mills, a large trading and investment company.

The third phase began in 1979 when an economic restructuring program was launched that would upgrade established industries and develop new ones that would utilize more capital, high technology, and skilled labor in the production of high-value manufactured goods and services for export. This policy was aimed at using Singapore's scarce labor resources more effectively and efficiently. The shift in emphasis stemmed from the tight labor market conditions and rising domestic costs of production as these would hurt the competitiveness of domestically-produced goods. Under the so-called Second Industrial Revolution, the government restructured its economy by upgrading the technology employed in the local manufacturing industries and by investing heavily in these industries. The government also followed a high-wage policy in order to reduce its dependence from labor-intensive manufacturing industries.

Singapore's industrialization program, however, met some difficulties in the mid-1980s as the economy experienced a recession. The Report of the Economic Committee headed by BG Lee Hsien Loong stated that the high costs of production severely affected the operations of multinational corporations (MNCs) in Singapore, which in turn was attributed mainly to the high-wage policy. Thus, the 1985-86 recession limited the extent in the implementation of the restructuring policy and significantly weakened the manufacturing production. Several policy measures were implemented including wage restraint and adoption of favorable investment incentives.

In the early 1990s, the government launched its vision of Singapore as a developed nation in a document called *The Next Lap* which envisioned Singapore to be in tough competition with advanced, developed nations towards the end of the century. Then, the government formulated a *Strategic Economic Plan* (SEP) which paved the way for the implementation of several specific program initiatives.[11] First, the *Manufacturing 2000* program aims to sustain manufacturing's share of GDP at more than 25 percent and its share of employment at more than 20 percent in the medium to long term.

---

[10] Poh-Kam Wong, Sock-Yong Phang, Jong-say Yong and Meng-Kng Chng, "Development of Internationally Competitive Indigenous Manufacturing Firms...," 1998.

[11] Poh-Kam Wong and Chee Yuen Ng, "Singapore's Industrial Policy...," 1997.

Second, the *International Business Hub* aims to enhance Singapore's position as a gateway to the Asia-Pacific region for business services like financial services, tourism, operational headquarters, logistics distribution, media/telecommunications, commodity trading, international arbitrage, exhibition and convention, tertiary education and training, and medical services.

Third, *Regionalization 2000* program aims to build an external economy which is closely linked to and which enhances the Singapore economy by participating in the growth of the Asian region.This program provides incentives and assistance for Singapore-based companies to invest in the region, and for Singapore to co-invest and co-manage large-scale industrial parks in the region.

Fourth, the *National Technology Plan* aims to develop Singapore into a center of excellence in select fields of science and technology through intensified research and development activities.

Fifth, the *IT2000 Vision* and the *National Information Infrastructure* initiatives aims to turn Singapore into an intelligent island through innovations in information technology (IT) and development of advanced telecommunications and information infrastructure.

Sixth, with the *Local Enterprises 2000* program, the government aims to promote the development of local enterprises through grants, loans, preferential interest rates, and tax incentives. In addition, the government utilizes the Local Industry Upgrading Program in which MNCs are asked to help upgrade the local companies which are their suppliers and business partners. Moreover, the government intends to help develop a group of promising local enterprises and turn them into future MNCs and industry leaders.

Seventh, the *Co-Investment Program* enables the Singapore government to co-invest in more technology-intensive and capital-intensive large scale projects like the semiconductor wafer fabrication industry, petrochemicals, and biotechnology. Finally, with the *Industry Cluster* Fund, the government established a S$2 billion fund aimed at promoting integrated industry clusters as exemplified by the co-investment program. Thus, the industrial policies cited above emphasize three main concerns, namely, internationalization, technological innovations, and creation and growth of industries.

Thailand

Several studies analyzed the extent of industrialization in Thailand.[12] Modern industrialization in Thailand began in the early 1960s. During the period from 1960-1971,

---

[12] These studies include Atchaka Sibinruang and Peter Brimble, in Seiji Naya (ed.), *Direct Foreign Investment Theories and Export Promotion:Policies and Experiences in Asia*, Southeast Asia Central Bank Research and Training Center, Kuala Lumpur, 1987, pp. 317-357; Jean-Christophe Simon, "The Thai Manufacturing Sector: New Patterns of Expansion," in Michael Parnwell (ed.), *Uneven Development in Thailand*, Aldershot, UK: Avebury, 1996, pp.82-108; Nipon Poapongsakorn and Belinda Fuller, "Industrial Location Policy in Thailand: Industrial Decentralization or Industrial Sprawl," in Seiichi Masuyama, Donna Vandenbrink and Siow Yue Chia (eds.), *Industrial Policies in East Asia*, Japan: Nomura Research Institute and Singapore: Institute of Southeast Asian Studies, 1997, pp.146-184; Patcharee Siroros and Wilaiwan Wannitikul, "International Competitiveness of Indigenous Firms: Case Studies of the Gems and Jewelry Industry and the Siam Cement Group," in Kazuo Takahashi (ed.), *Asia's Development Experiences – How Internationally Competitive National Manufacturing Firms Have Developed in Asia*, Tokyo, Japan: Foundation for Advanced Studies on International Development, 1998, pp.264-310; Nipon Poapongsakorn and Somkiat Tangkitvanich, "Industrial Restructuring in Thailand: a Critical Assessment", in Seiichi Masuyama, Donna Vandenbrink, and Siow Yue

import substitution was the main objective of Thailand's industrial policy-makers in order to reduce its dependence on imported consumer goods. In the 1960s, domestic manufacturing activities were concentrated on food processing as it accounted for a third of total manufactured products. Local industries were protected through higher tariffs on imported goods.

The ISI period coincided with the First and Second National Economic Development Plans, 1961-66 and 1967-71, respectively. These plans were implemented by government agencies like the Ministry of Finance which set import tariffs, the Ministry of Commerce which imposed quota restrictions, and the Board of Investment which promoted investment through government incentives like exemption from import duties on capital goods, lower or zero duties on imported raw materials and intermediate inputs, and exemption from corporate taxes. The government's protection of the domestic manufacturing sector resulted in different effective rates of protection – lower for machinery products, and moderate to high range for consumer products. On the other hand, resource-based activities were subject to export tariffs. Thus, Thailand's tariff structure was made favorable to the domestic manufacturing sector at the expense of the export sector.

By the end of the 1960s, the Thai economy began to falter and its balance of payments started to worsen due to rapid growth in the importation of machinery and raw materials, stagnation of primary exports, and the decline in foreign investment. Thus, the government adopted the Third National Development Plan (1972-77) which emphasized a change in its industrial policy towards promotion of manufactured exports, the deepening of the import substitution process for intermediate goods and raw materials, the promotion of small-scale and labor-intensive industries, and the dispersion of industries into the rural areas.

Throughout the 1970s and the first half of the 1980s, Thailand's external deficits persisted and worsened. The government responded by emphasizing the urgency of promoting exports of manufactured goods in the fourth and fifth plans (1977-1981 and 1982-1986, respectively) The government explicitly stated its commitment to promote exports of manufactured goods as the main source of growth. The fifth plan had strongly emphasized the restructuring of certain existing and new industries in order to achieve higher levels of efficiency and enhance the competitiveness in both external and internal markets. The sixth plan (1987-91) also called for the promotion of export-oriented industries, small-scale industries, rural industries located in areas outside Bangkok and its vicinity, agro-based industries, and basic industries like engineering, petrochemical, iron and steel industries. The seventh plan (1992-96) targeted the textile and garment industries although Thailand has lost its comparative advantage in labor-intensive industries. Thailand's eighth development plan was for the period from 1997-2001. Thailand claimed to be an emerging newly industrializing economy.

Thus, from the above discussions, Thailand's industrialization has been based on a series of 5-year development plans. However, its industrialization drive has met some criticisms, particularly with regard to inconsistencies between the development plans and strategies. As for the ISI phase, three inconsistencies were identified. First, there was incompatibility between making ISI as major industrialization strategy and calling for the promotion of labor-intensive industries. Second, the development plans called for the promotion and utilization of

Chia (eds.), *Industrial Restructuring in East Asia*, Japan: Nomura Research Institute and Singapore: Institute of Southeast Asian Studies, 2001, pp.109-138.

domestic raw materials, but the tariff structure discriminated against resource-based activities. Third, the development plans call for the promotion of household and small-scale industries, but the BOI favored large-scale, capital-intensive industries to support import substitution. As for the export-orientation phase, it was pointed out that inconsistency arose from the development plan of making exports as an engine of growth in the early 1970s but in reality, the trade regime remained largely the same (ie. anti-export bias) until the late 1970s given higher effective rates of protection for import-substituting industries.

The shift in Thailand's industrialization strategy from ISI to EOI has resulted in a changing structure of its merchandise exports in two ways. First, there was a shift away from primary commodities and towards manufactured goods. The year 1985 was very significant as exports of manufactured goods surpassed agricultural exports for the first time. Second, the exports of medium- and high-technology products surpassed exports of labor-intensive products for the first time in 1993.

The petroleum product industry registered a slower growth of 34 percent per year during the 1980-88 period. By 1993, it accounted for only 1.4 percent of GDP. On the other hand, the manufacturing sector grew at an average of about 10 percent per year during the period from 1960-1988. As the largest sector, manufacturing accounted for 26 percent of GDP in 1988 and 29 percent in 1993. Intermediate products like machinery, metal products, and iron and steel expanded rapidly. The textiles and garment products became the most important industry during the 1986-88 period. In 1989, the manufacturing industry expanded by 15 percent arising from the government's export-oriented policy, and also because of stable oil prices, interest rates and exchange rates. Moreover, Thailand has also developed supporting industries such as the construction of automotive engine plants and developing a major petrochemical complex that would provide inputs for the manufacturing sector. An important milestone in Thailand's manufacturing history was achieved when the 'Made in Thailand' Mitsubishi cars were exported to Canada, Portugal and Cyprus.

Indonesia

The Indonesian manufacturing sector has undergone four phases of development since the New Order in 1965.[13] The first phase was from 1967 to 1973 in which the Indonesian economy was driven mainly by liberalization and the return to normal conditions. Suharto's government inherited a badly damaged economy including an excess capacity, low level of foreign trade, and a 600 percent inflation rate. The new government undertook some economic liberalization measures which involved a shift in policy orientation away from heavy intervention towards a more market-oriented economy. These include liberalization of foreign exchange and trade policies, dismantling of the import licensing system, introduction

[13] Some of the more recent studies on Indonesian industrial development, policies and experiences include Hal Hill, "Indonesia's Industrial Policy and Performance: Orthodoxy Vindicated," Economic Development and Cultural Change, 1996, pp.147-174; Hal Hill, Indonesia's Industrial Transformation, Singapore: Institute of Southeast Asian Studies, 1997; Haryo Aswicahyono, "Transformation and Structural Change in Indonesia's Manufacturing Sector," in Mari Pangestu and Yuri Sato (eds.), Waves of Change in Indonesia's Manufacturing Industry, Tokyo: Institute of Developing Economies, 1997, pp.1-28; Karseno, Arief Ramelan, "Perspectives on Government Policy for Industrial Competitiveness in Indonesia," in Seiichi Masuyama, Donna Vandenbrink, and Siow Yue Chia (eds.), Industrial Policies in East Asia, Japan: Nomura Research Institute and Singapore: Institute of Southeast Asian Studies, 1997, pp.216-232.

of a new export bonus scheme, launching of foreign and domestic investment laws, rehabilitation of financial state banks, and introduction of a banking law. The economic reforms were very effective as inflation fell sharply to 17 percent in 1969, foreign exchange constraint was eased, and real manufacturing output expanded by 9 percent in 1968 and by 14 percent in 1969. The reforms continued until 1972 which included devaluation, unification of a multiple exchange rate system, simplification of export and import procedures, and elimination of international capital controls. However, despite these reform measures, major industrial sectors like textiles and automotive products received heavy protection.

The second phase in the development of the manufacturing sector in Indonesia was the petroleum years during the 1973-1982 period when the prices of crude oil rose significantly – first, in 1973-1974 and again, in 1978-1979. During this period, Indonesia followed an inward-oriented ISI regime. The oil boom led to a fundamental reappraisal of industrial policy objectives as the government took a more interventionist path through a more restrictive foreign investment policy. The more liberal foreign investment policy prior to the oil boom period generated significant inflows of FDI which in turn created resentment among Indonesian nationalists. This resentment reached its peak during the 1974 visit of former Japan's PM Tanaka in Indonesia. The massive oil bonanza also enabled the Indonesian government to intervene heavily through (i) an extension of credit subsidies to favored clients by the state banks, (ii) direct engagement in production by the state-owned enterprises particularly in upstream, capital-intensive industries like cement and fertilizer, and (iii) imposition of non-tariff barriers for imports, especially for planned heavy industries. Thus, the late 1970s was characterized with an extensive state-guided industrial intervention.

The third phase took place during the 1982-85 period following the decline in oil prices, which created a balance of payments crisis. Thus, it was realized that making oil exports as an engine of growth was limited and hence there was an urgency of shifting towards non-oil, manufacturing exports as sources of economic growth. Faced with economic difficulties, the government followed a prudent macroeconomic management including a re-scheduling in the development of capital-intensive industries, a significant devaluation of the rupiah by 27.5 percent in March 1983, and major banking reforms which included lifting of interest rate controls on state banks and credit ceilings. On the other hand, the government had become even more protectionist in terms of further restrictive trade and industrial policies through the increased use of NTBs over this period. In 1982, the government introduced a system called approved importers system which had become an instrument for quantitative restrictions on imports. Thus, the implementation of these protectionist measures resulted in a high-cost economy. Consequently, public discussions took place on the costs of protection, on pervasive regulations, and on inefficient state-owned companies.

In the fourth stage, from 1986 to the present, industrial policy has taken the form of deregulation and reforms. In 1986, Suharto's New Order government considered for the first time making non-oil exports and private sector industries as the main engines of growth in Indonesia. Thus, from an inward-looking strategy during the third phase, the government has shifted towards an outward-oriented economy in terms of trade and foreign investments. This change in policy stance resulted from the government's anticipated increase in global competition and from the successful export promotion experiences of high-performing East Asian economies like Taiwan, Hong Kong, South Korea and Singapore. The policy shift was implemented through a series of deregulatory measures including across-the-board reduction in nominal tariffs, and a reorganization of customs, parts and shipping operations. The government also adopted substantive trade reforms which resulted in the elimination of the import monopolies of plastic and steel, and cotton, and also in a more transparent quota allocation system for textile. Moreover, financial reforms were implemented in 1988 which resulted in increased competition among banks. In addition, both foreign and domestic investments were liberalized particularly for export-oriented FDI by allowing 95 percent foreign ownership and domestic distribution.

Conclusion

The five Southeast Asian economies followed an ISI-policy before switching to an EOI policy. The Philippines began the industrialization of the region through the creation of import-substituting industries in the late 1940s. A decade after, Malaysia, Singapore and Thailand followed the Philippine example while Indonesia joined in only two decades later. However, Singapore switched to an EOI-policy in the late 1960s given its separation from Malaysia in 1965, its small domestic market, and its lack of natural resources. This has proved to be successful for Singapore as it has resulted in rising trade, output, income and standards of living.

During the 1970s and the 1980s, other Southeast Asian economies relied less on ISI policy and began to follow the EOI policy adopted by East Asian economies like Singapore, Hong Kong, South Korea and Taiwan. Some factors which accounted for this change in industrialization policy include the limited success of ISI, the declining and fluctuating prices of primary commodities, and the consequent pursuit of export-diversification policy. The need to diversify is reflected in the changing structure of trade - away from primary and toward manufactured exports and the rising dependence on manufactured imports.

In order to promote an outward-oriented industrialization policy, the Southeast Asian governments have provided strong support through a package of incentives including tax exemptions, improvement of the investment climate and provision of industrial infrastructure including the establishment of industrial parks and export-processing zones which have offered a variety of fiscal and financial incentives to investors.

Questions for Discussion

1. The Southeast Asian economies have pursued two types of industrialization policy: (a) outward-oriented policy which promotes free and open trade and investments, and (b) an inward-looking policy which involves heavy government protection of the domestic manufacturing sector. Compare and contrast these policies in terms of their costs and benefits.
2. Despite efforts to promote and develop the agricultural sector in Southeast Asia, it has remained backward, stagnant and unproductive. On the other hand, the non-agricultural (manufacturing and services) sector has become modern, more developed and productive.
   (a) Explain why such structural dualism has existed in Southeast Asia.
   (b) Explain whether or not you would expect this dualism to persist.

3. In order to promote and develop the industrial sector in Southeast Asia, particularly the manufacturing sector, some countries have adopted import-substitution policies while others have followed export-oriented policies. Discuss why these countries differ in their approaches to industrialization.
4. "To industrialize or not to industrialize – is the policy issue. Various countries in Southeast Asia have taken up the challenge of industrialization by adopting strategies that would suit their own respective economies. Among Southeast Asian economies, Singapore has achieved a higher level of industrial development than others. It is therefore to the advantage of all Southeast Asian economies to follow the policies that Singapore has adopted." Do you agree with the given statements? Explain.

Suggested Materials for Case Studies:

Indonesia

Rock, Michael, 1999, "Reassessing the Effectiveness of Industrial Policy in Indonesia: Can the Neoliberals be Wrong?" *World Development,* Vol.27, No.4, pp.691-704.

Asia

Quibria, M.G., Shamsun Ahmed, Ted Tschang, Mari-Len Reyes-Macasaquit, 2003, "Digital Divide: Determinants and Policies with special reference to Asia," *Journal of Asian Economics,* Vol.13, No.6, pp.811-825.

REFERENCES

Antonio Jr., Emilio, 1997, "Industrial Policies in the Philippines: Growing Reliance on Market Mechanisms," in Seiichi Masuyama, Donna Vandenbrink, and Siow Yue Chia (eds.), *Industrial Policies in East Asia,* Japan: Nomura Research Institute and Singapore: Institute of Southeast Asian Studies, pp.233-252.

Aswicahyono, Haryo, 1997, "Transformation and Structural Change in Indonesia's Manufacturing Sector," in Mari Pangestu and Yuri Sato (eds.), *Waves of Change in Indonesia's Manufacturing Industry,* Tokyo: Institute of Developing Economies, pp.1-28.

Bagchi, Amiya Kumar, 1989, "Industrialization," in John Eatwell, Murray Milgate and Peter Newman (eds.), *Economic Development,* London and Basingstoke, UK: The Macmillan Press, pp.160-173.

Bank Negara, 1991, "The Accelerated Industrialization Drive," *Bank Negara Annual Report,* pp.53-63.

Bautista, Romeo, John Power and Associates, 1979, *Industrial Promotion Policies in the Philippines,* Manila: Philippine Institute for Development Studies.

Chia, Siow Yue, 1986, "Direct Foreign Investment and Industrialization in Singapore," in Chong-Yah Lim and Peter Lloyd (eds.), *Singapore Resources and Growth,* Singapore: Oxford University Press, pp.79-117.

Chia, Siow Yue, 2001, "Singapore: Towards a Knowledge-Based Economy," in Seiichi Masuyama, Donna Vandenbrink and Siow Yue Chia (eds.), *Industrial Restructuring in*

East Asia, Japan: Nomura Research Institute and Singapore: Institute of Southeast Asian Studies, pp.170-208.

Hill, Hal, 1996, "Indonesia's Industrial Policy and Performance: Orthodoxy Vindicated," *Economic Development and Cultural Change*, Vol.45, No.1, pp.147-174.

Hill, Hal, 1997, *Indonesia's Industrial Transformation,* Singapore: Institute of Southeast Asian Studies.

Jomo, Sundaram, 1990, *Growth and Structural Change in the Malaysian Economy*, London: Macmillan Press.

Jomo, Sundaram, Rajah Rasiah, Rokiah Alavi and Jaya Gopal, 1998, "Industrial Policy and the Emergence of Internationally Competitive Manufacturing Firms in Malaysia," in Kazuo Takahashi (ed.), *Asia's Development Experiences – How Internationally Competitive National Manufacturing Firms Have Developed in Asia*, Tokyo, Japan: Foundation for Advanced Studies on International Development, pp.178-261.

Kanapathy, Vijayakumari, 2001, "Industrial Restructuring in Malaysia: Policy Shifts and the Promotion of New Sources of Growth," in Seiichi Masuyama, Donna Vandenbrink, and Siow Yue Chia (eds.), *Industrial Restructuring in East Asia,* Japan: Nomura Research Institute and Singapore: Institute of Southeast Asian Studies, pp.139-165.

Karseno, Arief Ramelan, 1997, "Perspectives on Government Policy for Industrial Competitiveness in Indonesia," in Seiichi Masuyama, Donna Vandenbrink, and Siow Yue Chia (eds.), *Industrial Policies in East Asia*, Japan: Nomura Research Institute and Singapore: Institute of Southeast Asian Studies, pp.216-232.

Lim, Imran and Helen Nesadurai, 1997, "Managing the Malaysian Industrial Economy" in Seiichi Masuyama, Donna Vandenbrink, and Siow Yue Chia (eds.), *Industrial Policies in East Asia*, Japan: Nomura Research Institute and Singapore: Institute of Southeast Asian Studies, pp.185-215

Lim, Linda, 1995, "Foreign Investment, the State and Industrial Policy in Singapore," in Howard Stein (ed.), *Asian Industrialization and Africa,* St. Martin's Press, New York, pp.205-238.

Medalla, Erlinda, Gwendolyn Tecson, Romeo Bautista and John Power, 1995, *Catching Up with Asia's Tigers,* Vol.1, Main Report, Manila: Philippine Institute for Development Studies.

Myrdal, Gunnar, 1956, *An International Economy*, Harper and Bros., New York.

Poapongsakorn, Nipon and Belinda Fuller, 1997, "Industrial Location Policy in Thailand: Industrial Decentralization or Industrial Sprawl," in Seiichi Masuyama, Donna Vandenbrink and Siow Yue Chia (eds.), *Industrial Policies in East Asia*, Japan: Nomura Research Institute and Singapore: Institute of Southeast Asian Studies, pp.146-184.

Poapongsakorn, Nipon and Somkiat Tangkitvanich, 2001, "Industrial Restructuring in Thailand: a Critical Assessment", in Seiichi Masuyama, Donna Vandenbrink, and Siow Yue Chia (eds.), *Industrial Restructuring in East Asia*, Japan: Nomura Research Institute and Singapore: Institute of Southeast Asian Studies, pp.109-138.

Sibinruang, Atchaka and Peter Brimble, 1987, in Seiji Naya (ed.), *Direct Foreign Investment Theories and Export Promotion:Policies and Experiences in Asia*, Kuala Lumpur: Southeast Asia Central Bank Research and Training Center, pp. 317-357

Simon, Jean-Christophe, 1996, "The Thai Manufacturing Sector: New Patterns of Expansion," in Michael Parnwell (ed.), *Uneven Development in Thailand*, Aldershot, UK: Avebury, pp.82-108.

Siroros, Patcharee and Wilaiwan Wannitikul, 1998, "International Competitiveness of Indigenous Firms: Case Studies of the Gems and Jewelry Industry and the Siam Cement Group," in Kazuo Takahashi (ed.), *Asia's Development Experiences – How Internationally Competitive National Manufacturing Firms Have Developed in Asia*, Tokyo, Japan: Foundation for Advanced Studies on International Development, pp.264-310.

Saw, Swee Hock (ed.), 1980, *ASEAN Economies in Transition*, Singapore: Singapore University Press, pp.169-242.

Wong, Poh Kam and Chee Yuen Ng, 1997, "Singapore's Industrial Policy to the year 2000," in Seiichi Masuyama, Donna Vandenbrink and Siow Yue Chia (eds.), *Industrial Policies in East Asia*, Japan: Nomura Research Institute and Singapore: Institute of Southeast Asian Studies, pp. 121-141.

Wong, Poh-Kam, Sock-Yong Phang, Jong-Say Yong and Meng-Kng Chng, 1998, "Development of Internationally Competitive Indigenous Manufacturing Firms in Singapore," in Kazuo Takahashi (ed.), *Asia's Development Experiences – How Internationally Competitive National Manufacturing Firms Have Developed in Asia,* Tokyo, Japan: Foundation for Advanced Studies on International Development, pp. 372-447.

World Bank, 1976, The Philippines: Priorities and Prospects for Development. Washington DC: The World Bank.

In: Asian Economic and Political Issues, Volume 11
Editor: Harvey E. Roth, pp. 113-140
ISBN: 1-60021-192-5

Chapter 6

SOUTH KOREA-U.S. ECONOMIC RELATIONS: COOPERATION, FRICTION, AND PROSPECTS FOR A FREE TRADE AGREEMENT (FTA)

Mark E. Manyin
Analyst in Asian Affairs Foreign Affairs, Defense, and Trade Division

ABSTRACT

South Korea is a major economic partner for the United States. In 2004, trade between the two countries was over $70 billion, making South Korea the United States's seventh-largest trading partner — ahead of France and Italy — and its seventh-largest export market. In 2005, the U.S. was Korea's third-largest trading partner, second-largest export market, and its largest supplier of foreign direct investment (FDI).

Bilateral economic relations have advanced to the point that the two sides in February 2006 announced their intention to negotiate a bilateral free trade agreement (FTA), which they hope to complete by 2007. The announcement followed South Korean concessions in four areas: beef, automobiles, pharmaceuticals, and "screen quotas" limiting the amount of screen time that foreign films could be shown. The United States had said an FTA could not be launched unless Seoul demonstrated its ability to deliver compromises in these sectors. If an agreement is reached, it would be the United States's largest FTA since the completion of the North American Free Trade Agreement. To go into effect, FTAs must be approved by Congress and the Korean National Assembly. The FTA negotiation and ratification processes are likely to politicize bilateral trade disputes and produce spillovers between the economic and strategic aspects of the relationship, particularly if there are dramatic developments in the crisis over North Korea's nuclear weapons program.

Increased U.S.-South Korean economic interaction has been accompanied by numerous disagreements over trade and economic policies. The intensity of the disputes has diminished considerably since the late 1980s and early 1990s, in part because South Korea has enacted a set of sweeping market-oriented reforms as a *quid pro quo* for receiving a $58 billion package from the International Monetary Fund (IMF) following the near collapse of the South Korean economy in 1997. In recent years, the United States and South Korea appear to have become more adept at managing their trade disputes, so that they tend to be less acrimonious than they were in the 1980s and 1990s. This is due in part to the quarterly, working-level bilateral trade meetings that have been held since early 2001. Strategic factors, including South Korea's increased economic integration with North Korea, have become issues on the bilateral U.S.-South Korea economic front. In the FTA talks, South Korean officials have said they will try to secure preferential tariff treatment for goods made by South Korean firms in the Kaesong industrial zone, located inside North Korea. In 2003, China surpassed the United States as South Korea's largest trading partner. Many South Korean exports to China are believed to be intermediate goods that are incorporated into products sent to the United States.

This report summarizes the main issues in U.S.-South Korean economic relations, including South Korea's economic prospects and economic reforms, major bilateral economic disputes, and the pros and cons of a U.S. -South Korean FTA. The report will be updated periodically.

The United States and South Korea (known formally as the Republic of Korea, or ROK) have been allies since the United States intervened on the Korean Peninsula in 1950 and fought to repel a North Korean takeover of South Korea. Over 33,000 U.S. troops were killed and over 100,000 were wounded during the three-year conflict. In 1954, a year after the parties to the conflict signed an armistice agreement, the United States and South Korea signed a Mutual Defense Treaty, which provides that if either party is attacked by a third country, the other party will act to meet the common danger. The United States maintains about 34,000 troops in the ROK to supplement the 650,000-strong South Korean armed forces.[1] In recent years, strategic differences between Washington and Seoul — particularly over the optimal policies toward North Korea — have caused some in the United States to question the benefits of the alliance.

Beginning in the 1 960s, rapid economic growth in South Korea propelled it into the ranks of the world's largest industrialized countries. For over a decade, South Korea has been one of the United States's largest trading partners. Economic growth also has helped transform the ROK into a mid-level regional power that can influence U.S. policy in Northeast Asia, particularly the United States's approach toward North Korea.

Overviews of U.S.-South Korean Economic Relations

In 2004, trade between the South Korea and the United States was over $70 billion, making South Korea the United States's seventh-largest trading partner — ahead of France and Italy — and its seventh-largest export market. Trades from the first 11 months of 2005 were roughly on track to duplicate the 2004 results. (See Table 1 and Table 2) For some western states and U.S. sectors, the South Korean market is even more important, ranking number five for California's exporters (in 2004), number two for Oregon's exporters, and number four for all U.S. agricultural exporters. Major U.S. exports to South Korea include semiconductors, machinery (particularly semiconductor production machinery), aircraft, and agricultural products. South Korea is among United States's largest markets for agricultural products and beef.

[1] In October 2004, the U.S. and South Korea agreed to a phased withdrawal of 12,500 U.S. troops in South Korea, reducing U.S. in-country troop strength from 37,000 to about 24,000 by September 2008.

Table 1. Annual U.S.-South Korea Merchandise Trade Billions of U.S. Dollars

Year	U.S. Exports	U.S. Imports	Trade Balance	Total Trade
1990	14.40	18.49	-4.09	32.89
1995	25.38	24.18	1.20	49.56
2000	26.30	39.83	-13.53	66.13
2003	22.52	36.93	-14.41	59.45
2004	24.99	45.06	-20.07	70.05
Jan-Nov 2004	22.70	41.36	-18.66	64.06
Jan-Nov 2005	23.74	39.57	-15.83	63.31
Major U.S. Export Items	Semiconductor chips and manufacturing equipment; aircraft; corn and wheat; plastics			
Major U.S. Import Items	Cellular phones; semiconductor circuits; televisions and flat panel screens; cars; computer parts; construction vehicles			

Sources: 1990 and 1995 data from Global Trade Information Services. 2000-2005 data from U.S. International Trade Commission.

South Korea is far more dependent economically on the United States than the United States is on South Korea. In 2005, the United States was Korea's third-largest trading partner, second-largest export market, third-largest source of imports, and its largest supplier of foreign direct investment. In 2003, China for the first time displaced the United States from its perennial place as South Korea's number one trading partner. Preliminary data from the Bank of Korea for 2005 indicates that Japan overtook the United States to become South Korea's second-largest trade partner.

Table 2. Asymmetrical Economic Interdependence (2005)

	Total Trade	Export Market	Source of Imports	Source of FDI
for U.S., ROK ranks	#7	#7	#7	n.a.
for ROK, U.S. ranks	#3	#2	#3	#1
In 2003, China surpassed the U.S. as the ROK's largest trading partner. In 2005, Japan surpassed the U.S. to become the ROK's second-largest trading partner.				

Increased economic interaction has been accompanied by numerous disagreements over trade policies. The intensity of the disputes has diminished considerably since the late 1980s and early 1990s, in part because South Korea has enacted a set of sweeping market-oriented reforms as a *quid pro quo* for receiving a $58 billion package from the International Monetary Fund (IMF) following the near collapse of the South Korean economy in 1997. In particular, as a result of the reforms, South Korea has opened its doors to foreign investors, ushering in billions of dollars of foreign portfolio and foreign direct investment (FDI). The result is that foreign companies, including U.S. firms, now are significant shareholders in many prominent industrial conglomerates *(chaebol),* own an estimated 40% of the value of the shares traded on South Korea's stock exchange, and own about one-third of the Korean banking industry. After his election to one five-year term in 2002, South Korean President Roh Moo-hyun said that more extensive reforms were needed to help accomplish his goals of raising per capita gross domestic product (GDP) to $20,000 and of transforming South Korea into a major economic hub in Northeast Asia. Increasingly, South Koreans also are concerned about rising economic competition from Chinese manufacturers.

The United States and South Korea appear to have become more adept at managing their trade disputes, so that they tend to be less acrimonious than they were in the 1980s and 1990s. This may be partly due to the quarterly, working-level "trade action agenda" trade meetings that were initiated in early 2001. Both sides credit the meetings, which appear to be unique to the U.S.-South Korean trade relationship, with creating a more constructive dialogue by serving as "action-forcing" events.

U. S.-ROK economic relations have advanced to the point that the two sides on February 2, 2006, announced their intent to launch negotiations to form a bilateral free trade agreement (FTA). The announcement followed South Korean concessions in four areas: beef, automobiles, pharmaceuticals, and "screen quotas" limiting the amount of screen time that foreign films could be shown. United States Trade Representative (USTR) Robert Portman had said an FTA could not be launched unless Seoul demonstrated its ability to deliver compromises in these sectors. If an agreement is reached, it would be the United States's largest FTA since the completion of the North American Free Trade Agreement (NAFTA) in 1992. To go into effect, FTAs must be approved by Congress. (For more on the U. S.-South Korea FTA negotiations, see "U. S.-South Korea FTA Negotiations" below) At the February 2006 launch, the two sides expressed their interest in concluding negotiations by the beginning of 2007.

SOUTH KOREA'S ECONOMY

The 1997 Financial Crisis and IMF-Directed Reforms

South Korea's 1997 financial crisis was a seminal event in the country's history. During the autumn of 1997 — spurred in part by the bankruptcy of six of the country's top thirty industrial conglomerates *(chaebol)* and a sharp increase in repayments required on short-term foreign debt — investors lost confidence in the economy and capital fled the country. The Korean *won* lost half its value in the space of a few days, tumbling from 900 to 1900 *won* to the dollar. In a futile attempt to prop up the currency, the government's foreign currency reserves dropped to $4 billion, an amount insufficient to carry the country through another day. In December 1997, barely a year after joining the Organization for Economic Cooperation and Development (OECD), Seoul turned to the IMF for economic assistance. At virtually the same time, South Koreans elected longtime democracy activist Kim Dae Jung to the presidency, the first time since the early 1 960s that an opposition leader had won the country's highest office.

After negotiating for weeks over the details, on December 4, 1997, South Korea and the IMF agreed to a $58 billion support package. In return, Seoul agreed to tighten its fiscal and monetary policies and engage in far-reaching, market-oriented reforms of its financial and corporate sectors and of its labor market policies. South Korea also agreed to open its economy further to foreign goods and investors. The newly-elected Kim government adopted most of the structural reforms as its own.

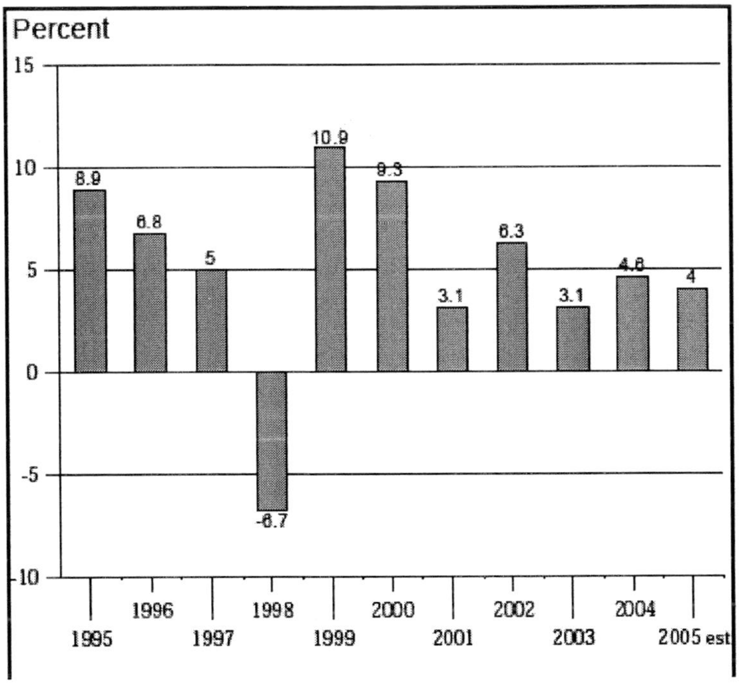

Source: Bank of Korea.

Figure 1. ROK Real GDP Growth, 1995-2005

Following the financial crisis, South Korea entered into a severe recession. In 1998, gross domestic product (GDP) contracted by 6.7% and unemployment nearly quadrupled, rising to 7.6% in 1998. The slowdown generated substantial anti-IMF and anti-American sentiment among many South Koreans.

Economic Events from 1999 2005

The economy rebounded in 1999 and 2000, growing by over 10% and 9%, respectively, and enabling the South Korean government to rapidly retire many of the debts it incurred in 1997.[2] In 2001, however, growth slowed considerably, dragged down by a combination of internal and external developments, including a decline in consumer and business confidence, the bursting of Korea's stock market bubble, rising oil prices, and a sharp falloff in exports to the United States and Japan, which entered economic downturns of their own. The government responded by lowering interest rates, unveiling an economic stimulus package, and easing the rules on the use of credit cards. These measures boosted consumer spending, which helped to double the growth rate from 3.1% in 2001 to 6.3% in 2002. Growth also was boosted by rapid economic integration with China. Domestic investment, however, remained low.

In 2003, overuse of personal credit cards led to the near-collapse of many financial firms and a sharp slowdown in economic growth, which fell back to 3.1%. Until the late 1 990s, the consumer sector of the economy had been largely untapped, with Korean lenders focusing on the corporate sector. Thus, when the government liberalized financial regulations and forced

Korea's giant conglomerates to curtail their borrowing in the aftermath of the 1997 crisis, banks and other financial institutions turned to consumers — at times recklessly — as a new source of profit. The number of credit card holders behind in their payments increased sharply, with an estimated 8% of the population in default in March 2004.[3] In 2003 and 2004, all eight of Korea's specialized credit-card issuers registered massive losses that collectively were more than double their assets. In most cases, insolvency was avoided only through bailouts and takeovers by affiliated members of the companies' respective *chaebol* groupings. Most of these moves appear to have been engineered, regulatorally enabled, and/or encouraged by the government, which feared a collapse of the financial system if the firms were allowed to fail. The government responded to the household debt crisis by tightening restrictions on credit card use and issuance, and by initiating a refinancing and forgiveness program for individual debtors.

For 2004, South Korea's economy grew by 4.6%, below the 6% growth rate the government had expected.[4] Much of the growth was driven by a surge in exports — particularly to China — which rose by over 30% from 2003. A sharp rise in oil prices (South Korea imports all of its oil) and lackluster domestic demand contributed to the slower-than-expected growth rate.

In early 2005, the government lowered its growth forecast from 5% to less than 4%, due in part to a slowdown in export growth. The government responded by unveiling a $6.5 billion fiscal stimulus policy. Beginning in the late spring, South Korean domestic production and demand began to increase, perhaps indicating a resolution of the credit card problem; despite rising energy prices (South Korea imports all of its oil), private spending rose by 3.2% in 2005, compared to a 0.5% contraction the year before. Toward the end of the year, the South Korean stock market and the *won* sharply appreciated in value, the latter against both the U.S. dollar and the Japanese *yen*. Despite this trend, South Korean exports continued to rise, albeit at a slower rate; exports rose by just over 12% in 2005, compared with a 31% growth rate in 2004. South Korea's merchandise trade surplus in 2005 was about $23 billion.[5] For 2006, the Ministry of Finance and Economy and the Bank of Korea forecast that South Korean growth will increase to the 5% range.

Economic Reforms

Financial Sector and Chaebol Reforms

Assessing Korea's economic reforms to date depends on one's perspective. If the point of comparison is the Korean economy in 1997, then the government's progress has been impressive. South Korea's economy today is far more transparent, open to foreign investors, and efficient than it was seven years ago. Progress has been particularly notable in opening the country to foreign direct investment (see below) and in reforming the financial sector. In

---

[2] In August 2001, Seoul paid off the last of the $19.5 billion it had borrowed from the IMF.

[3] Hye-Seung Seo, "South Korea Unveils Program To Help Ease Consumer Debt," *The Asian Wall Street Journal,* March 11, 2004.

[4] Gordon Fairclough, "South Korea Forecasts Growth Of Near 6% on Export Strength," *The Asian Wall Street Journal,* April 26, 2004.

[5] Ministry of Finance and Economy and the Korea Development Institute, *Republic of Korea Economic Bulletin,* Volume 28, No. 1, January 2006.

the years following the crisis, the government spent about $140 billion to bail out ailing banks and mutual funds.[6] This amount is approximately 25%-30% of the country's GDP, nearly twice the level required to save Mexico's financial system during its crisis in 1995. Notably, predictions that the government would have to spend substantially more funds have not come to pass, and Korea's banking sector as a whole has returned to profitability. By the end of 2001, non-performing loans (loans which are unlikely to be repaid) had fallen to 2.4% of total loans, compared with 16.4% in 1998. (In 2001, the percentage of non-performing loans for large banks in the United States was 1.5%.)

The Roh government has accelerated South Korea's efforts to re-privatize the banks that were nationalized in the aftermath of the 1997 crisis. By 2000, the nationalization program had brought about one-third of the banking industry's assets into government hands, and state ownership of the banking sector formed the crux of a major trade dispute with the United States and European Union, in which state-owned and state-controlled banks were accused of illegally subsidizing Hynix Semiconductor Inc., the world's third-largest producer of dynamic random access memory (DRAM) semiconductor chips. By the spring of 2004, however, sales of many of formerly state-owned banks had given foreign companies collectively a major stake in South Korea's financial sector, notwithstanding occasional statements by Korean politicians expressing misgivings about excessive non-Korean ownership. By 2005, foreigners owned about one-third of the assets in the Korean banking sector, including majority stakes in four of Korea's eight nation-wide banks.[7] In March 2004, Korea's Financial Supervisory Commission approved a $1.7 billion bid from Citigroup for a controlling stake in KorAm, Korea's seventh-largest bank.

If the yardstick used to assess South Korea's reforms is the U.S. economy, however, it becomes clear that Seoul has far to go if it is to make the economy truly responsive to market-oriented pressures and incentives. Progress has been particularly difficult in the government's attempts to pressure the *chaebol* to correct the problems revealed by the 1997 crisis, including excessively high debt levels, a heavy reliance on short-term debt, the lack of transparency, weak corporate governance, and corporate structures dominated by individual families rather than professional business managers. Although two of the largest *chaebol* — Daewoo and Hyundai — have been dismantled and debt-equity ratios for most of the top conglomerates have been reduced, corporate governance and cross-shareholdings within *chaebol* groupings remain major problems. The bailouts of struggling credit card affiliates in 2003 and 2004 seemed to many to indicate that the *chaebol* had not reformed their past practices of forcing their profitable enterprises to rescue failing ones. Also in 2003, a massive accounting scandal at SK Global, the trading unit of the country's fourth-largest *chaebol*, SK Group, revealed similar structural problems.[8]

[6] Francesco Guerrera, et. al., "Seoul Plans to Sell Most of Stake in Hana Bank," *Financial Times*, January 28, 2004.

[7] Foreigners also are significant shareholders in many prominent chaebol and own an estimated 40% of the value of the shares traded on South Korea's stock exchange.

[8] SK Global (now SK Networks)was found to have window-dressed its financial statements by over 7 trillion *won* (around $5.8 billion), for which several senior level executives, including SK Corp's chairman were convicted of breaching fiduciary responsibilities. The chairman served a three-month prison term. Following SK Global's restatement of its earnings, SK Corp led a rescue of its subsidiary despite the objections of most of SK Corp's foreign shareholders, led by Dubai-based Sovereign Asset Management. SK managers ultimately defeated Sovereign's efforts, and in July 2005, Sovereign sold its 15% stake in SK Corp.

Additionally, the reckless credit card lending activities of Korean credit card firms in 2003 and 2004 exposed the continued weaknesses in risk management and due diligence by Korean financial interests. One of the government's responses has been to accelerate plans to further restructure the financial industry by passing new laws allowing the consolidation of banking, insurance, asset management, and brokerage services. Some critics, however, worry that this cross-sectoral consolidation will accentuate the problem of cross-shareholding within *chaebol* groupings. Also, bailouts of the two largest credit card companies, LG Card and Samsung Card, in 2003, have raised fears that the "too big to fail" dynamic continues to persist in South Korea.

Foreign Direct Investment Reforms

As part of its commitment to the IMF in December 1997, Seoul pledged to eliminate most restrictions on foreign firms' long-term investments in local subsidiaries and controlling interests in local companies. The government of President Kim Dae Jung, who was elected during the nadir of Korea's financial crisis, moved aggressively to liberalize Korea's foreign investment regime. Partly as a response to Kim's reforms, and partly in response to the lower prices of Korean assets following the 1997 crisis, FDI flows increased markedly, soaring from $3.2 billion in 1996 to a peak of $15.7 billion in 2000. FDI fell off significantly from 2001-2003, before rising to $12.8 billion in 2004, the same year President Roh Moo-hyun's government began a policy of boosting FDI as a source of domestic growth.[9] Since the 1997 crisis, FDI commitments by U.S. companies have totaled nearly $20 billion. (See Figure 2.) A number of high-profile Korean companies have been taken over by foreign interests, notably General Motors' purchase of Daewoo Motors in 2002.[10] Citigroup's $2.4 billion purchase of KorAm Bank in March 2004 was the largest foreign direct investment in Korean history and Citigroup's largest investment outside North America.

Despite the increased openness to foreign ownership, a number of high-profile acquisitions by foreign companies have been either delayed or cancelled, due to nationalistic objections to the sale, disagreements over the sales price, and/or the discovery of previously undisclosed debts owed by the target Korean company. These delaying actions often have backfired, resulting in far lower eventual sale prices. A case in point was the protracted sale of Daewoo Motors. In June 2000, Daewoo Motor's creditors, many of them government-owned or controlled, reached a tentative agreement with Ford, which bid nearly $7 billion for the company. Negotiations became difficult, and after discovering billions of dollars in previously hidden liabilities (and taking a large loss from the Firestone tire recall), Ford withdrew its offer. General Motors, which initially had bid $4 billion, remained the only viable suitor. Negotiations with creditors and the government dragged on for over a year and a half, however. Finally, in May 2002, GM and Daewoo's creditors signed an agreement, by which GM acquired a controlling stake in Daewoo Motors for $400 million.

---

[9] In a March 4, 2004 speech to the American Chamber of Commerce of Korea, Minister of Finance and Economy Lee Hun-jai announced the new policy, saying, "foreign direct investment is important not just for short-term recovery of the Korean economy, but also for supporting longer-term growth potential." Andrew Ward, "Korea Moves to Win Back Foreign Business," *Financial Times,* March 5, 2004.

[10] Since then, GM Daewoo has become GM's manufacturing platform in Asia.

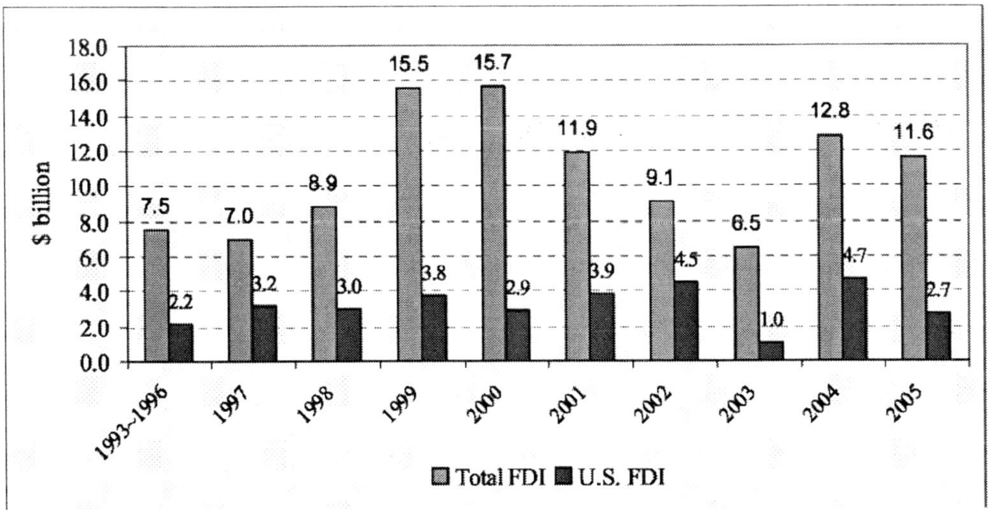

Source: ROK Ministry of Commerce, Industry, and Energy

Figure 2. Foreign Direct Investment into the ROK, 1993-2005

Many Koreans, however, have reacted with alarm to foreign investment and there has been growing discussion of restricting the takeover of Korean companies by foreigners. For instance, when Newbridge Capital sold its 50% stake in Korea First Bank in early 2005 at a high profit, it was accused of being a "foreign exploiter." The South Korean government attempted to limit or eliminate an investment treaty with Malaysia, Newbridge's home, that allowed the company to avoid paying Korean taxes on its gains. Newbridge bought Korea First Bank in 1999 and is credited in many circles with turning around the bank's fortunes. Part of the Korean government's apparent ambivalence to foreign investment, particularly in the financial sector, is that foreign multinationals often are more resistant to government pressure. Newbridge, for instance, reportedly resisted efforts by the South Korea's Financial Supervisory Commission to advance loans to two failing companies, Hynix and LG Credit.[11]

South Korea's Increased Economic Integration with China

As mentioned earlier, in 2003 China surpassed the United States as South Korea's number one trading partner (see Figure 3). South Korea has run trade surpluses with China for a number of years, in contrast to the increasingly large trade deficits it has run with Japan (see Figure 4). For several years, China has also been the number one destination for South Korean overseas direct investment, by a large margin. Many South Korean exports to China are intermediate goods used in the production of finished goods that ultimately are exported from China to other countries, including the United States. A growing number of Koreans are studying the Chinese language and traveling to China, and public opinion polls show that a growing number of Koreans have favorable views of China. These developments, combined with a sharp decline in favorable views of the United States, have led many American observers

[11] Edward Graham, "South Korea Should End its Corporate Xenophobia," *Financial Times,* August 4, 2005.

to worry that Chinese influence over South Korean policy is likely to rise in the future, at the expense of the United States.

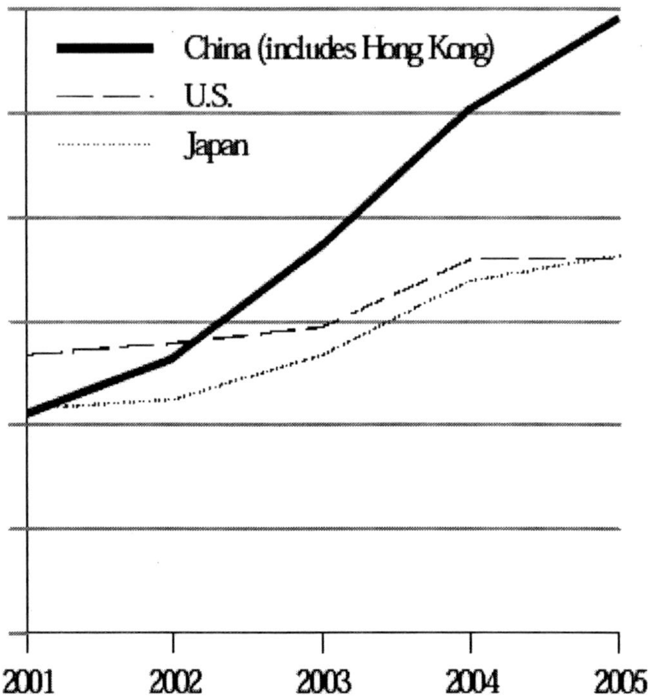

Sources: Korea International Trade Association, Bank of Korea.

Figure 3. ROK Trade with China, U.S., and Japan, 2001 -2005

Many South Koreans, however, have ambivalent views of China's growing economic importance. The increased competitiveness of many Chinese manufacturers has caused some consternation in some South Korean firms, pushing them to search overseas for lower-cost production bases. There are concerns that jobs, particularly in the manufacturing sector, will be lost to Chinese workers as South Korean foreign direct investment in China increases.

Improved Inter-Korean Economic Relations

In the past three years, South Korea has emerged as North Korea's second-most important economic partner, after China. Inter-Korean trade has more than doubled since 2000, to just over $1 billion in 2005 (see Figure 5).[12] South Korea runs a trade surplus with North Korea. From 1994-2004, Korea provided around $3 billion worth of economic and humanitarian aid to North Korea, most of which has come since the June 2000 summit between North Korean leader Kim Jong-il and then-South Korean President Kim Dae Jung. Since the summit, the two Koreas have reconnected inter-Korean roads, are close to reconnecting two rail lines, have expanded a tourism site in Mt. Kumgang (North Korea), and have completed construction of a pilot industrial zone in Kaesong (North Korea) for South Korean companies to erect factories using

[12] South Korean National Statistical Office; Korean Ministry of Unification.

North Korean labor. For 2006, there are plans to expand the Kaesong site beyond the 15 companies currently operating there, despite previous statements by South Korean government officials that resolving the North Korean nuclear crisis was a prerequisite for starting any "new" inter-Korean economic programs, presumably including the expansion of the Kaesong site beyond the pilot program. Additionally, as part of the six-party talks on North Korea's nuclear weapons programs, Seoul has proposed sending large amounts of electricity to North Korea, in exchange for concessions from Pyongyang.

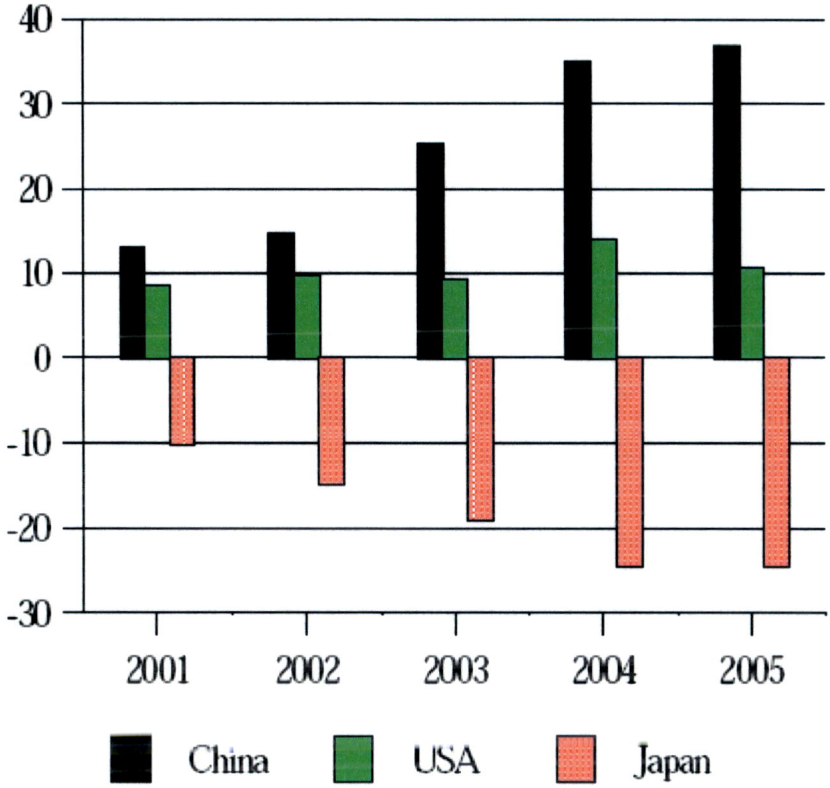

Source: Bank of Korea

Figure 4. ROK Trade Balances with Major Partners

The Kaesong Industrial Zone

The worsened economic situation for many South Korean small and medium sized enterprises (SMEs) is thought to be a major factor propelling President Roh Moo-hyun's economic initiatives with North Korea. In particular, the inter-Korean industrial zone in Kaesong (also spelled "Gaesong"), North Korea, just north of the demilitarized zone separating the two countries, is explicitly designed for use by SMEs, over 1,000 of which reportedly have expressed interest in participating. A pilot site at Kaesong, housing the factories of fifteen South Korean firms, opened in 2004, and in the summer of 2005 the two Koreas announced plans to expand the zone in 2006 and 2007.

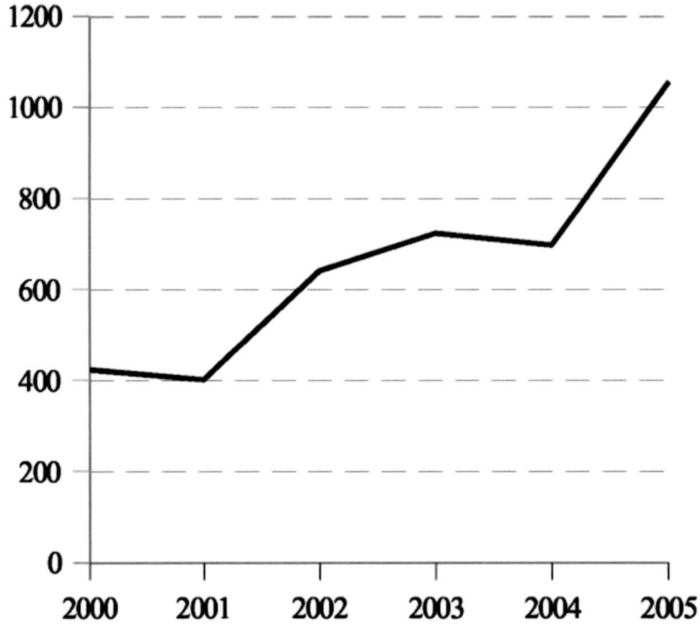

Source: Unification Ministry

Figure 5. North-South Korea Trade

The Kaesong industrial zone could become a contentious issue in the bilateral FTA talks. Since the zone opened, it has been South Korean policy to request that its FTA partners to allow exports from Kaesong to be considered "Made in Korea," thereby enabling these products to receive the preferential status conferred by the FTA.[13] On February 3, 2006, the Vice-Minister of South Korea's Ministry of Unification reportedly stated that Seoul plans to try to secure preferential tariff treatment for Kaesong-made goods in FTAs with the United States and Canada.[14] When questioned about this policy during the February 2, 2006 launch of the FTA, USTR Portman stated that the FTA would cover only products made in South Korea. At an economic press roundtable in Seoul on February 8, 2006, an unnamed official with the U.S. embassy said, "...the provisions of the FTA in our view will apply to goods originating within the territories of the two parties... .what qualifies as an originating good is something that will be settled in the chapter [of the FTA] called Rules of Origin."[15] The latter half of the statement appears to indicate that the Bush Administration may feel there is room for negotiation on this point.

[13] The Korea-Singapore FTA, due to take effect in March 2006, extends duty-free treatment to Kaesong-made goods. The Korea-EFTA (European Free Trade Association) FTA, signed in December 2005, extends duty-free treatment to Kaesong-made goods if over 60% of their content are materials of South Korean origin. In the discussions between South Korea and ASEAN (the Association of Southeast Asian Nations) over an FTA, the two sides agreed that in principle, no tariffs will be imposed on Kaesong-made goods. Ministry of Unification, "Goods Produced in the GIC Subject to No-Tariff in Several FTAs,"*Inter-Korean Issues Weekly,* Volume33, February 10, 2006.

[14] *Ibid.*

[15] US Embassy in Korea, "Questions and Answers from Economic Press Roundtable with Embassy Official," February 8, 2006.

Some analysts worry that improved inter-Korean economic relations are undermining the Bush Administration's policy of constricting the inflows of foreign currency that are thought to go to the North Korean elite, providing a critical base of support for North Korean leader Kim Jong-il. Alternatively, coordinated U.S. and South Korean policies could use economic leverage to pressure North Korea. In broad terms, the Bush Administration has stated that it supports South Korea's economic engagement with North Korea, including the Kaesong industrial zone.[16] In 2004 and 2005, the United States approved several export controls clearances that were required by U.S. law for South Korean firms to bring items — such as computer and telecommunications equipment — to Kaesong.[17]

MAJOR U.S. TRADE DISPUTES WITH SOUTH KOREA

Given the disparities in size and economic dependence, it is not surprising that the United States typically sets the agenda of U.S.-ROK trade talks. Since the 1997 financial crisis, these complaints have tended to be directed at regulations promulgated by "domestic" ministries, such as the Ministry of Health and Welfare, the Korean Food and Drug Administration, and the Ministry of Environment, that traditionally have had little contact with foreign governments or firms. One element of the U.S. strategy toward Korea appears to be attempting to raise the pressure on these ministries by pushing for the Korean Cabinet to focus on the issue.

In general, U.S. exporters and trade negotiators identify the lack of transparency of Korea's trading and regulatory systems as the most significant barriers to trade with Korea, in almost every major product sector. In 2004, the transparency issue became a stand-alone item in the quarterly trade action agenda meetings. Many U.S. government officials also complain that Seoul continues to use government regulations and standard-setting powers to discriminate against foreign firms in politically sensitive industries, such as automobiles and telecommunications. Another major cross-sectoral complaint is that restrictions in the Korean labor market, such as mandatory severance pay, raise the cost of investing and doing business. Finally, the United States and other countries have pressed South Korea to open further its agricultural market, which is among the most closed in the OECD.[18]

Below are brief descriptions of several major sector-specific disputes between the U.S. and South Korea.

Major Agriculture Issues

Despite South Korea's place as one of the top destinations for U.S. agricultural exports, U.S. government and agricultural industry officials contend that Seoul retains a number of tariff and non-tariff barriers that have stunted U.S. bilateral exports. South Korean agricultural tariffs are particularly high compared to the United States and most OECD

[16] See, for instance, Joint Declaration on the ROK-U.S. Alliance and Peace on the Korean Peninsula, White House Office of the Press Secretary, November 17, 2005.
[17] US Embassy in Korea, "Questions and Answers from Economic Press Roundtable with Embassy Official," February 8, 2006; January and February 2006 conversations with officials familiar with the Kaesong export control discussions.
[18] OECD, *Economic Survey - Korea 2004*.

members; according to USTR, South Korea's average applied agricultural tariffs are 52%, more than four times the U.S.'s average.[19] The completion of a comprehensive FTA therefore is to dramatically expand U.S. agricultural exporters' access to the Korean market; by one estimate, U.S. agricultural exports will increase by more than 200% within four years after a hypothetical FTA is implemented.[20] South Korea's farmers, while shrinking in terms of population and contribution to GDP, remain a politically powerful force in South Korea. At the February 2006 launch of the FTA, ROK Hyun-chong Kim said Seoul plans to spend over $100 million in adjustment assistance to South Korean farmers over the coming decade.

In recent years, the number and intensity of agricultural disputes on the U.S. trade agenda with South Korea appear to have diminished, as manufacturing and service sector issues have been emphasized. Two of the most contentious agricultural trade disputes over the past two years have involved beef and rice.

South Korea's Beef Ban

South Korea, along with Japan and other countries, banned U.S. beef imports in late December 2003, after the United States reported the discovery of a cow with bovine spongiform encephalopathy (BSE or "mad cow disease"). South Korea formerly was the third-largest foreign buyer of U.S. beef; the United States exported nearly $800 million worth of beef to South Korea in 2003.[21] Throughout 2004, USTR official said that FTA negotiations were unlikely to begin with South Korea while the ban was in place. During bilateral talks in January 2006, South Korea agreed to partially lift its ban. "Toward the end of March" 2006, South Korea will allow imports of U.S. boneless beef from cattle less than 30 months old. Boneless beef constituted about half of U.S. bilateral beef exports in 2003. Korean negotiators reportedly backed down from their desire to limit imports to boneless beef from cattle less than 20 months old. While welcoming the agreement, USTR Portman also said he was "extremely disappointed" that Korea did not fully open its market to all U.S. beef products.[22] The U.S.-ROK agreement came a month after Japan agreed in December 2005 to partially lift its ban. A week after the South Korean decision, Japan reimposed its ban after prohibited bone material was found in beef shipments from the United States. South Korea has not taken this step.

Rice

The South Korean government controls the purchase, distribution, and end-use of all imported rice. During the Uruguay Round of multilateral trade negotiations (1986-1993), South Korea was granted a 10-year grace period before opening its rice market to imports. In return for receiving this concession, South Korea agreed to allow minimum access for rice through the use of quotas. The grace period ended on the last day of 2004. Prior to that date, South Korea notified the WTO that it wished to extend the minimum access quota system rather than convert to tariffs. Under the Uruguay Round agreement, Seoul could do this only if

---

[19] USTR, *FTA: United States and Republic of Korea Economic and Strategic Benefits,* February 2, 2006.

[20] United States International Trade Commission (ITC), *U.S.-Korea FTA: The Economic Impact of Establishing a Free Trade Agreement (FTA) Between the United States and the Republic of Korea,* (Washington, DC, 2001), p. 5-1 - 5-2.

[21] USTR, *FTA: United States and Republic of Korea Opportunities for Agriculture,* February 2006.

[22] USDA Press Release No. 0004.06, "Johanns and Ustr Portman Welcome Progress to Reopen Korean Market to U.S. Beef," January 13, 2006; "U.S. Applauds Korea Beef Deal as First Step, Signals Additional Talks" *Inside US Trade,* January 20, 2006.

it obtained the consent of other WTO members, which could demand concessions to expand their quota. The United States availed itself of this right, and on December 30, 2004, U.S. and South Korean officials announced an agreement, under which Korea will double the amount of rice it imports over the next 10 years, provide guaranteed access for 50,000 MT of U.S. rice each year, and make imported rice available directly to Korean consumers. In November 2005, after months of delay and acrimonious debate, the Korean National Assembly ratified the rice deal. China and Thailand, two other parties to the rice negotiations, reportedly wished to see an end of the quota system in favor of tariffication, which presumably would be more advantageous to lower-cost rice producers such as themselves. In 2003, U.S. exporters sold 55,000 metric tons (MT) of rice — or about 28% of the 200,000 MT minimum access quota — to South Korea, behind China's exports of 115,000 MT.[23]

Other Issues

Automotive Trade [24]

Automotive trade is perennial issue in trade talks between the United States and South Korea, the world's fourth-largest producer of automobiles. For years, U.S. officials have argued that Korean tax and "Korea unique" certification practices discriminate against imports. In 2005, USTR Portman included automobiles in his list of four sectors that on which the United States would seek concessions from South Korea before agreeing to begin FTA negotiations. In announcing the intent to launch talks, Portman alluded to the South Korean Ministry of the Environment's decision in the fall of 2005 to grant auto makers with a low share of the Korean market an exemption, until 2009, from Korea's regulations on ultra-low emissions. Previously, the regulations would have applied in January 2007.

South Korean imports of foreign automobiles totaled fewer than 31,000 in 2005 — including about 5,800 U.S. vehicles — just over 3% of the South Korean market, up from less than 0.5% five years earlier (see Table 3). Most of the foreign cars sold in South Korea are luxury models. In contrast, South Korean auto manufacturers exported over 730,000 cars to the United States in 2005, capturing over 4% of the U.S. market. Nearly all of these vehicles were produced by Hyundai Motors, including vehicles produced by its subsidiary Kia, formerly Korea's second-largest independent manufacturer. USTR is pushing South Korea to lower its 8% tariff, which is more than three times the U.S. level of 2.5% on imported cars. Moreover, the United States continues to protest that South Korea's tariff, tax and regulatory structure unfairly penalize automobiles with larger-sized engines. Specifically, the Bush Administration has called on Korea to move from engine displacement taxation to a value-based taxation system, because the former assesses higher taxes on larger vehicles.[25] Periodically, some Members of Congress have introduced legislation calling on South Korea to end the practices that impede foreign market access and requesting various U.S. executive agencies to monitor Korea's progress on this issue. Two initiatives were H.Con.Res. 144 and S.Con.Res. 43, introduced in the 107th Congress, in May 2001.

---

[23] Inside US Trade, "Fight over Korean Rice Market Pits China Against U.S., Australia," June 11, 2004.
[24] This section written with Stephen Cooney, CRS Industry Analyst. For more on the United States auto industry, see CRS Report RL32883, *U.S. Automotive Industry: Recent History and Issues.*
[25] USTR, *2004 National Trade Estimate Report on Foreign Trade Barriers,* p.3 13.

For much of the post-Korean War era, South Korea's market was closed to the import of automobiles. It banned all automobile imports prior to 1989, and the ban on importation of automobiles from Japan was eliminated only in 1999. Gradually, the industry has opened up to foreign investment, though almost all cars sold in Korea are still locally produced.

In its October 1997 Super 301 report to Congress, the Clinton Administration designated Korea as a "Priority Foreign Country" for its barriers to foreign motor vehicles.[26] USTR subsequently initiated an investigation under Section 301 of the U.S. Trade Act of 1974, as amended, and issued a call for bilateral consultations to provide fair market access for foreign autos in Korea.[27] In 1998, the United States and South Korea signed a Memorandum of Understanding (MOU) on foreign access to Korea's auto market, which led the USTR to terminate the Section 301 investigation. Under the MOU, Seoul agreed to reduce its tariffs on motor vehicles from 80% to 8%, proactively address instances of anti-import activity in Korea, lower or eliminate many automobile taxes, create a new financing system to make it easier to purchase automobiles, and streamline its standards and certification procedures. Many of these steps — including lowering tariffs — have been implemented.

Furthermore, Seoul has largely abandoned its policy of allowing only Korean-owned auto companies to operate in South Korea. With Hyundai's purchase of Kia, Korea's second-largest producer, there is now only one Korean-owned motor vehicle manufacturer left, although it is dominant in the home market. In 2002, General Motors purchased the Daewoo Motor Company from the bankrupt Daewoo conglomerate. Two other smaller vehicle producers, Samsung and Ssangyong, have also come under the control of foreign investors.

Table 3. U.S.-ROK Automotive Trade
Vehicular Units, including Light Trucks

	2000	2001	2002	2003	2004	2005
Korean Auto Companies' Sales in the U.S. *Market Share*	473,400 *2.7%*	618,300 *3.6%*	650,300 *3.9%*	637,700 *3.8%*	688,670 *4.1%*	730,863 *4.3%*
Total Foreign Auto Companies' Sales in Korea* *Market Share*	4,400 *0.3%*	7,700 *0.5%*	16,100 *1.3%*	19,500 *1.9%*	23,345 *2.1%*	30,901 *3.3%*
U.S. Auto Companies' Sales in Korea* *Market Share*	1,700 *0.1%*	2,000 *0.1%*	4,700 *0.4%*	4,100 *0.4%*	5,415 *0.5%*	5,795 *0.7%*

Source: U.S. Department of Commerce

* Figures for foreign and U.S. companies' sales in South Korea do not include the sales of GM Daewoo Automotive Technologies, which has captured between 12% and 13% (104,000 - 128,000) of the Korean market since GM took over Daewoo in 2002.

[26] Super 301 (Section 310 of the 1974 Trade Act) requires the USTR to report to congress on "priority foreign countries" that practice unfair trade and "priority practices" that have the greatest effect on restricting U.S. exports. If agreement is not reached on the priority practices, the USTR is required to initiate a Section 301 case (see the following footnote). For more information, see Wayne Morrison, *Section 301 of the Trade Act of 1974,* CRS Report 98-454.

[27] Section 301 (sections 30 1-309 of the Trade Act of 1974) authorize the USTR to initiate investigations of foreign trade practices that allegedly discriminate against U.S. commerce. If a settlement with the foreign country is not reached following the initiation of the investigation, the USTR decides whether or not to retaliate, usually in the form of 100% tariffs on selected imports from the offending country. See CRS Report 98-454, *Section 301 of the*

Meanwhile, Korea's top automotive manufacturer has renewed an earlier effort to build cars in North America, as well as to import them. In May 2005, Hyundai Motors opened a new $1.1 billion plant in Montgomery, Alabama. The facility is expected to produce 300,000 vehicles annually and will employ approximately 2,000 workers. The plant's suppliers are expected to employ approximately 5,500 workers.[28] Hyundai's subsidiary Kia also is reported to be planning to open a U.S. production facility.

Pharmaceuticals

Korea is ranked in the world's top 15 pharmaceutical markets, with annual sales in the $4 billion range. In 2001, imports comprised approximately 30% of the total market, compared with an average of 50%-70% for other countries that do not have a significant research-based domestic industry. Korea's expenditures on pharmaceutical products is about $115 per person per year, less than half the $240 average for OECD countries.[29] The country has a nationalized health insurance system, which began to experience a negative cash flow in 1995. For years, the U.S. government has complained that a number of Korea's pharmaceutical policies are designed to protect the domestic Korean industry, which predominantly produces generic drugs.

Criticisms have mounted since 2001, when the Korean government implemented a series of emergency measures to fill the national health insurance fund's mounting deficit, estimated at the time to be over 4 trillion *won* ($3.3 billion). Recent complaints include the lack of transparency of the Korean Ministry of Health and Welfare, particularly the Ministry's allegedly poor record on consulting with and notifying companies about regulatory changes; the reimbursement scheme of the health insurance system, which allegedly gives price incentives for doctors to prescribe and patients to use Korean-made products; poor protection of intellectual property rights for medical patents; and the discriminatory nature of Seoul's requirements that foreign drugs must be retested on Koreans living in Korea, rather than on other ethnic Asians, as the United States has insisted. In a sign of pharmaceuticals' growing importance on the bilateral trade agenda, in January 2002, the two sides established a bilateral private sector health care reform working group. In 2005, USTR Portman said FTA negotiations would not be launched without progress on pharmaceutical issues. At the October 2005 trade action agenda meeting, the South Korean government agreed that no new drug reimbursement pricing policies would be introduced in the near future, agreed to set up an independent mechanism under which drug reimbursement decisions could be appealed, and clarified the reasons the Korean Food and Drug Administration was requiring drug manufacturers to submit large amounts of proprietary data as part of the drug approval process.

South Korea's "Screen Quotas"

Since 1966, South Korea has sought to protect its domestic film industry by mandating that movie theaters devote at least 146 days per year (or 40% of the calendar year) to showing domestic films. The issue was a major reason the United States and South Korea were unable to finalize negotiations over a bilateral investment treaty (BIT), which were initiated in the

Trade Act of 1974, as Amended: Its Operation and Issues Involving its Use by the United States, by Wayne Morrison.

[28] May 20, 2005 letter from Hyundai Motor Co.'s Washington, DC office.

late 1990s but were suspended in 1999.[30] Each country's motion picture industry has significant political clout; during South Korea's 2002 presidential elections, Roh was backed by several prominent South Korean actors. Nonetheless, for years Roh's administration pledged that it would reduce, if not eliminate, the quotas. For U.S. trade officials, the issue became a symbol of the Roh government's ability and capacity to make the difficult political concessions that would also come in FTA negotiations. On January 26, 2006, the day after the beef ban was partially lifted, South Korea's Prime Minister announced that the screen quotas would be cut in half, to 73 days a year. The following week, the two countries announced their intent to launch FTA talks. The growing popularity — both in South Korea and abroad — of South Korean films undoubtedly made Roh's concession more palatable.

South Korea's Alleged Currency Manipulation

In recent years, South Korea has been criticized for intervening in foreign currency markets by purchasing U.S. dollar assets to artificially lower the value of the Korean *won* against the U.S. dollar in order to boost exports. As of the end of November 2005, South Korea was the seventh largest foreign holder of U.S. treasury securities, holding 66.5 billion.[31]

As Figure 4 shows, the *won* generally has been appreciating against the dollar since 2001. The *won's* rise was particularly marked in late 2005 and early 2006, when it reached levels not seen since before the 1997 financial crisis. During the same period, the *won* has risen even more precipitously against the Japanese *yen.* This is particularly worrisome to many Korean exporters because they compete directly against more Japanese than U.S. companies and because many Korean manufacturers rely upon imports of intermediate goods from Japan.

Since the *won* began its gradual ascent in 2001, South Korean authorities have intervened episodically to slow the *won 's* rise, though the scale of the intervention has been far less than Japan and China's. The United States made currency intervention a major issue at the Asia Pacific Economic Cooperation (APEC) Finance Ministers and G-7 Finance Ministers meetings in September 2003. Shortly thereafter, South Korea appeared to ease off large-scale interventionist policies; South Korean government officials say that since early 2004, they have engaged in only minor intervention to "smooth" excessive currency volatility.[32] In response to the *won*'s spike since late 2005, although some Korean officials have said that their currency is overvalued, as of early 2006 they appear not to have intervened in currency markets in a large-scale way. Indeed, in early February 2006, South Korean Finance Ministry officials said they would like to loosen restrictions on *won*-denominated transactions overseas in order to make the *won* more widely traded.[33]

---

[29] American Chamber of Commerce in Korea, *Improving Korea 's Business Climate 2002,* p. 148.

[30] BITs are designed to improve the climate for foreign investors — typically by committing the signatories to prohibit discrimination against foreign investors — by establishing dispute settlement procedures and by protecting foreign investors from performance requirements, restrictions on transferring funds, and arbitrary expropriation. The United States has signed over 30 BITs, primarily with countries undergoing significant economic reforms.

[31] Department of the Treasury and the Federal Reserve Board, "Major Foreign Holders of Treasury Securities," [http://www.ustreas.gov/tic/mfh.txt]. Japan held $683 billion in U.S. treasury securities, China $250 billion, and the United Kingdom $223billion.

[32] Charles Roth, "South Korea to Use Reserves For Local Asset Management," *The Asian Wall Street Journal,* February 14, 2005.

[33] Laura Santini, "Won Bulls see Korean Currency as a Proxy for Asia's Growth," *The Asian Wall Street Journal,* February 7, 2006.

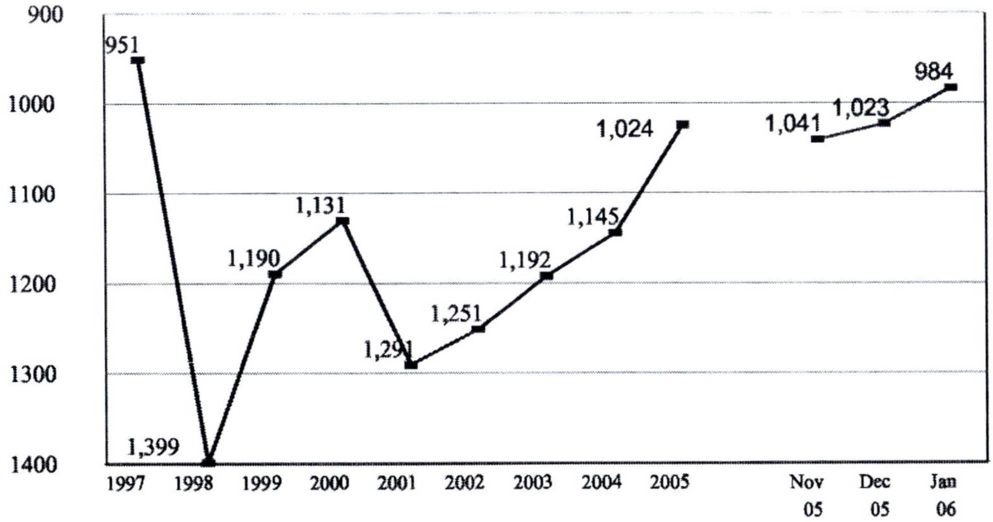

Figure 6. Won-Dollar Exchange Rate, 1997-2006 Source: Bank of Korea, Average Basic Rate. Y-Axis is Inverted.

In the future, the U.S. dollar and the market for U.S. Treasury securities could be affected by the South Korean government's launch of the Korean Investment Corporation (KIC) to manage a portion of South Korea's foreign exchange reserves, in July 2005. The KIC initially is managing $20 billion, and is expected to eventually manage $100 billion by 2012. The stated goals of the program are to invest South Korean foreign currency holdings more effectively. The program also aims to boost President Roh Moo-hyun's efforts to turn Korea into a major financial and commercial hub in Northeast Asia by helping boost Korea's asset management industry.

Some members of Congress have criticized Korea's currency policy. A "Fair Currency Act" (Lieberman) was introduced in Senate the last two Congresses (S. 377 in the 109th Congress and S. 1592 in the 108th Congress). If passed, they would require the U.S. government to monitor and take action against specific countries, including South Korea, that are "engaged most egregiously in currency manipulation."

Intellectual Property Rights Issues

Bilateral tensions often have arisen over U.S. allegations that Korea does not sufficiently protect intellectual property rights (IPRs). Since becoming a signatory to the World Trade Organization (WTO) Agreement on Trade-Related Aspects of Intellectual Property Rights (TRIPs) in 1994, USTR has moved Korea back and forth between the Special 301 "priority watch list" and the "watch list."[34] Most recently, in January 2005, USTR downgraded Korea to the "watch list" because of "significant steps" Seoul had taken to strengthen its IPR regime. USTR has cited South Korea's increased protection for recordings transmitted over the internet

[34] "Special 301" refers to Section 182 of the Trade Act of 1974. Since the start of the Special 301 provision in 1989, the USTR has issued annually a three-tier list of countries judged to have inadequate regimes for IPR protection, or to deny access: 1) *priority foreign countries* are deemed to be the worst violators, and are subject to Section 301 investigations and possible trade sanctions; 2) *priority watch list countries* are considered to have major deficiencies in their IPR regime, but do not currently warrant a Section 301 investigation; and 3) *watch list countries,* which maintain IPR practices that are of particular concern, but do not yet warrant higher level designations. See Wayne Morrison, *Section 301 of the Trade Act of 1974,* CRS Report 98-454.

and the launch in May 2004 of a "Pan-Government Comprehensive Plan For IPR Protection" headed by a Han Duksoo, a prominent official who has a Cabinet portfolio to promote the initiative. USTR also lists several items, such as copyright protection and DVD piracy, on which it would like to see Korea make additional progress.[35]

Telecommunications

In recent years, telecommunications has emerged as one of the most contentious trade issues between the United States and South Korea. With one of the world's highest rates of Internet usage, South Korea is often used as a market for telecommunications companies to test cutting-edge wireless products and technologies. The Roh government has designated next-generation mobile communications as one of ten "new growth engines" that will help Korea reach President Roh's 2003 goal of nearly doubling per capita GDP to $20,000 by the end of the decade. Perhaps to this end, the Korean government has attempted to set mandatory, single-technology standards for wireless telecommunications services. These efforts led USTR in April 2004 to name South Korea as a "key country of concern" in its annual report under Section 1377, which requires USTR to assess U.S. trading partners' compliance with international telecommunication agreements.

Specifically, for two years, USTR negotiated with the South Korean government over the Ministry of Information and Communication's (MoIC) plan to require all cell phone services to use only the so-called wireless Internet platform for interoperability (WIPI) for downloading information from the Internet. WIPI is a new platform developed by a Korean association funded by Electronics and Telecommunications Research Institute (ETRI), a government-funded institute. The requirement would have excluded users and developers of other operability platforms, such as the platform developed by San Diego-based Qualcomm, which is used by a leading Korean cellular service provider. In April 2004, Seoul and Washington announced they had reached a compromise that allows MoIC to implement WIPI, but also permits cellular phones to be made compatible with other standards.[36]

A similar dispute is over MoIC's issuance of a mandatory standard — to be located in the 2.3 gigahertz (GHz) bandwidth spectrum — for a new portable broadband Internet system used to transmit information from the Internet to laptops and other wireless equipment. USTR and U.S. companies charged that, under the influence of ETRI, the original, domestically-designed standard was designed to deliberately exclude foreign companies in favor of Samsung.[37] In June 2004, the Korean government announced that all license holders would have to use one of the several technologies compatible with a standard designed by the International Institute of Electrical and Electronics Engineers. USTR has criticized the decision as excluding companies that have developed other systems. USTR also has asked the Korean government to revise its restrictions on foreign ownership in the telecommunications sector.[38]

---

[35] USTR, *2005 Special 301 Report,* April 29, 2005.

[36] "U.S., Korea Reach Deal on Single Standard for Cell Phone Technology," *Inside US Trade,* April 30, 2004.

[37] USTR, "Results of 2004 Section 1377 Review of Telecommunications Trade Agreements," p. 5.

[38] USTR, *2005 National Trade Estimate Report on Foreign Trade Barriers (NTE),* p. 394-95

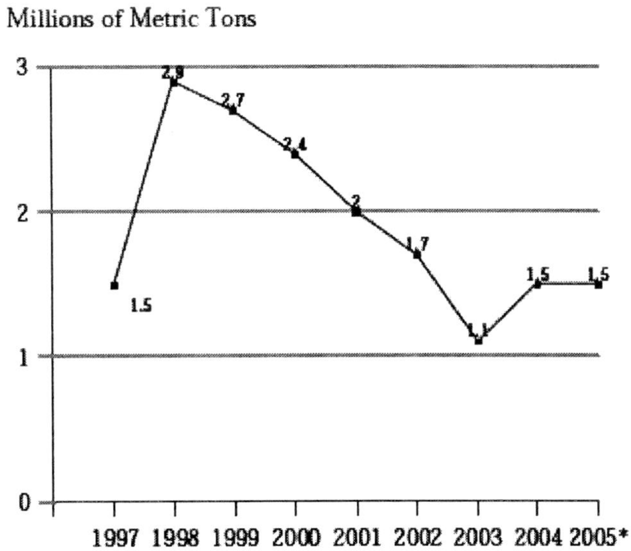

Source: U.S. Census Bureau; * January - November

Figure 7. Steel Imports from Korea, 1997-2004

Steel [39]

From 1998 through 2003, South Korean steel exports to the United States were one of the most politically charged items on the bilateral economic agenda, particularly since the 1997 Asian financial crisis. From 1997 to 1998, Korean shipments of steel to the U.S. nearly doubled, vaulting South Korea into the top five U.S. sources of steel imports. In 2003, imports from South Korea declined below pre-crisis levels, helping to defuse the issue. In the preceding five years, a number of anti-dumping cases were initiated against South Korean exporters, and Presidents Clinton and Bush each granted safeguard relief (under Section 201 of the Trade Act of 1974) for U.S. steel producers.[40] Korea and other countries challenged both Section 201 actions at the World Trade Organization, which ultimately ruled that the actions were inconsistent with global trading rules. In December 2003, President Bush terminated the safeguard tariffs he had established in March 2002.[41] In 2000, Korea also won a major WTO case involving anti-dumping duties the United States imposed against Korean exports of stainless steel plate in coils and stainless steel sheet and strip. Korea remains one of the leading exporters of steel to the United States by volume, at about 1.5 million metric tons annually in 2004-2005, but is now well behind the three leading Western Hemisphere

---

[39] This section written with Stephen Cooney, CRS Industry Analyst. For more, see CRS Report RL3 1748, *The American Steel Industry: A Changing Profile.*

[40] Section 201 relief, often referred to as "safeguard" or "escape clause" relief, is defined in sections 201-204 of the Trade Act of 1974, as amended (19 U.S.C. 225 1-2254). Safeguard relief provides for temporary duties, quotas, or other restrictions on imports that may be traded fairly, but that enter in such quantities as to cause or threaten to cause serious injury to a domestic industry. The relief is intended to give the domestic industry an opportunity to adjust to the new competition and remain competitive. Within six months after a Section 201 petition has been filed with the International Trade Commission, the ITC must conduct an investigation, determine if relief is warranted, and recommend appropriate remedial action from a specified range of options. The President then decides whether to implement the recommended measure, apply an alternative measure, or take no action at all.

[41] For more on the steel Section 201 case, see CRS Report RL32333, *Steel: Price and Availability Issues,* by Stephen Cooney.

suppliers (Canada, Mexico, Brazil), as well as China. The rise in steel prices since 2003 has to some extent defused this issue.

Assistance to Hynix Semiconductor

In 2001, a major trade dispute erupted between the United States and South Korea over allegations that the Seoul government was propping up Hynix Semiconductor, presently the world's third-largest producer of dynamic random access memory (DRAM) semiconductor chips. In 2001 and 2002, Hynix's leading creditors — most of which were owned by the Korean government — orchestrated a series of rescue packages that kept Hynix in business by enabling it to restructure its 8.6 trillion *won* (over $7 billion) in debt. In the United States, Micron Technology, the Idaho-based second largest producer of DRAMs, led a campaign against the support packages, arguing that they amounted to government-sponsored bailouts that allow Hynix to export at low prices and that they were a prime cause of the drastic plunge in global chip prices in 2001 and 2002. Micron, the last U. S.-based DRAM producer, eventually filed a countervailing duty case, which it won, resulting in a 44% punitive tariff being assessed against Hynix's exports to the United States. In a similar case, the European Union imposed a 34% countervailing duty against Hynix. Korea challenged both rulings in the WTO. A WTO panel was formed and in February 2005 ruled that the United States had failed to "properly demonstrate" that the Korean government had subsidized Hynix. The United States appealed in June 2005, the WTO's Appellate Body reversed the ruling, in part by using a definition of what government actions constitute a subsidy that is broader than the definition used by the panel.[42] Because Appellate Body decisions cannot be appealed, the United States's punitive tariffs will remain in place.

Meanwhile, Hynix has sold many of its non-semiconductor assets, introduced a program to upgrade its efficiency, completed its debt-workout program, and has overtaken Idaho-based Micron to become the world's second-largest chipmaker.

South Korea's Performance in the Doha Development Agenda

In the current round of multilateral trade talks, the Doha Development Agenda, USTR officials consistently have praised South Korea for attempting to bridge the differences between the developed and developing countries, particularly on non-agricultural market access issues such as industrial tariffs and services. Seoul also has been criticized consistently for resisting agricultural liberalization in the negotiations. Korea's tariffs on agricultural products, except rice, average 66%, compared with a 7.5% average for tariffs on industrial products.[43]

Korea's Complaints Against U.S. Anti-Dumping and CVD Practices

For over a decade, South Korea has chafed at the United States's use of anti-dumping and countervailing duty (CVD) laws to raise tariffs on Korean exports. According to one study, in July 2000 the five CVD and 18 anti-dumping orders against South Korean exports covered approximately $2.5 billion, or over 7%, of U.S. imports from South Korea in 1999. Moreover, these tariff hikes have tended to be concentrated in a handful of Korean industries —

[42] "WTO Appellate Body Finds U.S. Can Keep Duties on Korean DRAMS," *Inside US Trade,* July 1, 2005.
[43] USTR, *2004 National Trade Estimate Report on Foreign Trade Barriers,* p.290.

semiconductors, steel, televisions, and telecommunications equipment — that have considerable political influence in Seoul.

During the Uruguay Round (1986-1993) of the General Agreement on Tariffs and Trade (GATT, the WTO's predecessor organization), Korea was one of several countries demanding revisions to global anti-dumping rules, changes the United States opposed because of concerns that they would constrain U.S. anti-dumping investigators. South Korea, joined most prominently by Japan, has taken up this issue again in the Doha Development Agenda talks, against U.S. opposition.[44]

In recent years, Seoul has become more assertive in using the WTO to challenge United States's trade practices. In 1999 and 2000, Seoul took the U.S. to the WTO over allegedly discriminatory U.S. anti-dumping duties placed on Korean exports of steel and semiconductors. Korea won both of the steel cases it initiated.

U.S. Visa Policies

South Koreans' complaints about U.S. visa policies tend to fall into two categories.[45] First, some Korean government officials, Korean businesses, the American Chamber of Commerce in Korea, and Korean-Americans have questioned why South Korea is not a participant in the U.S. Visa Waiver Permanent Program, under which foreigners traveling from certain countries are permitted to travel to the United States for up to ninety days without having the immigration documents normally required for entry.[46] Among the statutory requirements for countries to participate in the U.S. visa waiver program is that the country must have a low nonimmigrant visa refusal rate for two years — averaging no more than 2% over both years and not exceeding 2.5% in any one year. According to State Department officials, South Korea's visa refusal rates have consistently been over this threshold. According to one report, in 2005 the rate was slightly below 4%.[47] U.S. State Department officials attribute the rise in Korea's refusal rates since 1997 to the increased number of Koreans illegally seeking to find work in the United States. Since the United States put in place new visa procedures after the September 11, 2001 terrorist attacks, all South Koreans who want to visit the United States must interview for a visa at the U.S. Embassy in Seoul. Reportedly, the U.S. consular section in Seoul has become the busiest largest U.S. nonimmigrant visa processing post in the world, processing an average of almost 2,000 visas per day.[48] During his November 2005 summit with President Roh in South Korea, President Bush announced that the United States would work with Seoul to develop a "roadmap to assist Korea in meeting the requirements for membership" in the visa waiver program, a move that has been supported by a number of groups in the United States.[49]

---

[44] In his address at the December 2005 Doha Development Round ministerial in Hong Kong, South Korean Trade Minister Kim said that a "tangible outcome" in anti-dumping was "indispensable" for South Korea. Statement by Mr Hyun Chong Kim Minister for Trade, World Trade Organization Ministerial Conference Sixth Session Hong Kong, WT/MIN(05)/ST/19 14 December 2005 (05-5992).

[45] For more on U.S. visa policies, see CRS Report RL3 1512, *Visa Issuances: Policy, Issues, and Legislation,* by Ruth Wasem.

[46] For more on the visa waiver program, see CRS Report RL3 222 1, *Visa Waiver Program,* by Alison Siskin.

[47] Balbina Y. Hwang, "Including South Korea in the U.S. Visa Waiver Program," Heritage Foundation Backgrounder #1872, July 25, 2005.

[48] *Ibid.*

[49] "Joint Declaration on the ROK-U.S. Alliance and Peace on the Korean Peninsula," White House Office of the Press Secretary, November 17, 2005.

The second category of complaints is lodged against U.S. visa policies implemented since the September 2001 terrorist attacks on the United States, particularly requirements for mandatory interviews, fingerprinting, and greater scrutiny of business travelers for possible technology transfer risks. Like citizens of many other countries, Koreans particularly have objected to the fingerprinting, which some Koreans have likened to requirements imposed upon them during Japan's thirty-five-year occupation of the Korean Peninsula in the first half of the 20th Century.

A U.S.-SOUTH KOREA FREE TRADE AGREEMENT?

Beginning in 2004, the South Korean Foreign Ministry began proposing the idea of a U.S.-ROK FTA. At first, the Bush Administration reportedly was cool to the idea. In late 2004, presentations by South Korean Trade Minister Hyun-chong Kim apparently made an impression on key U.S. policymakers, particularly then-USTR Robert Zoellick, such that in January 2005 the two sides began a six-month bilateral process of the logistics, benefits, and risks of an FTA. At the end of this review, in June 2005, U.S. Trade Representative Robert Portman reportedly told Trade Minister Hyun-chong Kim that it was premature to launch actual negotiations until key outstanding issues were resolved. These included South Korea's alleged barriers to imports of automobiles and pharmaceuticals, its ban on imports of U.S. beef, and its "screen quotas" that served to restrict the showing of foreign films."[50] Many U.S. officials said that Korea's action on these issues was a litmus test for whether Seoul is politically capable of making the compromises the United States will expect in an FTA agreement. By the end of January 2006, South Korea had offered concessions in all four sectors, paving the way for the two sides to announce their intention to launch FTA talks the following month.

As part of President Roh's goal of transforming South Korea into an economic hub, and in an effort to keep pace with Japan and China — which have initiated several bilateral and regional trading arrangements — Seoul has pursued a number of FTAs and similar arrangements, signing FTAs with Chile (signed in 2003), Singapore (2005), the European Free Trade Association[51] (2005), and a framework economic agreement with ASEAN, the Association of Southeast Asian Nations (2005). Thailand has opted out of ROK-ASEAN agreement, due to South Korea's continuation of its restrictions on imports of rice. Additionally, South Korea has launched FTA talks with Japan (though these have been stalled since late 2004) and Canada. Joint FTA studies are underway with Mexico, India, and the Mercosur countries (the Mercado Común del Sur consists of Brazil, Argentina, Paraguay, and Uruguay).

Arguments for and Against an FTA

A U.S.-ROK FTA is championed by the American business community in Korea, and many Korean businesses operating in the United States. The National Association of Manufacturers has identified South Korea as a one of the "top five candidate countries" for a

[50] "Portman Says U.S. Not Ready to Launch FTA Talks with Korea," *Inside US Trade*, June 10, 2005.
[51] EFTA is comprised of Iceland, Norway, Switzerland, and Liechtenstein.

future trade agreement. In previous Congresses, Senator Max Baucus introduced legislation (S. 944 in the 107th Congress and S. 1869 in 106th Congress) authorizing FTA negotiations with Seoul. No legislative action was taken on either attempt. On September 8, 2005, following a meeting of the Congressional Oversight Group that consults with USTR, House Ways and Means Chairman Bill Thomas reportedly said that the possibility of an FTA with Korea is "exciting," and noted many of the economic reforms Seoul has carried out in recent years.[52] A number of Members of Congress from both parties spoke during the February 2006 launch of the FTA on Capitol Hill and expressed their support for an FTA.

On the economic front, the biggest beneficiaries of an FTA likely would be those export industries in both countries that currently face relatively high initial trade barriers to their products. In a 2001 study undertaken at the request of the Senate Finance Committee, the International Trade Commission (ITC) estimated that within four years after implementation of a hypothetical FTA, U.S. bilateral agricultural exports would increase by more than 200%. For Korea, the ITC projected that textiles and apparel exporters would see their shipments to the U.S. rise by 125%.[53] Thus, the report implied that the FTA's potential benefits would be greatly diluted if these politically sensitive sectors were excluded.[54] After four years, U.S. exports to Korea were estimated to increase by 54% while South Korean exports to the U.S. would rise by 21%. Overall, an FTA would raise U.S. GDP by a projected 0.2%, while Korean GDP would rise by 0.7%.[55] An earlier study by the Institute for International Economics (IIE), found similar effects for the U.S. economy, but had a wider band for the increase on Korean GDP, which was projected in the 0.4%-2.0% range.

As in the ITC study, the IIE report found that most of the benefits to U.S. firms would derive from increased access to Korea's market. In contrast, the IIE projected that most of Korea's gains from an FTA would stem not from preferential access to the U.S. market but from improvements in the allocative efficiency of the Korean economy brought about by the trade reforms required by an FTA.[56] The figures cited from both studies derived from "static" models that focused on the effects of tariff liberalization, rather than the more dynamic (but harder to quantify) aftereffects. Thus, some economists say these numbers underestimate the likely gains to both sides; one of the major long-term benefits from an FTA may be less the rise in bilateral trade itself, and more the gains realized from further accelerating and cementing South Korea's market-oriented reform process.[57]

Many proponents of a U.S.-ROK FTA contend that an agreement will boost U.S. strategic interests. Some have called for an FTA as a way to reinforce the U.S.-South Korea alliance, which many believe to be under significant stress due to differences over how to deal with North Korea and the size and role of the U.S. troop presence in South Korea.[58] A related argument is that an FTA with South Korea will help counter China's growing economic and political influence in South Korea particularly, and in East Asia generally, developments

[52] "Thomas Endorses Korea, Egypt FTAs," *Inside US Trade*, September 9, 2005.

[53] United States International Trade Commission (ITC), *U.S.-Korea FTA: The Economic Impact of Establishing a Free Trade Agreement (FTA) Between the United States and the Republic of Korea*, (Washington, DC, 2001), p. 5 1 5 2.

[54] For a similar argument, see Choi and Schott, *Free Trade*, p.80.

[55] ITC, *U.S.-Korea FTA*, p. x-xi.

[56] See Choi and Schott, *Free Trade*, p. 79-82

[57] Presentation by Edward M. Graham at *Sustaining the Alliance U.S.-Korean Relations in the New Asia*, February 1, 2006 conference, American Enterprise Institute.

which some believe are hampering U.S. interests. Some — including Senator Baucus — have coupled this contention with criticism of the Bush Administration's trade policy of negotiating FTAs with politically important but relatively economically insignificant countries and of neglecting U.S. economic relations with Asia.[59]

Opposition to a prospective U.S.-ROK FTA is expected to come from U.S. import-competing groups, particularly clothing manufacturers, that have benefitted from relatively high trade barriers. U.S. industries and companies that allege trade barriers have made it difficult to penetrate the Korean market, such as U.S. automobile manufacturers, also are expected to cast doubt on the wisdom of concluding an FTA with South Korea. On the day the FTA was launched, Representative Sander Levin issued a statement that the Bush Administration "must stand up" for the U.S. auto industry in the FTA talks.[60] On the issue of agriculture, at the February 2006 press conference announcing the intent to launch FTA talks, USTR Portman said the FTA would be "comprehensive" — a euphemism referring to the inclusion of agriculture. Trade Minister Kim said that although there is no pre-agreement to exclude sensitive agricultural sectors, he also said that all FTAs include some exceptions or staged implementation periods on sensitive sectors.[61]

FTA negotiations are expected to be complicated by the expiration of trade promotion authority (TPA), also known as "fast track negotiating authority," in June 2007.[62] If negotiations are not finalized by this date and TPA is not renewed, the implementing legislation for a U.S.-Korea FTA could be considered under normal congressional procedures, potentially giving Congress greater scope to review and ask for changes in specific portions of an agreement.

Skepticism, at times mixed with outright opposition, may also come from U.S. companies and trade experts contending that South Korea has a mixed record at best in implementing previous agreements due in part to staunch resistance by South Korean import-competing industries. Indeed, disagreements between the United States and South Korea prevented the two countries from finalizing negotiations over a bilateral investment treaty (BIT)[63] The major stumbling block is Korea's so-called "screen quotas." If the two countries could not conclude a BIT, which is far less comprehensive than an FTA, many skeptics wonder if they will realistically be able to complete an FTA.

---

[58] Balbina Y. Hwang and Anthony B. Kim, "Beyond the U.S. — South Korea Alliance: Reinvigorating Economic Relations," *Heritage Foundation Backgrounder,* No. 1853, May 18, 2005.

[59] Senate Committee on Finance Press Release, "Speech of U.S. Senator Max Baucus at the First Annual Asia Forum 'Toward a Strong Asia Trade Policy,'" September 21, 2004. For more on the Bush Administration's pursuit of FTAs, see CRS Report RL3 1356, *Free Trade Agreements: Impact on U.S. Trade and Implications for U.S. Trade Policy,* by William Cooper, and CRS Report RS2 1657, *U.S. Trade Policy and Changing Domestic and Foreign Priorities: A Historical Overview,* by Ray Ahearn.

[60] February 2, 2006 Press Release, "In Negotiating a Korean Trade Agreement Bush Administration Must Stand up for U.S. Automotive Sector."

[61] "U.S., Korea Announce FTA, Hope to Complete Talks by End of Year," *Inside US Trade* February 3, 2006.

[62] Under TPA, Congress agrees to consider trade agreements which the President has negotiated, on a fast-track basis - without amendment and with limited debate. For more, see CRS Report RS22237, *Trade Promotion (Fast-Track) Authority in the Trade Act of 2002,* by Lenore Sek.

[63] BITs are designed to improve the climate for foreign investors — typically by committing the signatories to prohibit discrimination against foreign investors — by establishing dispute settlement procedures and by protecting foreign investors from performance requirements, restrictions on transferring funds, and arbitrary expropriation. The United States has signed over 30 BITs, primarily with countries undergoing significant economic reforms. The U.S. and South Korea last held formal negotiations in 1999.

One danger of launching FTA talks is that differences over strategic issues — particularly in dealing with North Korea — could negatively affect the negotiations or the consideration of the agreement in Congress and/or the National Assembly. South Korea's policy of emphasizing bilateral reconciliation with North Korea generally has meant that Seoul has not supported U.S. actual and rhetorical efforts to pressure North Korea. As mentioned above, although the U.S. has supported the Kaesong industrial zone project inside North Korea, South Korea's attempts to allow Kaesong-made products to have preferential tariff status into the United States could be contentious. The interplay between the FTA talks and developments with North Korea also could bring greater scrutiny to the relationship between South Korean firms and North Korean enterprises. For instance, many South Korean banks reviewed their connections to Banco Delta Asia following the September 2005 decision by the U.S. Treasury Department to warn U.S. financial institutions not to deal with the Macau bank because of its alleged laundering counterfeit U.S. currency produced in North Korea. Since the fall of 2005, North Korea has said it will not return to the six-party talks unless these "sanctions" are lifted. North Korea's human rights abuses also could become intertwined with the FTA talks if human rights advocates decide to criticize the dealings of South Korean firms with North Korean enterprises.

Additionally, if the FTA talks fail or become exceptionally bitter, they could damage the U.S.-South Korean alliance. Many observers believe that in recent years the economic side of the relationship has been the alliance's strong suit, for four reasons. First, the creation of a robust dispute resolution body in the WTO in the mid-1990s has helped depoliticize many bilateral disputes. Second, the economic reforms pursued by South Korean since the 1997 economic crisis have helped resolved some of the two countries' systemic disputes and on many disputes have given the United States allies at the top of South Korea's government. Third, as mentioned earlier, the two sides have become more adept at managing disputes. Finally, the economic relationship has benefitted from the good fortune of few, if any, transcendent economic disputes over the past five years.

The launch of the FTA is likely to change three of these four factors, at least while the agreement is being negotiated and then debated in Congress and the National Assembly. The WTO dispute resolution system likely will retain its depoliticizing role, but many interests in the United States are likely to shine a spotlight on the incomplete areas of South Korea's reforms, rather than the areas of progress. The quarterly working-level trade meetings that have helped stabilize the economic relationship are likely to be superseded by the FTA talks. Lastly, by definition, the FTA is likely to politicize nearly every aspect of the bilateral relationship, particularly if the agreement reaches the ratification stage in the two countries' legislatures. The South Korean media and National Assembly often carefully and publicly scrutinize their government's economic negotiations with the United States for signs that Korean officials compromised too heavily. In early 2005, for instance, the National Assembly launched a corruption investigation of individuals who negotiated the deals with the United States and other countries to allow greater imports of foreign rice into South Korea. Due to the size of the Korean market, U.S. companies may demand more concessions than they have in other recent FTA negotiations, such as those with Australia and Thailand. If so, this is likely to be perceived as unfair inside South Korea.

In: Asian Economic and Political Issues, Volume 11
Editor: Harvey E. Roth, pp. 141-165
ISBN: 1-60021-192-5

Chapter 7

REGIONAL ECONOMIC INTEGRATION IN SOUTHEAST ASIA: CASE OF ASEAN[1]

Teofilo C. Daquila

ABSTRACT

This chapter examines the regional integration process that has taken place in Southeast Asia through the ASEAN regional grouping. It analyzes the initiatives that have been undertaken by ASEAN to foster closer regional economic integration. It also identifies and explains the different factors which have affected the ASEAN integration process. Finally, it identifies ASEAN's linkages with the global economy at the multilateral, regional and bilateral levels including the present and future schemes which may impact on the ASEAN regional grouping.

INTRODUCTION

The governance of international trade on a multilateral level rests mainly with the GATT and its contracting parties, and now the WTO and its members. As the only international body which deals with the rules of trade between nations, the WTO is centered on its agreements, the legal ground-rules for international commerce and for trade policy. The agreements aim mainly to help trade flow as freely as possible, to achieve further liberalization gradually through negotiation, and to set up an impartial means of settling disputes.[2] The multilateral trading system is based on a set of fundamental principles which include non-discrimination, freer trade, predictable policies, encouraging competition, and extra-provisions for less-developed countries.

---

[1] Earlier versions of this chapter were presented as invited conference papers at the following institutions: Chulalongkorn University (2001, 2002), Vienna Institute for International Economic Studies (2003), and published as a journal article written jointly with Le Huu Huy, titled "Singapore and ASEAN in the Global Economy: The Case of Free Trade Agreements," in the *Asian Survey*, Vol.43, No.6, pp.908-928.

[2] See WTO website: http://www.wto.org.

Article 1 of the GATT establishes the central requirement that signatory governments shall extend unconditionally to all contracting parties (members) any advantage, favor, privilege, rules and procedures that they give to products originating in or destined for any other country.[3] Thus, under this 'most-favored nation' (MFN) clause, no country is to give special trading advantages to another or to discriminate against it: all are on equal basis and share the benefits of any moves towards lower trade barriers.[4] However, there are exceptions to this MFN clause such as Article XXIV of the GATT 1947, which is the principal agreement dealing with customs unions and free trade areas – a provision on regional trading agreements (RTAs). It provides a number of rules governing such agreements, including notification and review by the contracting parties acting jointly. Agreements must meet the "substantially-all-trade" requirement, and members of a regional agreement must have a trade policy with respect to third countries that is not on the whole higher or more restrictive than the individual policies prior to the agreement.[5]

Multilateral trade liberalization in the postwar period has been paralleled by a process of integration through regional agreements.[6] Nearly all of the WTO members have concluded RTAs with other countries. In the period 1948-1994, GATT contracting parties notified 108 RTAs relating to trade in goods, of which 38 in the five years ending 1994.[7] However, during this period, the West European countries were parties in 76 out of 108 instances. During the 1995-1999 period, 67 additional RTAs were notified, some of which in the area of trade in services. Out of 194 RTAs notified to the GATT/WTO, 107 are presently in force. These RTAs have at times been concluded by countries in the same geographic region, and in other cases, have involved countries in different regions. These RTAs include the European Community, the European Free Trade Area (EFTA), NAFTA, Mercosur, Australia-New Zealand CER, and the ASEAN Free Trade Area (AFTA).

This chapter broadly seeks to analyze the regional integration process that has taken place in ASEAN. The following section provides an analysis of the initiatives that have been undertaken by ASEAN to foster closer regional economic integration. The third section identifies and explains the different factors which have affected the regional integration process in ASEAN. The fourth section identifies ASEAN's linkages with the global economy, namely, at the multilateral, regional and bilateral levels including a discussion of the present and future schemes which may impact on the ASEAN regional grouping.

---

[3] WTO, *Regionalism and the World Trading System*, Geneva: World Trading Organization, 1995, p.5.

[4] WTO, *Trading Into the Future,* Geneva: World Trading Organization.

[5] WTO, *Regionalism …*, 1995, p.7.

[6] For an interesting discussion of the co-existence between multilateralism and regionalism, see Sung-Hoon Park, "East Asian Economic Integration – Finding a Balance between Regionalism and Multilateralism", EIAS Briefing Paper, February 2002, Brussels: European Institute for Asian Studies. Among others, he discussed instances in which regionalism is viewed as a stumbling block or a building block to multilateralism. For an earlier discussion of the same subject matter with reference to ASEAN, see Mohamed Ariff, "Economic Regionalism versus Multilateralism: Dilemmas for Southeast Asia?" Paper presented at ISEAS 30th anniversary conference on Southeast Asia in the 21st Century: Challenges of Globalization, Singapore, 1998.

[7] WTO website: http:*//www.wto.org/wto/develop/regional.htm* – Regional Integration and the Multilateral Trading System, printed on 01 October 1, 1999.

ASEAN ECONOMIC INTEGRATION

To promote closer economic cooperation/integration, ASEAN has undertaken both widening and deepening economic activities.[8]

Enlargement

The ASEAN region expanded from ASEAN-5 in 1967 to ASEAN-6 in 1984 to include Brunei. In 1995, the admission of Vietnam enlarged the region to ASEAN-7 and then to ASEAN-9 in 1997 with the entry of Laos and Myanmar. The grouping saw its fifth enlargement in 1999 to ASEAN-10 with the inclusion of Cambodia. On a positive note, the expansion of the ASEAN region brings together some 550 million people and a regional income of about US$550 billion. The huge regional market and the rising per capita income of the ASEAN people offer tremendous trade and investment opportunities for the rest of the world. However, the expansion of ASEAN to include non-democratic countries was met with criticisms and harsh attitudes from the other countries. Unlike the EU which prescribes democratization as a prerequisite for membership admission, the ASEAN regional grouping does not impose this criterion following its policy of non-interference in domestic affairs.

Trade Liberalization

ASEAN has pursued efforts aimed at liberalizing trade through tariff reductions and lessening/elimination of non-tariff barriers. These measures (were already discussed in chapter 6) include Preferential Trading Arrangements (PTAs), the Common Effective Preferential Tariff (CEPT) scheme, and AFTA.

ASEAN has also undertaken measures to liberalize trade in services. As the region grows and per capita income increases, the ASEAN people demand more goods and services. More services and institutions have been created to meet this rising demand, which is reflected in the growing importance of the services sector, particularly, in financial services, transportation and communications. The ASEAN Framework Agreement on Services was signed by the ASEAN Trade and Industry ministers in December 1995 to liberalize trade in services in seven sectors: air transport, business services, construction, financial services, maritime transport, telecommunications and tourism. During the 4th ASEAN informal summit meeting in Singapore in November 2000, the leaders signed the e-ASEAN Framework Agreement which provides for the liberalization of intra-regional trade in information and communications technology (ICT) products and services by eliminating duties and non-tariff

[8] For a discussion of these regional initiatives, see Teofilo Daquila, "Towards Strengthening ASEAN Integration: Challenges, Strategies and Prospects", in Apirat Petchsiri, Alfred Kellerman, Charit Tingsabadh and Pornsan Watananguhn (eds.), *Strengthening ASEAN Integration: Lessons from the EU's Rule of Law*, Thailand: Chulalongkorn University's Interdisciplinary Department of European Studies, the Center for European Studies, and TMC Asser Institute of the Netherlands, 2001, pp.77-87. For more recent analysis, see Teofilo Daquila, "ASEAN Economic Performance: Revisiting the Past, Looking to the Future," *Harvard Asia Quarterly*, Mass.: Harvard University, Vol. 6, No.3, 2002, pp.9-14 , online exclusive.

barriers in three stages - 2003, 2004 and 2005, for the original members. For Cambodia, Laos, Myanmar and Vietnam, the three stages will take effect in 2008, 2009 and 2010.

Investment Liberalization

ASEAN has also undertaken measures to liberalize foreign direct investment (FDI). First is the ASEAN Investment Area (AIA) scheme which will encourage greater private sector participation in welcoming foreign investors. The second initiative is known as the ASEAN Industrial Cooperation (AICO) scheme which allows joint ventures between ASEAN nationals and foreign investors whose products or services will be given tariff preferences. Third is a type of Growth Triangle sub-regional cooperation scheme like the Singapore-Johor (Malaysia)-Riau (Indonesia) growth triangle, popularly known as SIJORI. This scheme exemplifies the positive synergy of factor endowments and comparative advantage, whereby Singapore provides excellent infrastructure and skilled labor, while Johor and Riau provide land and lower-cost labor. The success of the SIJORI growth triangle has led to its expansion to include other parts of Indonesia and Malaysia, which is an indication of its positive spillover effects. This concept has been replicated in other parts of the ASEAN region. including (i) the East ASEAN Growth Area (EAGA) scheme which involves Brunei, Indonesia, Malaysia and the southern Philippines, and (ii) the inter-state areas along the West-East Corridor (WEC) of the Mekong Basin in Vietnam, Laos, Cambodia and North-eastern Thailand under the ASEAN Mekong Basin Development Cooperation scheme.

Financial Cooperation

There are also developments arising from the recent economic crisis which provide lessons for ASEAN in terms of the need to strengthen their financial co-operation. Some of the proposed strategies include the use of domestic currencies in trade settlements and the setting up of the Asian Monetary Fund (AMF) by Japan. The proposed establishment of the AMF, to be capitalized at US$100 billion, aims to provide immediate financial assistance to crisis-hit countries in the future. However, the United States dismissed the proposal, fearing that it would diminish the effectiveness of the IMF and its policies in Asia, and the AMF proposal was rejected in the fifth APEC meeting in Manila. However, Malaysia's former PM Mahathir brought up the AMF idea again during the World Economic Forum in Singapore in 1999 and a modified version of the AMF proposal was discussed in the informal summit meeting of the ASEAN Finance Ministers in Manila in 1999. More recently, a network of bilateral swap arrangements among ASEAN countries, China, Japan and the Republic of Korea has been negotiated to assist ASEAN members in times of temporary balance-of-payments crises. Following the agreement on the Chiang Mai Initiatives (CMI), ASEAN agreed to enlarge the size of the ASEAN Swap Agreement to US$1 billion effective in November 2000. Substantial agreements on the bilateral swap arrangements have been reached between Korea and Japan, Malaysia and Japan, and Thailand and Japan.

FACTORS AFFECTING ASEAN REGIONAL INTEGRATION

Intra-ASEAN economic cooperation has proceeded very slowly particularly during the 1967-75 period. However, during the 1976 to 1992 period, some changes in the ASEAN machinery and more frequent summit meetings had improved the extent of economic cooperation. It was also during this period that specific areas and actions of economic cooperation were identified. However, it was only in 1992 following the Singapore Declaration that ASEAN heads of government formally decided to achieve AFTA and agreed on the enhancement of economic cooperation.

What then are the things that have worked in ASEAN, or equivalently, the strong points of ASEAN economic integration? What are those things that did not work, or equivalently, the weak points of economic integration?[9]

First is the ASEAN institutional machinery. In 1967, the individual member states of ASEAN were hesitant to accord it with strong powers over the members, preferring a high level of individual sovereignty.[10] Thus, this resulted in an organizationally loose structure which avoided the trappings of a strong regional organization. The supreme decision-making authority was vested on the Foreign Ministers of the five ASEAN states during the annual ministerial meetings held in the capital cities of member countries on a rotational basis. The initial structure consisted of the Annual Ministerial Meetings, the ASEAN standing committee, ad hoc and permanent committees and the national secretariats. The decentralized and overlapping bureaucratic structure generated some obstacles for ASEAN as an organization like delays, and many suggestions were never considered nor realized. Moreover, there was no high level body directly in charge of making decisions and executing economic policies. Thus, the narrow structure of the initial ASEAN machinery was one of the contributory factors to the low level of economic cooperation particularly during the 1967-1975. Having realized this, the institutional structure was expanded in 1976 during the Bali summit to include economic and other ministers, as well as the establishment of an ASEAN Secretariat in Jakarta to provide a central administrative and coordinating body. The ASEAN Economic Ministerial Meetings has been the decision-making organ for economic matters. Since 1976, the supreme decision-making authority is the ASEAN Heads of Government Meeting, also known as the ASEAN Summits, which were held as and when necessary.

Second is the consensus style. As ASEAN was established on loose foundations, it has developed and evolved through a cumulative, gradual process whose decisions and actions have been carried out on a consensus style, popularly known as the 'ASEAN way" of doing things which relies to a large extent on the personal approach in contrast to the more legalistic and structural ways in the western countries. The consensus approach is embodied in two Malay terms: *musyawarah,* the process of decision-making through discussion and consultation, and *mufakat*, the unanimous decision that is arrived at.[11] The consensus approach is viewed as a weak point of ASEAN as decision-making has been delayed due to differences in attitudes and views of member countries, and differences in their levels of

---

[9] For discussion of these problems, see Teofilo Daquila, "The ASEAN Experience of Economic Cooperation," Paper presented at "The East African Forum on the East African Community: Economic Aspects of Integration," organized by Friedrich Ebert Foundation, 27-29 Sept 1999, Kampala, Uganda.

[10] For an excellent analysis of ASEAN's organizational structure, see Paul Davidson, *ASEAN: The Evolving Legal Framework for Economic Cooperation*, Singapore: Times Academic Press, 2002, pp.14-50.

development and economic structures. However, some have argued that the consensus approach brings the ASEAN member countries closer and that direct conflicts have been avoided. But even when a consensus has been reached, not all members are obliged to participate in the decision since ASEAN allows bilateral and other types of cooperative arrangements (like sub-regional growth areas). In other cases, ASEAN provides for a membership-minus-x principle in which only able members can implement the agreement at the time while other members may join when they are able to do so. In light of the impact of the Asian financial crisis in 1997/98, outgoing ASEAN Secretary-General Rodolfo Severino has suggested that ASEAN needs to move away from a 'relationship-based' way of doing things and creating wealth to one that was more rules-based and market-driven.[12] Within ASEAN, a rationalization of the framework for economic cooperation and the development of rules to set the guidelines within which this cooperation can take place is occurring.[13]

Third is political commitment. During the 1967-1992 period, there were only four irregular summit meetings which took place in Bali (1976), Kuala Lumpur (1977), Manila (1987) and Singapore (1992). The holding of only four and irregular summits within 25 years since its formation in 1967 was an indication of the lack of political commitment. Having learned from this shortcoming, the summit meeting has been institutionalized since 1992 to take place once every three years with informal meetings in between. Outgoing ASEAN secretary-general Rodolfo Severino called for more political commitment within ASEAN in order to achieve greater economic integration. He said that ASEAN "seems to have stuck in framework agreements, work programs and master plans."

Fourth, the problems associated with various schemes and instruments of economic cooperation in industry, banking and finance, agriculture and trade. The early scheme of industrial cooperation through the ASEAN Industrial Projects (AIP) was relatively ineffective because of lack of feasibility studies, lack of financing, lack of political commitment, lack of private sector participation, and rigidity in equity requirements. Given these shortcomings, other schemes like AIC and AIJV had evolved through time providing for flexibility in the requirements allowing the participation of foreign investors and the private sector. On trade cooperation, the low utilization rate and hence the ineffectiveness of the PTAs was attributed to various problems such as a long exclusion list, too detailed disaggregation and inclusion of irrelevant items. With these shortcomings and having realized the need to enhance economic cooperation in the midst of rising protectionism in other parts of the world (like EU and NAFTA), the ASEAN heads of government agreed and committed in 1992 to carry out deeper and meaningful trade liberalization measures through CEPT to pave the way for AFTA in the year 2003.

Fifth, the dominance of national interests over regional interests also accounts for the low level of regional economic integration. ASEAN's economic performance has been shaped to a large extent by the national economic policies of their respective governments particularly on trade and FDI.

---

[11] Paul Davidson, *ASEAN: The Evolving Legal Framework...*, 2002, p.41.

[12] Paul Davidson, *ASEAN: The Evolving Legal Framework...*, 2002, p.43.

[13] Paul Davidson, *ASEAN:The Evolving Legal Framework...*,2002, p.158-159. Some examples of the agreements which are forming the "rules" of an evolving legal framework are: The Framework Agreement for Enhancing ASEAN Economic Cooperation, the Agreement on the Common Effective Preferential Tariff (CEPT) scheme for the ASEAN Free Trade Area, the ASEAN Industrial Cooperation Scheme, the ASEAN Investment Area, the ASEAN Framework Agreement on Services, and the ASEAN Framework Agreement on Intellectual Property Cooperation.

On the trade front, ASEAN economies have largely embraced free trade, but with varying degrees of openness as reflected by the differences in their tariff structures, the extent of protectionism and trade liberalization measures. Being a highly open export-oriented economy, Singapore has the lowest tariffs. Thailand has the highest tariffs, due to its ISI policy which protects domestic manufacturing industries. Indonesia, Malaysia and the Philippines have tariff structures somewhere between Singapore and Thailand. More open economies like Singapore have preferred a faster pace of tariff cuts than the more closed economies like Indonesia and Thailand. However, since most ASEAN countries rely on tariffs as a major source of government revenues, tariff reductions have proceeded slowly.

On the investment front, ASEAN governments have opened their economies to FDI to various degrees. With no natural resources and a limited domestic market, Singapore is the most reliant upon FDI. The Philippines, Indonesia, Malaysia and Thailand have natural resources and much larger domestic markets, and therefore could afford to be less dependent upon FDI. Indonesia and Malaysia are oil and gas producers and have benefited substantially from the oil price hikes in the 1970s. However, declining oil prices combined with the fact that oil is a non-renewable resource have convinced both Indonesia and Malaysia to diversify their economies and increase their dependence on FDI. Over the years, ASEAN governments have followed Singapore's experiences by relaxing regulations on investments and foreign equity ownership for export firms. Most ASEAN governments now allow 100% foreign ownership as long as the business produces mainly for exports.

ASEAN AND THE GLOBAL ECONOMY

ASEAN has been more historically dependent on countries/groupings outside the region particularly Japan, the United States and the European Union for trade, FDI, technology and foreign aid. For example, while intra-EU trade hovers around 50-60 percent of its global trade, intra-ASEAN trade has been around 15-20 percent of its global trade. As such, ASEAN has been linked more to the global economy particularly in the areas of liberalization, facilitation and cooperation through multilateral, regional and bilateral schemes.

Multilateral Links

ASEAN has been linked to the WTO. In ASEAN, Singapore hosted the first WTO meeting in December 1996. It brought together ministers and representatives of member countries. It was a very significant gathering as they came up with a crucial document known as the 'Information Technology Agreement' which will liberalize the information technology industry on a global scale. The WTO meeting is a victory of consensus and compromise between the North and South.

The WTO replaced the General Agreement on Tariffs and Trade (GATT) as a result of the Uruguay Round multilateral trade negotiation which lasted for seven years (1986-1993). The WTO aims to implement the results of this round, namely, (a) that member countries implement tariff reductions commitments in industrial products, (b) that quotas on agricultural imports and imports of textiles and apparel are replaced with less restrictive tariffs, (c) that the Multi-Fibre Agreement will be dismantled, (d) that trade in textiles and clothing will be integrated into the normal GATT rules, and (e) that the dispute settlement mechanism be strengthened. These trade liberalization measures have certainly brought both benefits and costs to the ASEAN region as it will compete with other countries in some products particularly in agricultural and textile products but can complement in other manufactures.

The WTO has also taken initiatives to liberalize trade in services. In 1995, the export of services was valued at US$1,234 billion. The EU is the largest service exporter with a share of 46 per cent. Accounting for a share of 17 percent, the United States offered to liberalize its financial sector by giving foreign companies unrestricted market access not only to existing operations of foreign companies but also to all foreign institutions and to new or expanded financial services. The ASEAN region accounted for 5.4 percent (US$67 billion) of the global exports of services. Singapore and Thailand were the main beneficiaries as they shared 44 percent and 22 percent of the region's service exports, respectively. The Philippines, Malaysia and Indonesia accounted for 14 percent, 10 percent and 9 percent, respectively.

Extra-Regional Links

ASEAN has been linked to the global economy through its membership in regional fora like the Asia-Pacific Economic Cooperation (APEC) and the Asia-Europe Meeting (ASEM). Through APEC, the ASEAN countries have been involved with two of its major trading and investment partners namely, Japan and the United States. In APEC, ASEAN has been considered as the cornerstone for the successful implementation of an open-regionalism strategy that would pave the way for the successful achievement of the goal of Bogor Declaration which is to free trade and investments in the region in 2010 for developed countries and 2020 for developing countries. In 1996, APEC leaders agreed to back a global deal which will eliminate most tariffs on information technology products by the year 2000 including computers, semi-conductors, software and telecommunications equipment. The global information technology package is worth US$500 billion on a global scale, with APEC members accounting for 80 percent of the total trade. ASEAN should be proactive and should lead APEC in realising this goal. APEC should complement, and not compete with the WTO.

ASEAN has also been linked with the European Union through the Asia-Europe Meeting (ASEM), which is a trans-atlantic and trans-pacific regional forum initiated by Singapore's former PM Goh Chok Tong. The first meeting was held in Bangkok in March 1996. As it brought together leaders of the ASEAN, EU-15, China, Japan and Korea, it was an important step towards more meaningful and enhanced relationship between Asia and Europe. ASEAN is also considered as the cornerstone of ASEM and it should continue to do so. ASEAN should push for the institutionalization of the summit meeting to put a greater political commitment and dedication from all leaders involved.

Bilateral Links Through FTAs

Given the slow pace of trade liberalization undertaken by the WTO on a multilateral level[14] and by ASEAN on a regional basis, and in light of the uncertainties arising from global developments, some ASEAN countries have undertaken or are considering bilateral Free Trade Agreements (FTAs) with countries outside the ASEAN. Singapore has concluded FTAs with New Zealand, Japan, EFTA, Australia and the United States. Singapore also has on-going negotiations with Mexico, Canada, Korea, Jordan and India. Other countries are also interested in FTAs. As for Malaysia, its Minister for International Trade and Industry announced that the Malaysian government is already studying the costs and benefits of forging bilateral FTAs, but those which are focused on services like telecommunications. The United States has also proposed FTAs each with Thailand and the Philippines. Australia is also negotiating an FTA with Thailand. Inspired by Japan-Singapore FTA, President Gloria Arroyo had officially proposed the establishment of an FTA during her third visit to Japan on 4 December 2002.[15]

Singapore's Bilateral FTA's

Singapore's bilateral FTA's can be grouped into three categories, namely, completed FTAs, on-going FTAs, and future FTAs (see Fig.8.1). On the first category, Singapore has completed its negotiations for an FTA each with New Zealand, Japan, the European Free Trade Area (EFTA), Australia and the United States. The *Agreement between New Zealand and Singapore on a Closer Economic Partnership (ANZSCEP)* was the first FTA concluded by Singapore in August 2000 after six rounds of negotiations. It was signed by New Zealand's Prime Minister (PM) Helen Clark and Singapore's former PM Goh Chok Tong on November 14, 2000, and has been implemented since January 2001. It was the second FTA for Singapore after AFTA. Launched in October 2000, the *Agreement between Japan and the Republic of Singapore for a New-Age Economic Partnership (JSEPA)* was concluded in October 2001 after 12 rounds of substantive negotiations. It was signed on January 13, 2002 by the Japanese PM Junichiro Koizumi and former PM Goh and went into effect on November 30, 2002.[16]

With the initiative floated in December 2000, the *EFTA-Singapore Free Trade Agreement* (ESFTA) was signed on June 26, 2002 by Singapore's former Trade and Industry

[14] In his speech titled "Regionalism in Place of or Together with Multilateralism" delivered before the Economic Society of Singapore on 9 July 1992, Professor Rolf Langhammer identified three strands of a weakening multilateralism. First, there was the decline of the American superpower in politics and of the loss of the functions of a "leading economy" in economics. Second, apart from lacking sanction mechanism, he cites two additional weaknesses: GATT mixes allocation targets and distribution targets by giving special and differential treatment to developing countries. Third, the heterogeneity of membership in the GATT has increased with the number of members increasing to more than one hundred, [*which hampers decision-making*].

[15] It is expected that the proposed Japan-Philippines FTA would go beyond the usual FTA to maximize the many areas of complementarity between them. President Arroyo cited examples like Japan can utilize Filipino health care workers given Japan's aging population and Japanese high tech firms can hire skilled young Filipino workers. For details, see *Philippine Star* online issue December 4, 2002: http://www.philstar.com/philstar/print.asp?article=103628.

Minister Brigadier-General (BG) George Yeo and Ministers of EFTA, after three rounds of negotiations. The agreement came into force on January 1, 2003.[17]

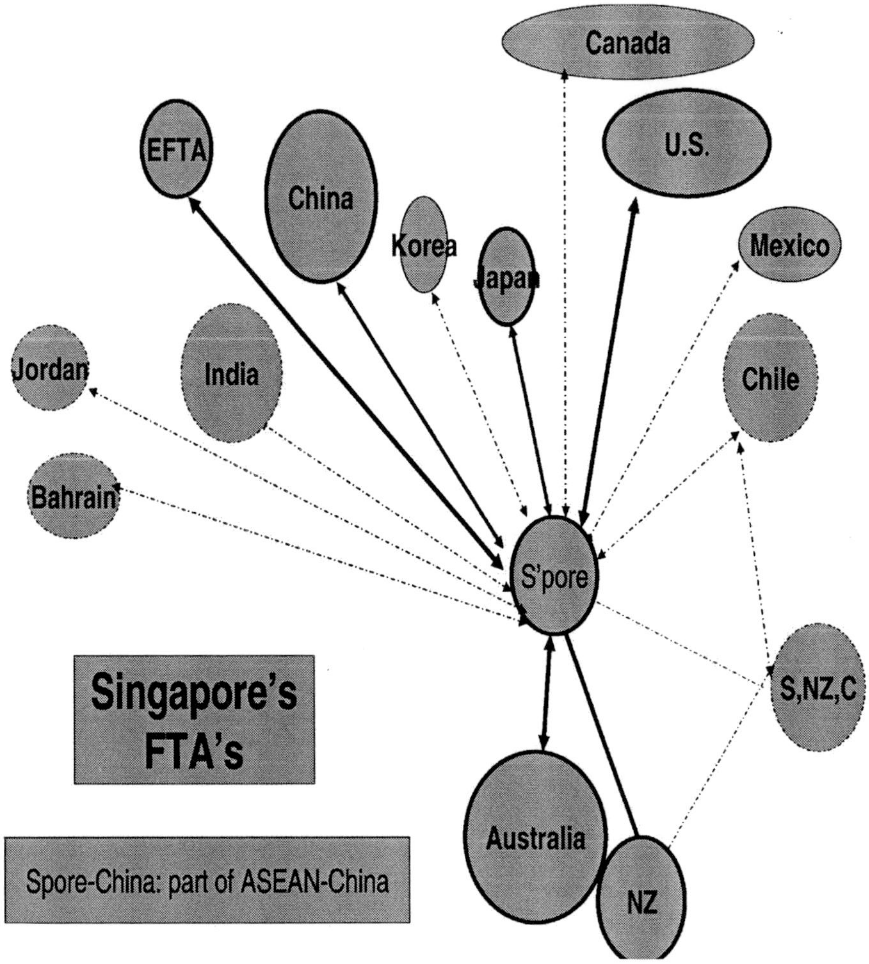

Figure 8.1. Singapore's Free Trade Agreements (FTAs)

During the APEC Summit 2000 in Brunei, former US President Bill Clinton and Singapore's former PM Goh agreed to commence negotiations towards the establishment of the *United States-Singapore Free Trade Agreement* (USSFTA). After several rounds of lengthy negotiations during a two-year period, some 50 negotiators from the Singapore side, led by Singapore's Ambassador-at-large, Professor Tommy Koh, had 'traversed thousands of miles locked in talks – in Washington, Singapore and London.'[18] The deal was completed in January 2003 with President George Bush formally notifying the US Congress that he intends

[16] The JSEPA comprises provisions for liberalization and facilitation, partnership and cooperation, and dispute settlement, among others. For more discussion, see section titled "JSEPA: a backdoor for Japanese products?"

[17] The ESFTA is EFTA's 19th FTA and Singapore's 3rd after FTAs with New Zealand and Japan. It is a historical achievement given that it is the first FTA between Europe and Asia which is expected to hasten economic linkages between the two continents. EFTA consists of Switzerland, Iceland, Liechtenstein and Norway.

[18] See The Straits Times, "How the FTA was won," November 23, 2002, p.28.

to enter into an FTA with Singapore. It is the first FTA of the US with Asia.[19] The agreement passed smoothly through the US Congress. It came into force by the start of the year 2004. As Singapore is a regional hub for many American companies, the bilateral deal is viewed as a model for trade liberalization throughout the region which could pave the way for multilateral liberalization.

On the second category of FTAs, Singapore has on-going bilateral trade discussions with Canada and Mexico. On June 5, 2000, Canada's former International Trade Minister Pierre Pettigrew and Singapore's former Trade and Industry Minister BG George Yeo announced the possibility of negotiating *Canada-Singapore Free Trade Agreement* (CSFTA) between the two countries. Three rounds of negotiations were already completed on a range of issues such as trade in goods, services, financial services, investment, government procurement, dispute settlement, and competition.[20] On September 13, 1999, Mexico's former President Ernesto Zedillo Ponce de Leon and Singapore's former PM Goh agreed in-principle to negotiate *Mexico-Singapore Free Trade Agreement* (MSFTA) which could draw the two regions (Latin America and Southeast Asia) closer together. Having completed four rounds of negotiations since July 2000, progress has been made covering areas like trade in goods and services, investment, and government procurement.

On the third category of FTAs, Singapore plans to commence bilateral talks with South Korea, India and the European Union. The Trade Ministers of Singapore and Korea jointly announced on November 14, 2002 about the creation of a study group to look into the scope of the *Korea-Singapore Free Trade Agreement* (KSFTA). The joint study group, consisting of government officials, businessmen and academics, commenced in January 2003.[21] South Korea was Singapore's eighth largest trading partner in 2002. Singapore's exports to Korea included S$734 million of integrated circuits and S$466 million of computers, disk drives, printers and peripherals in the period from January to September 2002.[22] While the Korean-Chile trade pact dragged on for three years because of agricultural concerns, the KSFTA is expected to be completed at a faster pace given Singapore's experience and know-hows in FTA negotiations.

In April 2002, India's former PM Atal Behari Vajpayee and Singapore's former PM Goh agreed to set up a study group consisting of senior Singapore and Indian officials to look into establishing a comprehensive economic partnership agreement which is expected to be far more wide-ranging than the regular free trade deals.[23] During his visit to Singapore in February 2003, India's former Deputy PM Lal Khrisna Advani said that "Singapore evokes

[19] Singapore was the US 11th largest trading partner with total two-way trade in goods and services valued at US$38.8 billion in 2001. See The Straits Times, "Bush gives go-ahead for FTA pact with S'pore," February 1, 2003, p.A12.

[20] Having been asked about the relationship between APEC and FTAs, BG Yeo stated that the proposed CSFTA will help both sides of the Pacific closer together to achieve the APEC's Bogor vision of free trade and investments. In a symposium about Singapore's FTAs on March 7, 2003, Mr. Aubeck Kam, a director in Singapore's Ministry of Trade and Industry, pointed out that the proliferation of FTAs across the Asia-Pacific region could serve as building blocks to achieve the Bogor goals of free and open trade and investments in the region.

[21] See The Straits Times, "Spore-Seoul free trade talks to begin next year," November 15, 2002.

[22] The Straits Times, "Spore-Seoul free trade...," p.A38.

[23] Trade between the two countries has been growing rapidly and hit an all-time high of S$6.9 billion last year. Singapore's former PM Goh Chok Tong stated that the EPA is expected to provide access for Indian companies in the ASEAN region while giving greater confidence to Singapore companies that want to invest in India. The agreement is expected to be sealed between the two countries within a year. See The Straits Times, "S'pore, India for economic partnership," April 9, 2002, p.1.

admiration for the manner that it transformed its economy thanks to the vision of its leaders and enterprise of its people" and that "we *[Indians]* are exerting to replicate these attributes in our country" to make India a developed nation by 2020.[24] PM Goh visited India in April 2003 during which negotiations for the *India-Singapore Comprehensive Economic Cooperation* was launched.

Danish PM Anders Fogh Rasmussen told Singapore's former PM Goh Chok Tong during his visit to Copenhagen that he is in favor of an FTA between Singapore and the EU.[25] As Professor Jayakumar, Singapore's former Foreign Affairs Minister, stated, "Singapore remained convinced that one way to forge stronger links [*between ASEAN and the EU*] was through the conclusion of an EU-ASEAN free trade pact ... and ... that the clinching of a Singapore-EU free trade deal could be a first step towards a wider pact with ASEAN."[26] He further noted that "while the EU side was not yet ready to enter into free-trade agreements with Singapore or the *[ASEAN]* bloc as a whole, ASEAN's series of free-trade arrangements with China, India, Japan, Korea and the United States, struck a resonance with the Europeans."[27]

Given the benefits and potential opportunities offered by FTAs, Singapore, New Zealand and Chile have even moved on to a higher plane by jointly announcing a new trilateral FTA initiative during the APEC summit held in Los Cabos, Mexico in October 2002.[28] It was described as "a win-win situation" by New Zealand's PM Helen Clark, "path-breaking" by Singapore's former Trade and Industry Minister BG George Yeo, and "difficult but could be overcome" by Chile's President Ricardo Lagos.[29] It is viewed as a pioneering attempt at linking the Americas and the Asia-Pacific region to liberalize trade consistently with APEC and the WTO. This agreement will also pave the way for the three partners to access the three regions to which they belong – Latin America, Asia and the Pacific.

The Pros and Cons of Singapore's FTAs

In theory, FTAs come into effect when two or more countries come together and negotiate towards the removal of trade restrictions on goods and services against each other. FTA signatories enjoy the benefits which include the removal of tariff and non-tariff barriers which will lead to foreign exchange savings. Moreover, FTAs will give members greater access to their respective markets and therefore create a larger internal market which increases the degree of competition among FTA suppliers. A larger internal market also creates opportunities for exploitation of scale economies by allowing for a higher degree of specialization in production. The free flow of goods and services will allow countries to

[24] The Vajpayee's government undertook some landmark decisions in its push for economic liberalization. These included a program for the road network connecting the major metropolitan centers, a drive to develop the IT software industry, and a new plan to interlink the major rivers in India, and most importantly, the creation of a feeling of confidence and optimism that India can be a front-ranking nation. See The Straits Times, "S'pore and India plan talks on free-trade pact," February 4, 2003.

[25] Denmark is one of the 15 EU countries which has been studying the possibility of a Singapore-EU FTA. See The Straits Times, "Denmark backs Singapore-EU free trade pact," April 18, 2002, p.6.

[26] The Business Times, "EU, ASEAN pledge to boost trade, political ties," February 24, 2003.

[27] The Straits Times, "EU and ASEAN ministers pledge closer trade and intelligence ties," January 29, 2003, p.A6.

[28] The Straits Times, "Singapore, NZ and Chile go for 3-way trade talks," October 28, 2002.

[29] The Straits Times, "Singapore, NZ and Chile..." p.A18.

further capitalize on their comparative strengths and hence the optimal allocation of resources. On the strategic front, establishing FTAs could also help to anchor the presence of the signatories in their respective territories or regions. Moreover, FTAs could also be forged for geopolitical reasons like serving as a confidence measure to promote harmony towards closer political integration.

While Singapore has always advocated the promotion of free trade on multilateral and regional levels, various factors have contributed to Singapore's bilateral trade policy. *First,* the pace of ASEAN regional integration is too slow, below what Singapore expects for its own benefit and for the prosperity of ASEAN. In particular, ASEAN countries have struggled among themselves to bring down their tariffs to achieve the ASEAN Free Trade Area (AFTA) by 2003.[30] Moreover, AFTA has lost its momentum due to the Asian financial crisis of 1997 and political disarray in countries like Indonesia and the Philippines.

Having been a founding member of ASEAN, Singapore is indeed committed to AFTA. However, in view of the slow-moving regional integration process, it is imperative for Singapore to seek fulfillment of its objectives through bilateral channels, to complement Singapore's multilateral and regional trade liberalization initiatives. Singapore's former PM Goh said that "those who can run faster should run faster…and should not be restrained by those who don't want to run at all."[31] Singapore's economic viability depends on its geo-strategic position as the port of call in the Asia-Pacific linking Europe, the Middle East, the African continent, the South Asian continent, through to the Pacific islands and the Americas. It is important to view Singapore's status as a bustling port of call. In reality, Singapore's port faces increasing competition from the developments of other port facilities in Thailand, Hong Kong, China and particularly Malaysia.[32]

Second, ASEAN has been slow in building free-trade linkages with the United States, Japan and the EU. In his meeting with the editors of 11 Asian newspapers at the *Istana* [Singapore's Presidential Palace], former PM Goh said that "we would like ASEAN to move faster; I'm impatient because I believe ASEAN is taking a lot of time in just looking at ASEAN, whereas it should be looking outside ASEAN."[33] PM Goh's view is valid since trade outside the regional grouping (extra-ASEAN) has been far more significant at around 70-75 percent of ASEAN's global trade during the past 2-3 decades. However, because of the weak economic conditions in Japan, US and the EU, ASEAN should latch on with the rising economies of India and China to avail of the benefits and opportunities from their linkages.[34]

---

[30] The Agreement for Common Effective Preferential Tariff (CEPT) scheme leading to AFTA was implemented on January 1, 1993. The original members of ASEAN were expected to achieve the AFTA required tariff rates of 0-5% by the year 2003. During its 15th meeting, the AFTA Council announced that each of the original five members (Indonesia, Malaysia, the Philippines, Singapore and Thailand) had reduced tariffs to 0-5% on at least 90% of its tariff lines in the inclusion list. The newer ASEAN members are given a longer period to achieve this reduction in light of their current level of economic development. Each member of ASEAN has a 10-year time frame of tariff reduction program under AFTA. Vietnam is targeted to fully implement AFTA in 2006, while the target year for Laos and Myanmar is 2008, and 2010 for Cambodia

[31] Asian Economic News, "Singapore free trade pact worrisome, Mahathir says," March 5, 2001.

[32] Singapore has faced growing competition from the Malaysian Port of Tanjung Pelepas (PTP) which lured away Danish Maersk Sealand in 2000 and Taiwan's largest shipping company, Evergreen Marine in 2002. See The Straits Times, "PSA's cargo volume down 8.9% last year," January 19, 2002.

[33] The Straits Times, "ASEAN 'slow' on free-trade links," May 3, 2002, p.1.

[34] Despite being fierce competitor in some sectors, China's growth and prosperity will benefit ASEAN in some ways. ***First,*** ASEAN can zoom in on China's growing middle-class who will demand more foreign goods and more foreign tours. For example, Singapore's booming two-way trade with China posted a significant increase of 39.5 percent in non-oil domestic exports in 2002 to S$6.2 billion, with petrochemicals, electronics and

Third, there has been greater progress in the trade liberalization and enlargement activities in the Western Hemisphere such as the creation of the North American Free Trade Agreement (NAFTA) which encompasses the US, Canada and Mexico; the widening of the EU to include some Central and Eastern European countries; and the establishment of the Free Trade Area of Americas (FTAA) in 2005 to include North, South and Central Americas. These developments were emphasized in a speech delivered by Ms. Ng Bee Kim, director of Singapore's Ministry of Trade and Industry (MTI) and Singapore's chief negotiator for EFTA-Singapore FTA:

> We argued that with the worldwide trend towards FTAs, we could not afford to be left out of the game. The EU, already a huge FTA in itself, was in the process of enlargement. The EU also has FTAs with many Central and East European, African and South American countries. The US, Canada and Mexico have NAFTA. And then you have the massive and ambitious Free Trade Area of the Americas (or FTAA), whereby more than 30 North and South American countries intend to form the world's largest FTA. We felt that these compelling developments merited a refinement of our trade policy. If, through FTAs, everyone else was part of a selective club where the members got special trading privileges, then Singapore had better ensure that we had membership too. Otherwise, our *[Singapore's]* companies would be seriously disadvantaged.[35]

Fourth, Singapore's FTAs are expected to serve both economic and strategic interests. On the economic front, FTAs could provide certain predictability for Singapore businessmen and investors, lower barriers to trade and investment, and open up considerable opportunities for Singapore's business community. As Ms Ng Bee Kim of Singapore's Ministry of Trade and Industry declared:

> FTAs could achieve the following: Reduced tariffs would save costs for our exporters. Our companies could be guaranteed access to the services markets of other countries. All other sorts of barriers that our companies faced in selling goods and services to foreign markets could be reduced or eliminated. Having solid investment rules would also be an added attraction for MNCs to set up shop and invest in Singapore, creating jobs for our people in the process.[36]

Fifth, Singapore's FTAs could promote the liberalization and integration of regional markets and hasten global free trade within the context of the WTO. On January 17, 2000, Singapore's former Minister of Trade and Industry, BG George Yeo, was asked if

---

precision engineering products as main exports to China. ***Second,*** ASEAN exports to China are already bigger than the region's exports to any other part of the world as pointed out by Mr Tharman Shanmugaratnam, Singapore's Senior Minister of State for Trade and Industry and Education. ***Third,*** the number of tourists from China who visited ASEAN had increased by 30-35 percent a year including 400,000 Chinese visitors to Malaysia in 2001. Tourist arrivals in Singapore from China in October 2002 rose by 35.4 percent. Vietnam received over 700,000 Chinese tourists in 2002. ***Fourth***, Malaysia's former PM Dr Mahathir Mohamad said that there would be some products that China cannot produce that ASEAN could capitalize on like the potential huge demand for paper and palm oil products. (See The Straits Times, "ASEAN must latch on to China's growth," May 7, 2002, p.A6, and The Straits Times, "Chinese tourists heading for Southeast Asia," December 14, 2002, p.A2),

[35] Taken from her speech delivered in a seminar on FTAs organized by the Icelandic Chambers of Commerce, June 24, 2002. See Singapore's MTI website:
< *http://www.mti.gov.sg/public/FTA/frm_FTA_Default.asp?sid=37&cid=1183* >

[36] See Singapore's MTI website:
< *http://www.mti.gov.sg/public/FTA/frm_FTA_Default.asp?sid=37&cid=1183* >

Singapore's pursuit of bilateral FTAs reflects Singapore's dissatisfaction with the pace of global trade liberalization. He replied that 'to some extent, yes" and warned that the failure of the WTO Ministerial Meeting in Seattle may cause the momentum of trade liberalization to falter and embolden protectionist measures.[37] Also, when asked in a Singapore symposium about how Singapore's pursuit of bilateral FTAs may affect Singapore's WTO commitments, Mr. Raymond Lim, Singapore's Minister of State for Foreign Affairs and Trade and Industry, said that 'both are equally important and resources are dedicated to both, and that they are not mutually exclusive.'[38] On another occasion, Mr. Lim emphasized that the pursuit of bilateral arrangements is parallel and complementary to the multilateral system.[39] Moreover, Mr. Chan Beng Seng, Deputy Director of Singapore's Ministry of Trade and Industry, maintained that Singapore would always focus on multilateral trade negotiations whereas FTAs would constitute a complementary and dynamic force. Mr. Khaw Boon Wan, former head of Singapore's Trade and Industry Ministry, also believed that suitably designed regional and bilateral pacts could stimulate further global trade liberalization in the WTO.[40]

Singapore's FTAs also contain a strategic angle. Establishing FTAs with various countries around the world could help to anchor the presence of these countries in the region, and keep Singapore and ASEAN on their radar screen. This is especially important for a small nation like Singapore.

However, Singapore's dual move towards AFTA and FTAs has been quite controversial among its ASEAN fellows. There have been concerns that such FTAs may undermine the strength of AFTA and complicate future negotiations of ASEAN with other strategic partners like China and Japan. Malaysia's Foreign Minister Syed Hamid Albar said that "when we do something outside the ASEAN context which could weaken the organization, we must think twice."[41] Mr. Jose Ampeso, a Filipino diplomat who was formerly based at the Philippine Embassy in Singapore, stressed that a FTA, like the one between Singapore and Japan, could undermine the strength of AFTA as the rest of ASEAN would perceive Singapore as Japan's favorite trading partner.

Singapore's go-it-alone move has been viewed by others as against the spirit of ASEAN. While no sanctions are imposed on Singapore's participation in trade negotiation with countries outside the ASEAN regional grouping, Singapore should not ignore the political, social, cultural and economic implications of its policies including FTAs. For instance, Malaysia has expressed its criticisms against Singapore's FTA policy.[42] According to the Malaysian Foreign Minister, Syed Hamid Albar, "Singapore may not have done anything wrong in legal terms but morally, the *[Singapore]* Republic's action showed that it had

---

[37] See The Business Times, "Bilateral pacts could have catalytic effects: BG Yeo," January 18, 2000.

[38] "Singapore's position has always been that FTAs create the 'competitive dynamics' towards greater liberalization. Moreover, FTAs represent 'competitive liberalization' rather than "competitive protectionism." See The Straits Times, "S'pore values both WTO deals, FTAs," February 21, 2003, p.A18.

[39] Speech delivered in an International Symposium on "FTAs: JSEPA and Beyond," organized by the Japan Economic Foundation and the Singapore Institute of International Affairs, held in Singapore on March 7, 2003.

[40] Hardev Kaur, "Amid globalization trend, Pacific Rim sees a bellweather on bilateral trade," *The WorldPaper,* [accessed 21 April 2003] < http://www.worldpaper.com/2001/may01/tradeblocs4.html >

[41] Hardev Kaur, "By reaching out."

[42] Prior to her independence in 1965, Singapore was part of the Federation of Malaya. Singapore is connected to Malaysia in the north by a causeway carrying road, rail and water supply links. Malaysia has always been Singapore's major trading partner. However, their relationship has been strained because of various historical

undermined friendship in ASEAN."[43] Moreover, a Malaysian newspaper, *Berita Harian Malaysia*, argued that Singapore's FTA with non-ASEAN countries could "provide a third route or back door for them to penetrate AFTA markets."[44]

More interestingly during a lunch talk before the members of the Singapore International Chamber of Commerce, Malaysia's Minister of International Trade and Industry, Rafidah Aziz, highlighted that Singapore's special trade pacts with several countries are not FTAs but bilateral agreements.[45] In her opinion, there is a huge difference between an FTA and a bilateral agreement. An FTA involves tariff negotiations, but a bilateral agreement does not as it is only concerned with trade facilitation and the promotion of trade.[46] With her definition of bilateral trade agreement, Ms Rafidah said that "all of us do that" which presumably refers to all trading nations in the world including ASEAN. She further argued that if trade negotiation is undertaken by an ASEAN member country including offers of tariff cuts to a non-ASEAN country, the same offers should be made to the rest of ASEAN and this could therefore nullify the benefit of having bilateral FTAs because the rest of ASEAN could also benefit.[47] She further stated that the non-ASEAN country being offered concessions cannot come into ASEAN through the bilateral agreement because of the ASEAN local content rule of at least 40 percent. When asked what if Singapore's bilateral trade pacts with various countries had tariff negotiations, she said that "... they [Singapore and her bilateral partners] have to go back to ASEAN provisions, and the ASEAN Secretariat will alert them on this ... then whatever provisions in the Act will then apply."[48]

However, by now, it should be clear that Singapore's bilateral trade agreements do in fact involve trade negotiations and tariff cuts. With the passing of time, Malaysia's earlier stance against Singapore's bilateral FTAs has changed given Ms. Rafidah Aziz's announcement that the Malaysian government is already studying the costs and benefits of forging bilateral FTAs, but those which are focused on services like telecommunications. Malaysia's former PM Dr. Mahathir Mohamad also announced during his visit to Tokyo in December 2002 that his country would be having an FTA with Japan.[49] The proliferation of FTAs and their benefits and opportunities may have led to Malaysia's policy-makers taking a second look at bilateral pacts.

disputes over several overlapping territorial claims, border customs and the negotiation of a new agreement for Malaysia to supply water to Singapore.

[43] The Hindu, "Malaysia Cautions on Trade Pacts," November 23, 2000.

[44] The Business Times, "Singapore won't be back door to AFTA," May 3, 2001.

[45] The Business Times, "S'pore's trade pacts are not FTAs," October 12, 2001.

[46] The Business Times, "S'pore's trade pacts," p.7.

[47] The Business Times, "S'pore's trade pacts," p.7.

[48].According to Ms Rafidah Aziz, a FTA would be subject to rules agreed by the ASEAN countries under the two regional arrangements – the Common Effective Preferential Treatment (CEPT) scheme and the ASEAN Investment Area (AIA). The CEPT scheme enables tariff negotiations under AFTA. See The Business Times, "S'pore's trade pacts," p.7

[49] The Business Times, "The paradox of Asia's FTAs," December 18, 2002. Japan is Malaysia's second most important trading partner after the United States. Bilateral trade between Japan and Malaysia reached a total of RM99 billion (S$46 billion) in 2001. Japan is also the second largest foreign investor in Malaysia. See The Straits Times, "Malaysia aims for first free-trade deal with Japan," December 13, 2002, p.A22.

Towards ASEAN's Bilateral FTAs

Given the different stages of policy developments among ASEAN countries, the convergence towards full trade liberalization could be a long way to go unless ASEAN countries, either individually or jointly, do something. In this context, aimed at complementing her regional and global trade liberalization policies, Singapore, as discussed in the previous section, has concluded several FTAs, has on-going trade negotiations, and intends to establish more FTAs. For example, the Singapore–US bilateral FTA is expected to benefit not only Singapore but also the other ASEAN countries, like Indonesia, as Singapore's exports to the US can make use of ASEAN-manufactured components.[50] As such, Singapore's FTA could create a win-win environment for ASEAN with more trade opportunities as well as economic and political stability. While the process for ASEAN regional integration is irreversible, AFTA members will benefit from Singapore's bilateral FTAs once they are catalyzed by such an impetus to restructure their economies and external trade to cope with the new challenges of a globally competitive world.

It is interesting to observe that other ASEAN countries are also keen in forging FTAs. As stated earlier, Malaysia is now considering to form a bilateral FTA with Japan. Also inspired by the Japan-Singapore FTA, Philippine President Gloria Arroyo officially proposed the establishment of a FTA during her third visit to Japan on December 4, 2002.[51] The United States has also proposed bilateral FTAs each with Thailand and the Philippines. Australia is also working towards commencing negotiations for an FTA with Thailand. In addition to planned FTAs between some ASEAN member countries and non-ASEAN countries, the ASEAN regional grouping itself is keen in establishing FTAs with countries outside the regional grouping like China, US and India because of the potential benefits and opportunities offered by FTAs.

During the ASEAN-China summit in November 2000, China's former Premier Zhu Rongji first proposed the establishment of the *ASEAN-China Free Trade Area* (ACFTA). It was mainly for strategic and economic reasons.[52] At the November 2001 ASEAN+China Summit, the leaders agreed to start negotiations for the ACFTA and to establish it within 10 years. After six rounds of negotiations, the Framework Agreement on Comprehensive Economic Cooperation between ASEAN and the People's Republic of China was signed by the leaders on November 4, 2002 in Phnom Penh, Cambodia. The agreement includes provisions for cooperation in economic liberalization as well as economic cooperation. The central liberalization element in the agreement is the "early harvest" in which ASEAN and China are committed to reduce tariffs for early harvest products mainly agricultural products. Tariffs on these products will be eliminated over three years, beginning January 1, 2004.

---

50 The Straits Times, "FTA 'customs union' to benefit Southeast Asia," March 17, 2002

51 It is expected that the proposed Japan-Philippines FTA could be beyond the usual FTA to maximize the many areas of complementarity between them. President Arroyo cited examples like Japan can utilize Filipino health care workers given Japan's aging population and Japanese high tech firms can hire skilled young Filipino workers. For details, see "Arroyo pushes free trade with Japan," *Philippine Star,* December 4, 2002:

52 Razeen Sally stated that "both political and economic factors lie behind the new form of regionalism – the formation of bilateral FTAs. China views FTAs as a means to exercise strategic leadership in the East Asian region. The economic motivation are mostly defensive. With the WTO being stuck in the drift and deadlock over the past few years, there is a race to secure preferential access to the markets of the major powers, and to defuse trade tension by locking into strong bilateral and regional partnerships." See The Straits Times, "Asia gets onto bandwagon of regionalism," January 28, 2003, p.16.

When concluded, ACFTA will be the largest FTA in the world with a regional GDP of US$2 trillion. It is expected that ASEAN could attract FDI in the region to serve the Chinese market. Moreover, with a huge market of 1.2 billion people, China promises an export boom for ASEAN as the latter's exports to China was estimated to grow by almost 50 percent.

Within days after the ASEAN-China FTA was formally inked, the United States announced the *Enterprise for ASEAN Initiative* (EAI) which could give ASEAN countries broader access to the US market. It will be based on the high standards set in the US-Singapore FTA. The EAI offers prospects of bilateral free trade pacts between the US and ASEAN countries which are WTO members. Should the EAI be implemented, ASEAN countries could penetrate the US markets more for its goods and services. However, Dr Frank-Jurgen Richter, the World Economic Forum's director for Asia, argued that the US's EAI initiative was mainly to counterbalance a rising China and that the US does not want to be left out in the cold. Moreover, given that APEC's free trade agenda is not moving as fast as it should, he predicts that APEC will be set back by the EAI – the US may believe that it can achieve more with the ASEAN economies through the EAI than with a sluggish APEC.[53]

Japanese PM Junichiro Koizume and the ASEAN leaders signed the *ASEAN-Japan Comprehensive Economic Partnership* (AJCEP) deal during the 8th ASEAN summit in Cambodia on November 10, 2002. According to Mr. Tsugami, a senior fellow at Japan's Research Institute of Economy, Trade and Industry (RIETI), this announcement was viewed as Japan's immediate response to the launching of the China-ASEAN FTA negotiation exactly a year ago which caught many Japanese political and business leaders by surprise.[54] It was a shocking news to Japan and that some sentiments which prevailed in Japan then were the fear that China might exclude Japan from the East Asian economic development and political circle, the question of why ASEAN countries abandon their "balancing diplomacy between major powers in the region," and the fear that Japan could be further left behind from the East Asian move because of the delay in the much needed domestic reforms.[55]

Japan and ASEAN have a combined population of 590 million (11 percent of the world's total population) and a combined GDP of US$4.9 trillion (18 percent of the world's total GDP). Unlike China's push for free trade, the AJCEP focuses on human resource development and investment promotion. Unlike ASEAN-China FTA, Japan's proposal will be implemented based on bilateral deals as any ASEAN member could commence talks with Japan to form a bilateral pact. Japan has already concluded an FTA with Singapore, and intends to form similar arrangements with Thailand, the Philippines, Indonesia and Malaysia.

India's former PM Atal Behari Vajpayee offered to commence negotiations for an *ASEAN-India Free Trade Area* (AIFTA) which could be completed in 10 years. He announced this proposal on November 5, 2002, a day after the signing of the ASEAN-China FTA. It was a surprised but welcome offer given that India is a relatively closed economy

---

[53] The Business Times, "The paradox of Asia's FTAs," December 18, 2002.

[54] Toshiya Tsugami, "On ASEAN-China Free Trade Agreement – a personal view from Japan," Presented at a symposium on "FTAs: JSEPA and Beyond", organized by the Japan Economic Foundation and Singapore Institute of International Affairs, Singapore, March 7, 2003.

[55] However, several counter-sentiments were cited as follows: (a) that it was Japan who shocked China first with its idea of launching "Japan-Korea FTA" in 1998 and JSEPA in 1999, (b) that it is not fair for Japan to complain to ASEAN for their "China shift" because Japan is shifting towards China more rapidly, (c) that ASEAN's move does not mean ignoring its "balancing diplomacy" but more of an indication to Japan to accelerate its economic reforms, and (d) that China does not intend to leave Japan as evidenced by the proposed formation of a trilateral FTA among Japan, China and Korea.

with high tariffs for its imports. Using an analogy, Singapore's former PM Goh Chok Tong said that the ASEAN jumbo jet is now ready to take off with one wing in the making in the East through agreements with China and Japan, and with India providing the second wing. Bilateral trade between India and ASEAN is expected to double within ten years from its present level of US$10 billion. Moreover, ASEAN is a strategic partner for India as it could provide a link to Northeast Asia. India could somehow provide a balance between ASEAN and Northeast Asia.

TOWARDS ASEAN OR EAST ASIAN ECONOMIC COMMUNITY?

In the future, the ASEAN regional grouping can form a common market to be known as *ASEAN Economic Community (AEC)* or an *East Asian Economic Community (EAEC)*. Singapore's former PM Goh proposed for the establishment of an AEC by 2020 during the 8th ASEAN summit in Cambodia in November 2002.[56] His proposal, along the lines of the European Economic Community, received a strong support from Thailand's PM Thaksin Shinawatra. As a single market with 500 million people, the AEC could allow the 10 member countries to enjoy free movement of goods and services, and a free movement of factors of production including capital and labor particularly professionals. Having had a number of economic initiatives on trade, tourism and services, the AEC could serve as the end vision for all these agreements. It is expected that the AEC could help in bridging the economic gap between and among ASEAN members which include high-income countries like Singapore, Brunei and Malaysia and lower-income ones like Laos, Cambodia and Myanmar.

Alternatively, the ASEAN+3 countries comprising 10 ASEAN countries, Japan, China and South Korea, can form an *East Asian Economic Community* (EAEC).[57] They can move away from being merely dialogue partners towards becoming more economically integrated. This could initially be in the form of an *East Asian Free Trade Area* (EAFTA), an idea which was first proposed by the East Asian Vision Group in its report presented during the ASEAN+3 summit in Brunei in November 2001. EAFTA could be achieved in 2006 as suggested by Mr. Noboru Hatakeyama, Chairman and CEO of Japan Economic Foundation.[58] He suggested that the ASEAN+3 Economic Ministers should recommend to their Leaders to commence the actual study on EAFTA from 2003 and enter into negotiation from 2004 with the goal of concluding it by the end of 2006. However, Professor Chia Siow Yue, former director of the Institute of Southeast Asian Studies, argued during the open forum on Singapore's FTAs, that Mr Hatakeyama's suggestion is very optimistic but not realistic. She further raised the idea that the more likely scenario is the one proposed by Mr. Long Yongtu, Vice Minister of China's Ministry of Foreign Trade and Economic Cooperation (MOFTEC), for the establishment of an East Asia Comprehensive Economic Partnership which includes

56 ASEAN and the EU are two different groups. For example, intra-regional trade in the former has hovered around 20-25 percent of ASEAN's global trade in the last two decades, while in the latter, intra-regional trade historically has been around 50-60 percent of EU's global trade. Despite this difference, ASEAN could learn from the EU on the different stages of its regional economic integration.

57 China, Japan and South Korea are currently ASEAN's dialogue partners under the ASEAN+3 framework. For an excellent discussion of this framework, including its origins, evolution and potentials, see Richard Stubbs, "ASEAN plus three: emerging East Asian regionalism?" *Asian Survey,* Vol.42, No.3, 2002.

trade facilitation and economic cooperation rather than trade liberalization. Whatever form it may take initially, the ASEAN+3 grouping should work towards becoming more fully integrated as a common market in the long-run.

The formation of an East Asian bloc is justified on several grounds. First, the integration of Southeast Asia with Northeast Asia could become one of the driving forces in the global economy as it provides a market of more than 2 billion people (a third of the world's population) and a fifth of global trade. Second, with China being ASEAN's fifth largest trading partner and emerging giant, economic ties with ASEAN for Japan and South Korea could be a means to counteract China's growing economic power. Third, the ASEAN regional grouping could be losing its attractiveness to foreign investors in light of China's rising economic might.[59]

Given all the existing regional agreements and FTAs, what is the best way to arrive at EAFTA? Dr Chulsu Kim, President of Korea's Sejong University, suggested a number of alternative scenarios for the process leading to EAFTA. These include (a) negotiating a region-wide FTA directly among all countries in the region, (b) phasing in EAFTA through the formation of various bilateral FTAs between ASEAN and Northeast Asian countries, and (c) forming a trilateral FTA among China, Japan and Korea and then move in the direction of consolidating with ASEAN.[60]

But what is the probability of forming an East Asian regional economic grouping. For one, Razeen Sally believes that an East Asian bloc forming around either China and/or Japan seems plausible given that the East Asian countries have relatively liberal trade policies and are reasonably well-integrated into the global economy.[61] However, he pointed out that the East Asian countries are hugely different in terms of their outward-orientation with Singapore and Hong Kong being free ports, with South Korea and Taiwan having liberalized substantially in recent years, with Thailand's protectionism remaining high, with Indonesia and the Philippines being mired in political and economic instability, with Myanmar, Vietnam, Cambodia and Laos having higher levels of protection, with Japan having a defensive trade policy particularly its agricultural sector, and with China narrowing the trade policy gap with other developing countries bringing average tariffs down to Southeast Asian and Latin American levels of around 10 percent.[62] These differences in their trade policy regimes and in their levels of development could certainly provide enormous challenges for the East Asian countries to form together as a regional economic grouping. In addition, there are some political and bilateral disputes which have to be settled like the historical hostility

---

[58] Noboru Hatakeyama, "EAFTA not a dream, but a reality," Presented at the symposium on "FTAs; JSEPA and Beyond," Singapore, March 7, 2003.

[59] In recent years, China's buoyant economic performance has diverted FDI away from ASEAN. In 2001, ASEAN attracted only US$13.1 billion which paled in comparison with China's US$47 billion. See The Straits Times, "ASEAN may become an East Asia grouping," Oct 12, 2002, p.28. On the contrary, however, a study by Singapore's Ministry of Trade and Industry reported that FDI in ASEAN and China have moved in tandem during the 1989 to 2001 period – that is, "the trends and patterns of global FDI flows to ASEAN and China have not shown that growth in China's FDI has been at the expense of ASEAN. Moreover, Japan, US and the EU have consistently invested more in ASEAN than in China, except in 1998." See The Straits Times, "China's rise has not been at ASEAN's expense," November 19,2002, p.A16. The results were also published by Friedrich Wu and Kok Keong Puah, "Foreign Direct Investment in China and Southeast Asia: Has ASEAN been losing out?" *Journal of Asian Business,* Vol.18, No.3, 2002.

[60] See Chulsu Kim, "Towards an East Asia Free Trade Agreement," delivered at the symposium on "FTAs: JSEPA and Beyond," Singapore, March 7, 2003.

[61] The Straits Times, "Asia gets onto bandwagon of regionalism," January 28, 2003, p.16.

[62] The Straits Times, "Asia gets," p.16.

between Japan and South Korea, disputes among countries of the ASEAN, and the political implications of the Taiwan issue.[63] While Malaysia has been supportive of an East Asian bloc,[64] other ASEAN countries view it differently. Singapore's position, for example, is that it will be more advantageous for ASEAN to maintain separate trade deals each with China, Japan and South Korea, instead of a joint agreement with them.[65] The main reason is that ASEAN might be overwhelmed by the combined power of the three giant economies and this may lead to the marginalization of the ASEAN economies particularly the smaller and poorer new members (Vietnam, Cambodia, Laos and Myanmar).

CONCLUSION

The regional integration process in ASEAN has evolved gradually during the past four decades. To move towards closer economic integration, ASEAN has undertaken both widening and deepening economic activities. While the enlargement process from five to ten members has resulted in a two-tier grouping, the development gaps between the higher and lower income countries can be narrowed down through several mechanisms including the provision of financial and technical assistance to the lower income countries and by encouraging more trade and investments in them.

ASEAN has also followed trade and investment liberalization measures aimed at improving the competitiveness of their economies and increasing the pace of regional integration. On the trade front, these measures, which include PTAs and CEPT, have been implemented towards achieving AFTA. While the PTAs proved to be ineffective because of the low utilization rate, the CEPT has enabled ASEAN to move towards a higher plane with the reduction of tariffs to 0-5 percent for ASEAN-6 on at least 90 percent of its tariff lines in the inclusion list. However, intra-ASEAN trade has remained low at 20-25 percent of its global trade, with much of this being accounted for by trade between Singapore, Malaysia and Indonesia. This fact is attributed to various factors including the favorable treatment given to imports of capital goods from developed countries, the different pace of industrialization among ASEAN countries, and the greater significance of extra-ASEAN economic ties particularly with Japan, the US and the EU.

On the investment front, ASEAN has undertaken measures to promote and encourage FDI including regional initiatives like the ASEAN Investment Area (AIA) and the ASEAN Industrial Cooperation (AICO) and sub-regional schemes like growth areas. Past regional schemes like AIP, AIC and AIJV had proved to be less successful.

Thus, despite regional and sub-regional initiatives, ASEAN economic integration has proceeded at a snail pace because of some factors which include, among others, a weak organizational structure, the consensus decision-making approach, lack of political commitment, the ineffectiveness of regional economic initiatives, the dominance of national over regional economic interests, and the significance of outside linkages.

---

63 The Korea Herald, "Toward an East Asian economic community," February 27, 2003.

64 Having advocated the idea of an East Asia economic grouping long time ago, Malaysia's PM Mahathir Mohamad resurrected it further during the 1997/98 economic crisis when he suggested the formation of an Asian monetary system towards a stable Asian currency. He brought up the idea again in Brunei in September 2001. See The Straits Times, "ASEAN may become an East Asia grouping," Oct 12, 2002, p.28.

65 The Straits Times, "ASEAN may become...," p.28.

With extra-regional being more significant than intra-regional economic linkages, ASEAN has implemented various multilateral and regional strategies to support the principles and objectives of the WTO, APEC and ASEM. However, with the growing importance of bilateral FTAs, some countries in ASEAN, led by Singapore, have completed or are planning to form FTAs with countries outside the grouping. As a free trader and a vocal champion of free trade, Singapore has supported and will continue to support the promotion of free and open trade at the multilateral level through the WTO and at the regional level through ASEAN, APEC and ASEM.

However, the failure of the WTO Ministerial Meeting in Seattle, the delays in the implementation of tariff cuts among ASEAN countries, and the slow progress of APEC's initiatives have encouraged Singapore to forge FTAs with both developed and developing countries outside the ASEAN grouping. Moreover, Singapore has weighed the likely negative consequences of the proliferation of FTAs and further regional integration efforts that are taking place in Europe and America which could provide a global imbalance in favor of the trans-atlantic regions of the world. Singapore, ASEAN, Asia, and the Asia-Pacific could be left behind if nothing is done from the Asian side. Singapore has courageously taken the initiative of negotiating FTAs.

Having been viewed as parallel and complementary to the global and regional initiatives, FTAs has economic and strategic rationale for Singapore. FTAs can generate substantial foreign exchange savings for Singapore's exporters, guarantee Singapore companies access to the goods and services markets of the partner countries, help to anchor Singapore in the radar of its partner countries like New Zealand, EFTA, Japan, Australia, United States, Canada, Mexico, India and Korea, and build bridges to the regions to which these countries represent including Asia, Oceania, America and Europe.

Singapore's FTA policy, however, has been met with criticisms particularly during its early phase. It was viewed as against the ASEAN spirit, and could provide a backdoor for goods from her partner countries to enter ASEAN duty-free. From Singapore's point of view, FTAs could serve as a trailblazer which other ASEAN countries could join. Indeed, over a period of two years since her first FTA was concluded with Japan, the criticisms against Singapore's FTAs have subsided. In fact, other ASEAN countries, and even the ASEAN grouping itself, have expressed keen interest in establishing FTAs with other countries like China, the United States, Japan and India. Aimed at promoting trade and investments between the bilateral partners, these FTAs are and must be consistent with the WTO, can be WTO-plus and pursue open regionalism to achieve open and free trade and investment in the future.

Questions for Discussion

1. Some countries in the world form regional economic groupings such as the Association of Southeast Asian Nations (ASEAN), the North American Free Trade Agreement (NAFTA), the European Union (EU), the Australia-New Zealand Closer Economic Relations (CER) and the Southern Common Market (MERCOSUR), to name a few. Why do countries form regional groups?
2. The EU is expanding further to include some central and eastern European countries. By the year 2005, the Free Trade Area of the Americas (FTAAs) will be formed to

include northern, central and southern American countries. It is also predicted that regional trading agreements could reach up to 300 by the year 2005. Discuss the consequences and implications of this trend in the ASEAN context.
3. ASEAN was formed in 1967 by five founding members, namely, Indonesia, Malaysia, the Philippines, Singapore and Thailand. Brunei joined in 1984. Other new members were admitted such as Vietnam (1995), Laos and Myanmar (1997) and Cambodia (1999). Discuss the benefits and costs of ASEAN enlargement to old and new members.
4. Despite its formation in 1967, the ASEAN regional economic integration has proceeded at a very slow pace. Why?
5. Explain clearly whether you agree or disagree with the following statement: "It is in the interest of all Asian states to conclude bilateral trade deals because multilateral talks at the WTO are moving slowly."

SUGGESTED MATERIALS FOR CASE STUDIES:

Blackhurst, Richard, 1997, "The WTO and the Global Economy," *The World Economy,* Vol.20, No.5, pp. 527-544.

Ong, Eng Chuan, 2003, "Anchor East Asian Free Trade in ASEAN," *The Washington Quarterly,* Vol.26, No.2, pp.57-72.

REFERENCES

Ariff, Mohamed, 1998, "Economic Regionalism versus Multilateralism: Dilemmas for Southeast Asia?" Paper presented at ISEAS 30th anniversary conference on Southeast Asia in the 21st Century: Challenges of Globalization, Singapore.

Asian Economic News, 2001, "Singapore Free Trade Pact Worrisome, Mahathir says," March 5.

Daquila, Teofilo C. 1999, "The ASEAN Experience of Economic Cooperation," Paper presented at "The East African Forum on the East African Community: Economic Aspects of Integration," organized by Friedrich Ebert Foundation, 27-29 September, Kampala, Uganda.

Daquila, Teofilo C. 2001, "Towards Strengthening ASEAN Integration: Challenges, Strategies and Prospects," in Apirat Petchsiri, Alfred Kellerman, Charit Tingsabadh and Pornsan Watananguhn (eds.), *Strengthening ASEAN Integration: Lessons from the EU's Rule of Law*, Thailand: Chulalongkorn University's Interdisciplinary Department of European Studies, the Center for European Studies, and TMC Asser Institute of the Netherlands, pp.77-87.

Daquila, Teofilo C. 2002, "ASEAN Economic Performance: Revisiting the Past, Looking to the Future," *Harvard Asia Quarterly,* Mass.: Harvard University, Vol. 6, No.3, pp.9-14 , online exclusive.

Daquila, Teofilo C. and Le Huu Huy, 2003, "Singapore and ASEAN in the Global Economy: Case of Free Trade Agreements," *Asian Survey* (USA: University of California, Berkeley), Vol.XLIII, No.6, pp.908-928.

Davidson, Paul, 2002, *ASEAN: The Evolving Legal Framework for Economic Cooperation*, Singapore: Times Academic Press, pp.14-50.

Hatakeyama, Noboru, 2003, "EAFTA not a dream, but a reality," Presented at the symposium on "FTAs; JSEPA and Beyond," Singapore, March 7.

Kim, Chulsu, 2003, "Towards an East Asia Free Trade Agreement," Paper delivered at the symposium on "FTAs: JSEPA and Beyond," Singapore, March 7.

Langhammer, Rolf, 1992, "Regionalism in Place of or Together with Multilateralism" delivered before the Economic Society of Singapore, July 9.

Park, Sung-Hoon, 2002, "East Asian Economic Integration – Finding a Balance between Regionalism and Multilateralism," EIAS Briefing Paper, Brussels: European Institute for Asian Studies.

Philippine Star, "Arroyo Pushes Free Trade with Japan," December 4, 2002.

Stubbs, Richard, 2002, "ASEAN Plus Three: Emerging East Asian Regionalism?" *Asian Survey,* Vol.42, No.3, pp. 440 – 455.

The Business Times (BT)

- "Bilateral pacts could have catalytic effects: BG Yeo," January 18, 2000.
- "Singapore won't be back door to AFTA," May 3, 2001.
- "S'pore's trade pacts are not FTAs," October 12, 2001
- "The paradox of Asia's FTAs," December 18, 2002.
- "FTA with India next on S'pore agenda: BG Yeo," January 30, 2003.
- "Singapore, Australia sign free trade agreement," February 17, 2003.
- "Singapore seals FTA deals with Australia," February 18, 2003.
- "EU, ASEAN pledge to boost trade, political ties," February 24, 2003.

The Hindu, "Malaysia Cautions on Trade Pacts," November 23, 2000.

The Korea Herald, "Toward an East Asian Economic Community," February 27, 2003.

The Straits Times (ST)

- "PSA's cargo volume down 8.9% last year", January 19, 2002.
- "Asia gets onto bandwagon of regionalism," January 28, 2002, p.16.
- "FTA 'customs union' to benefit Southeast Asia, March 17, 2002.
- "S'pore, India for economic partnership," April 9, 2002, p.1.
- "Denmark backs Singapore-EU free trade pact," April 18, 2002, p.6.
- "ASEAN 'slow' on free-trade links," May 3, 2002, p.1.
- "ASEAN must latch on to China's growth," May 7, 2002, p.A6.
- "ASEAN may become an East Asia grouping," Oct 12, 2002, p.28.
- "Singapore, NZ and Chile go for 3-way trade talks," October 28, 2002.
- "Spore-Seoul free trade talks to begin next year," November 15, 2002
- "China's rise has not been at ASEAN's expense," November 19, 2002, p.A16.
- "How the FTA was won," November 23, 2002, p.28.
- "Chinese tourists heading for Southeast Asia," December 14, 2002, p.A2),
- "Malaysia aims for first free-trade deal with Japan," December 13, 2002, p.A22.
- "Asia gets onto bandwagon of regionalism," January 28, 2003, p.16.
- "EU and ASEAN ministers pledge closer trade and intelligence ties," January 29, 2003, p.A6.

- "Bush gives go-ahead for FTA pact with S'pore," February 1, 2003, p.A12.
- "S'pore and India plan talks on free-trade pact," February 4, 2003.
- "S'pore values both WTO deals, FTAs", February 21, 2003, p.A18.

Tsugami, Toshiya, 2003, "On ASEAN-China Free Trade Agreement – a personal view from Japan," Presented at a symposium on "FTAs: JSEPA and Beyond", organized by the Japan Economic Foundation and Singapore Institute of International Affairs, Singapore, March 7.

Wu, Friedrich and Kok Keong Puah, 2003, "Foreign Direct Investment in China and Southeast Asia: Has ASEAN been losing out?" *Journal of Asian Business,* Vol.19, No.1.

INTERNET SOURCES:

Kaur, Hardev, 2003, "Amid globalization trend, Pacific Rim sees a bellweather on bilateral trade," *The WorldPaper,* [accessed 21 April] < *http://www.worldpaper.com/2001/may01/tradeblocs4.html*

Philippine Star, December 4, 2002: *<http://www.philstar.com/philstar/print.asp?article=103628>*

Singapore's MTI website: [accessed January 14, 2003] < *http://www.mti.gov.sg/public/FTA/frm_FTA_Default.asp?sid=37&cid=1183* >

WTO website: http:*//www.wto.org.*

WTO, 1995, *Regionalism and the World Trading System*, Geneva: World Trading Organization.

WTO website: *http://www.wto.org/wto/develop/regional.htm* – Regional Integration and the Multilateral Trading System, printed on 01 October 1, 1999.

In: Asian Economic and Political Issues, Volume 11 ISBN: 1-60021-192-5
Editor: Harvey E. Roth, pp. 167-189

Chapter 8

FOREIGN TRADE IN SOUTHEAST ASIA: THEORIES, POLICIES AND AFTA

Teofilo C. Daquila

ABSTRACT

This chapter examines the trade sector in Southeast Asian economies. It discusses the theories of trade including the absolute advantage, comparative advantage, Heckscher-Ohlin model, and competitive advantage. Some illustrations of these concepts in the context of Southeast Asia are discussed. This is followed by a discussion of the various trade policies including tariffs and non-tariff barriers. This chapter also analyzes the geographical and industrial patterns of Southeast Asia's exports and imports. Finally, it discusses the trade liberalization schemes followed by the Southeast Asian economies including the creation of the ASEAN Free Trade Area (AFTA).

INTRODUCTION

The appropriate role of trade and trade policy in economic development has been controversial for a long period of time. Greenaway and Morgan (1998) provides an excellent review of the core theoretical canons on trade policy and economic development.[1] As they stated further, based on multi-country and country-specific studies, the empirical evidence on the relationship between trade strategy and economic performance has been viewed from several different angles. First, some address the relationships between exports and economic growth on the assumption that more outward-oriented trade strategies are associated with higher exports. Second, some address the relationship between liberalization and exports - which is a narrower focus. Third, some attempts to use 'composite indicators of trade strategy and link these to indicators of economic performance.

[1] See David Greenaway and Wyn Morgan, "Trade Orientation and Economic Development: Theory and Evidence," in David Sapsford and John-ren Chen (eds), *Development Economics and Policy,* London, UK: Macmillan Press, 1988, pp.113-132.

In the case of Southeast Asian economies, exports have played a significant role in their economic development and transformation. Fukuda and Toya (1995) reported that the successful promotion of exports has been primarily responsible for rapid industrialization in the Asian newly-industrialized economies and even in the case of Southeast Asian countries.[2] This was true particularly for Thailand and Malaysia in the late 1980s when the growth rate of exports was more than twice as large as the rate of GNP growth between 1987 and 1990. The contribution of exports was less conspicuous in the Philippines and Indonesia, but their export-GNP ratios were higher than the Latin American countries, and even went up steadily in the late 1980s.

The remainder of this chapter is organized as follows. The next section discusses the various theories of trade. The third section describes briefly some trade policies. The fourth and fifth sections provide an analysis of the industrial and geographical trends and patterns of trade in Southeast Asia, respectively. The sixth section traces the trade liberalization policies in Southeast Asia focusing on the ASEAN Free Trade Area (AFTA).

Theories of Trade

Among the different theories of trade, this section discusses only four theories and are illustrated in the context of Southeast Asia. The first three are absolute advantage, comparative advantage and the Heckscher-Ohlin model.[3] The fourth model is based on the competitive advantage framework.

Absolute Advantage

Adam Smith postulated that two nations could trade based on absolute advantage. When one country (I) produces more efficiently than another country (II) in producing one good (X), then country I has an absolute advantage in the production of that good X. When Country II produces more efficiently than country I in producing the second good (Y), then country II has an absolute advantage in the production of good Y. Thus, country I will specialize in the production of good X and country II will specialize in the production of good Y. Both countries I and II can gain by exchanging part of their output for these goods. Trade is thus created. Through specialization, resources are used efficiently as they are re-allocated away from inefficient towards efficient commodity. Through trade, more output of both goods can be produced.

Assume that we have two countries; namely, Singapore and Indonesia. Because of labor conditions, Singapore is more efficient in the production of computers but inefficient in the production of textiles. Thus, Singapore has an absolute advantage in the production of computers. On the other hand, Indonesia is more efficient in the production of textiles but inefficient in the production of computers. Thus, Indonesia has an absolute advantage in the

---

[2] See Shin-ichi Fukuda and Hideki Toya, "Conditional Convergence in East Asian Countries: The Role of Exports in Economic Growth," in Takatoshi Ito and Anne O. Krueger (eds), *Growth Theories in Light of the East Asian Experience,* Chicago, USA: The University of Chicago Press, 1995, pp.247-265.

[3] For a complete discussion of these three trade theories, see Dominick Salvatore, *International Economics*, New York: Macmillan Publishing Co., 1990.

production of textiles. Both Singapore and Indonesia would gain by each producing the good of its absolute advantage and exchange them. Singapore would specialize in the production of computers by manufacturing more of them and exchange them for textiles manufactured in Indonesia. Consequently, more of computers and textiles would be manufactured and both countries would gain from trading.

To illustrate, consider the following example in Table 1. Assume that one hour of labor produces 6 units of computer in Singapore but only three in Indonesia. On the other hand, one hour of labor produces 6 yards of textiles in Indonesia, but only three in Singapore. Hence, Singapore is more efficient than Indonesia in the production of computers. Indonesia is more efficient than Singapore in the production of textiles. Both countries would gain by trading.

Table 1. Absolute Advantage

	Singapore	Indonesia
Computers (units/man-hour)	6	3
Textiles (yards/man-hour)	3	6

Comparative Advantage

In his book titled "Principles of Political Economy and Taxation" published in 1817, David Ricardo presented a very important concept called the law of comparative advantage, which has many practical applications. According to this law, if country I is more efficient than country II in the production of both goods X and Y, it still benefits to trade, as long as country II is not equally less productive in the production of both goods. Each country should specialize, produce and export the good in which it has a comparative advantage.

This is illustrated in Table 2. Singapore has absolute advantage in both lines of production as it produces higher computer and textile output than Indonesia. However, in terms of comparative advantage, Singaporean labor is twice as productive as Indonesian labor in the production of computers, but only one and a half times as productive as Indonesia in textiles. Equivalently, Indonesian labor is half as productive as Singaporean labor in computer production, but two-thirds as productive as Singaporean labor in textiles. Singapore's absolute advantage is greater in the production of computers and Indonesia's absolute advantage is greater in the production of textiles. Thus, we say that Singapore has a comparative advantage in the production of computers while Indonesia has a comparative advantage in the production of textiles. Singapore and Indonesia would need to specialize in the production of computers and textiles, respectively. Both would gain by trading.

Table 2. Comparative Advantage

	Singapore	Indonesia
Computers (units/man-hour)	6	3
Textiles (yards/man-hour)	3	2

The law of comparative advantage could also be explained in the context of opportunity costs. The opportunity cost of the first good (X) is the cost of a second commodity (Y) that needs to be given up in order to release sufficient resources to produce one additional unit of the first commodity (X). Without trade, Singapore needs to give up ½ of a unit of textile to produce one unit of computer domestically. Thus, the opportunity cost of a computer is one-half of a unit of textile (1C = ½ T in Singapore). This is shown in Table 3. Without trade, Indonesia needs to give up two-thirds of a unit of textile to produce one unit of computer domestically. Thus, the opportunity cost of a computer is two-thirds of a unit of textile (1C = 2/3 T in Indonesia). Hence, Singapore has the lower opportunity cost of computer in terms of the amount of textiles that has to be given up. Singapore would have a comparative (cost) advantage in the production of computers and Indonesia, in textiles. Singapore needs to specialize in the production of computers and exchange some of it for Indonesia's textiles.

Table 3. Comparative Advantage (Opportunity costs of one unit of computer)

	Singapore	Indonesia
Computers (units/man-hour)	6/6 = 1	3/3 = 1
Textiles (yards/man-hour)	3/6 = 0.5	2/3 = 0.67
Opportunity cost	1C = 0.5 T	1 C = 0.67 T

Heckscher-Ohlin Trade Model

According to this theory, nations trade as a result of the differences in their factor endowments; namely, labor and capital. The theory states that capital-abundant countries will produce and export capital-intensive goods and labor-abundant countries will produce and export labor-intensive goods.

But what is the meaning of factor abundance? There are two alternative definitions. The first definition is in terms of factor prices. Country I is capital-abundant if the price of its capital (P_C) relative to the price of its labor (P_L) is lower than that in Country II.

$$\frac{P_{C,I}}{P_{L,I}} < \frac{P_{C,II}}{P_{L,II}}$$

It also follows that if capital is cheaper in country I than in country II, then country I is abundant in capital. If labor is cheaper in country II than in country I, then country II is abundant in labor. As such country I will produce and export capital-intensive good while country II will produce and export labor-intensive goods. Some countries in Southeast Asia are more capital abundant such as Singapore and Malaysia, others are more labor abundant such as Indonesia, the Philippines and Thailand, with a population of about 205 million, 74 million and 62 million, respectively. Thus, according to this theory, the price ratio of capital to labor in Singapore is lower than that of Indonesia. As a result of this difference in factor intensity, Singapore will produce and export capital-intensive goods like computers while Indonesia will produce and export labor-intensive goods like textiles.

The second definition is stated in terms of the physical endowments of labor and capital. Country I is abundant in capital if the ratio of capital to labor is larger in country I than in country II.

$$\frac{C_I}{L_I} < \frac{C_{II}}{L_{II}}$$

where C_I and L_I are the total amounts of capital and labor , respectively, in country I and C_{II} and L_{II} are the total amount of capital and labor, respectively, in country II. This definition implies that from the production side, there is a bias in country I (the capital-rich country) towards producing capital-intensive good X. The opportunity cost of producing good X is lower in country I than in country II. For labor-abundant country II, there is a bias from the production side towards producing labor-intensive good Y as the opportunity cost of producing it is lower than in country I. From the demand side, demand in country I will be biased towards the capital-intensive good X and as such, in isolation, good X will be more expensive in country I than in country II. Demand in country II will be biased towards labor-intensive good Y and as such, in isolation, good Y will become more expensive in country II than in country I. With trade, country I will export labor-intensive good Y and country II will export capital-intensive good Y on the assumption that demand factors offset the production bias.

Therefore, the two definitions of factor abundance – first, based on price ratios of capital to labor, and second, based on the physical endowments of capital and labor – do not give equivalent theoretical results. It is only in the context of the first definition of factor abundance that a capital-abundant country will produce and export capital-intensive goods and that labor-abundant country will produce and export labor-abundant goods.

Theory of Competitive Advantage

Economists use "competitiveness" in various ways. One is purely macroeconomic in which the lack of competitiveness is treated as a real exchange rate problem which arises when a country at full employment runs a "persistent (and unwelcome) current account deficit which would in due course require adjustment, usually via a mixture of deflation and depreciation."[4] In this context, competitiveness is measured in terms of relative price and/or cost indices.

A broader definition of competitiveness used by most analysts is the one which focuses on structural factors affecting medium- to long-term economic performance such as productivity, innovation, skills and so on.[5] In this context, Porter (1990) developed a new paradigm which takes into account the changes in the nature of competition, and which challenges the traditional theory of comparative advantage.[6] As described by Singaravelu and Loh, Porter's theory of national competitive advantage consists of various determinants as

---

[4] A. Boltho, "The Assessment: International Competitiveness," *Oxford Review of Economic Policy*, Vol.12, No.3, 1996, p.2, as cited in Sanjaya Lall, "Competitiveness Indices and Developing Countries: An Economic Evaluation of the Global Competitiveness Report," *World Development*, Vol.29. No.9, 2001, pp.1503.

[5] J. Fagerberg, "Technology and Competitiveness," *Oxford Review of Economic Policy*, Vol.12, No.3, 1996, pp.39-51, as cited in Lall (2001: 1503).

[6] For an excellent analysis of Porter's theory of competititive advantage and its application to Southeast Asia, see Ananda Singaravelu and Loh Shen Lee, "Competitive Advantage: The US and ASEAN," in Tan Teck Meng, Low Aik Meng, John Williams and John Webster (eds), *US-ASEAN Relations: Implications for Business*, Nanyang Business Report Series, Singapore: Prentice Hall, 1997, pp.73-97.

shown in Fig. 1. It has four sets of variables which affect the ability of a firm to establish and sustain its competitive advantage in the global markets. These include factor conditions, demand conditions, related and supporting industries, and firm strategy, structure and rivalry. Factor conditions refer to a country's position in terms of factors of production like skilled labor or infrastructure which are necessary to compete in a given industry.

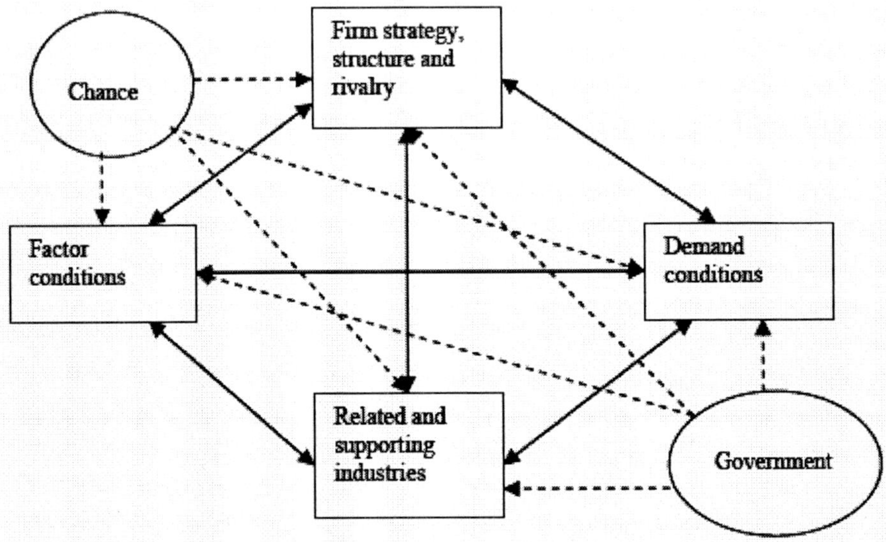

Source: Porter, 1990, as shown in Singaravelu and Loh (1997:184).

Figure 1. The Porter Diamond of Competitive Advantage

Demand conditions refer to the nature of domestic demand for the industry's product or service. Related and supporting industries refer to the presence or absence of supplier and related industries in a country which are internationally competitive. Firm strategy, structure and rivalry are concerned with the conditions in a country that govern the ways companies are created, organized and managed, and the nature of domestic rivalry. These four sets of conditions interact with one another and that they also interact with government influence and chance. Government influence is evident in the policies that impact each of these determinants. Chance is concerned with developments and events which are outside of the control of a firm and sometimes, the government.

Using his framework, an index labelled as the *Business Competitiveness Index* (BCI) was first introduced in *The Global Competitiveness Report 2000.*[7] The argument is that an economy cannot be competitive unless firms doing business there are competitive, whether they are domestic companies or affiliates of foreign companies.[8] However, the sophistication

---

[7] For an excellent discussion of competitiveness and its measurement, see Xavier Sala-i-Martin, Executive Summary, *Global Competitiveness Report 2003-2004,* p.xi-xxiv. However, Sanjaya Lall (2001:1501-1525) assesses the index used in this report and finds several deficiencies including broad definitions, biased approach, flawed methodology, and vague qualitative measures. He further argues that these weak theoretical and empirical foundations reduce the value of the indices for analytical or policy purposes.

[8] The concept of national competitiveness is, however, viewed as elusive by Paul Krugman. In his article titled "Competitiveness: A Dangerous Obsession" (Foreign Affairs, 1994: 28-45), Krugman stated that when we say

and productivity of companies is linked with the quality of the national business environment. As such, the BCI index is measured based on two sub-indices: (a) the sophistication of company operations and strategy, and (b) the quality of the national business environment.

How competitive are the Southeast Asian economies with other Asian economies? Table 4 shows the BCI for the top 10 and for some Asian countries based on a survey of 102 countries conducted by the World Economic Forum in collaboration with its 104 partner institutes. Among Asian countries, Singapore ranked 8th. It even ranked 4th in terms of the quality of the national business environment. Among Southeast Asian countries, Malaysia (26) and Thailand (31) are far much more competitive than Indonesia (60) and the Philippines (65). The Philippines ranked 74th in terms of the quality of the national business environment.

Table 4. The Business Competitiveness Index

Country	BCI ranking	Company operations and strategy ranking	Quality of the national business environment ranking
Finland	1	4	1
United States	2	2	2
Sweden	3	3	5
Denmark	4	7	3
Germany	5	1	9
United Kingdom	6	8	6
Switzerland	7	5	8
Singapore	**8**	**12**	**4**
Netherlands	9	10	11
France	10	9	14
		BCI for Asian countries	
Japan	12	6	20
Taiwan	15	16	16
Hong Kong	19	22	15
Korea	23	19	25
Malaysia	**26**	**26**	**24**
Thailand	**31**	**31**	**32**
India	37	40	36
China	46	42	44
Vietnam	**50**	**53**	**48**
Indonesia	**60**	**62**	**61**
Philippines	**65**	**48**	**74**

Source: Cited in Xavier Sala-I-Martin, "Executive Summary," The Global Competitiveness Report, Switzerland: World Economic Forum, 2003-2004, pp.xviii-xx. The BCI Index was measured based on a survey of 102 countries.

A second measure of competitiveness is the Growth Competitiveness Index (GCI) which was developed by Jeffrey D. Sachs and John McArthur. This index determines the capacity of the national economy to achieve sustained economic growth over the medium and long-term

that a corporation is uncompetitive, we mean that its market position is unsustainable – that unless it improves its performance, it will cease to exist. He further argues that countries, on the other hand, do not go out of business as they may be happy or unhappy with their economic performance, but they have no well-defined bottom line.

term. The GCI is based on three sub-indices, namely, the macroeconomic environment, the quality of public institutions, and technology. How competitive are Southeast Asian economies with other Asian economies? Table 5 shows the GCI in 2003 for the top 10 countries and for some Asian countries based on a survey of 102 countries conducted by the World Economic Forum in collaboration with its 104 partner institutes. Among Asian countries, Taiwan ranked 5th, followed by Singapore. Singapore ranked 1st in terms of macroeconomic environment, but in terms of technology index, Taiwan, Japan and Korea ranked better than Singapore. Among Southeast Asian countries, Malaysia (29) and Thailand (32) are again far much more competitive than the Philippines (66) Indonesia (72). In terms of the quality of public institutions, Indonesia ranked 76th while the Philippines ranked 85th.

Table 5. The Growth Competitiveness Index, 2003

Countries	GCI Ranking	Macroeconomic environment index	Public institutions index	Technology index
Finland	1	2	2	2
United states	2	14	17	1
Sweden	3	8	7	4
Denmark	4	5	1	8
Taiwan	5	18	21	3
Singapore	**6**	**1**	**6**	**12**
Switzerland	7	6	8	7
Iceland	8	16	3	15
Norway	9	4	16	13
Australia	10	7	4	19
GCI for Asian Countries				
Japan	11	24	30	5
Korea	18	23	36	6
Hong Kong	24	15	10	37
Malaysia	**29**	**27**	**34**	**20**
Thailand	**32**	**26**	**37**	**39**
China	44	25	52	65
India	56	52	55	64
Vietnam	**60**	**45**	**61**	**73**
Philippines	**66**	**60**	**85**	**56**
Indonesia	**72**	**64**	**76**	**78**

Source: As in Table.4, pp.xi-xvii. The GCI Index was measured based on a survey of 102 countries.

TRADE POLICIES

The flow of international trade is limited by various trade policies through restrictions and regulations generally known as trade or commercial policies which include tariffs and non-tariff trade barriers (NTBs). The General Agreement on Tariffs and Trade (GATT) was established in 1947 to achieve a substantial reduction of tariffs and NTBs to trade and thus to secure freer access of countries to to international markets.[9] While tariffs have been declining over the years, particularly on manufactured goods, nations worldwide have been dependent on NTBs which include quotas, voluntary export restraints (VERs), and technical, administrative and other regulations.[10]

A **tariff** is a tax or duty which is imposed on a commodity that crosses national boundaries. Tariffs can be imposed on imported or exported commodity. Import tariffs are the more common source of tax revenues particularly for the lower income countries in Southeast Asia. The more developed countries like Singapore relies more on personal and corporate income taxes as the major source of revenue. Export tariffs are commonly imposed by developing countries on their traditional primary commodities including agricultural commodities. The average tariff rates in ASEAN have declined substantially by as much as 51 percent since 1986.[11] In the context of the regional trade liberalization initiatives (discussed further in section 6 of this chapter), after ten years since 1993, the ASEAN Free Trade Area (AFTA) has been virtually realized. Regional tariffs on 99.60 percent of products in the CEPT Inclusion List (IL) of ASEAN-6 (Brunei Darussalam, Indonesia, Malaysia, the Philippines, Singapore and Thailand) are now within the 0-5 percent range, compared to 96.2 percent in 2002.[12] The average CEPT rate for ASEAN-6 has gone down from 12.8 percent in 1993 to 2.4 percent in 2003.

Import quotas are the most important non-tariff trade barrier which restricts the quantity of the imported commodity. They are usually imposed to protect the domestic industry like agriculture or manufacturing and/or for balance of payments purposes. For example, the European Union (EU) countries have imposed quotas on textiles imported from Southeast Asian countries. The EU and Vietnam have signed a 3-year agreement that gives Vietnam an increase in textile and clothing quotas worth 200 million euros (about US$215 million) a year.[13] In return, Vietnam is committed to lower its customs duties for EU imports of textile and clothing products progressively to 20 percent for clothing, 12 percent for fabrics, 7 percent for yarns and 5 percent for fibers by 2005.[14]

Voluntary export restraints (VER) is another type of non-tariff barrier whereby the importing nation induces another nation to "voluntarily" reduce its exports of a commodity. Should the exporting nation export of this commodity, the viabillity of the commodity in the importing nation will be affected, not only in terms of domestic production, but also employment in that industry. VERs have been negotiated by developed countries like the United States since the 1950s to restrict imports of textiles, cars, steel and other commodities from Japan and other exporting countries. In 1984, the US was able to negotiate VERs with major steel exporters which set its imports to about 20 percent of the US steel market which in turn was able to save some 35,000-40,000 jobs. However, with Japan signing a free trade

---

[9] Amelia Santos-Paulino, "The Effects of Trade Liberalization on Imports in Selected Developing Countries," *World Development*, Vol.30, No.6, 2002, p.959.

[10] For a complete discussion of the various types of trade policies, see Dominick Salvatore, *International Economics*, New York: Macmillan Publishing Co., 1990, pp.207-286.

[11] See Cludia Azarcon, "Comparative Tariff Policies of ASEAN Member Countries," *Journal of Philippine Development*, Number 43, Vol.24, No.1, First Semester, 1997, pp.93-135.

[12] ASEAN Secretariat, "Joint Media Statement," released during the 17th meeting of the AFTA Council, September 1, 2003, Phnom Penh, Cambodia, September 1, 2003. The acronym CEPT refers to Common Effective Preferential Tariffs, a scheme introduced since 1993 towards trade liberalization in the ASEAN region.

[13] *Textile World Asia*, "EU and Vietnam sign quota agreement," Spring 2003. (See http://www.textileworldasia.com/News.htm?CD=1846&ID=5025)

[14] *Textile World Asia*, "EU and Vietnam ..."

agreement (FTA) with Mexico, Japan will be able to export more cars and steel to the United States and Europe via Mexico.[15] As part of the agreement, Mexico will import Japanese vehicle parts and steel to assemble cars and electronic appliances for export to the US and Europe.

Technical, administrative and other regulations are other forms of NTB which include safety regulations, health regulations, and labelling requirements. Some examples of these standards are as follows: (i) an EU ban since 1989 on US exports of meat products from animals treated with growth-promoting hormones, which has effectively blocked U.S. meat (mainly beef) exports valued at about $100 million annually, (ii) an EU prohibition against US exports of poultry meat because the EU will not recognize as safe the U.S. processors' system for washing carcasses in chlorinated water, (iii) Korean border clearance procedures that can delay imported perishable products for several weeks, compared with several days elsewhere in Asia, and (iv) an EU decision, effective November 1, 1997, that human foods must be labeled to indicate whether they were produced from genetically modified corn and soybeans.[16]

International cartel is an organization of international producers who agree to restrict production and exports of a commodity to maximize profits. The Organization of Petroleum Exporting Countries (OPEC) is an example. It decided to restrict its output and exports of oil and this led to a four-fold increase in the world price of crude oil in 1973-74. Southeast Asian countries, particularly the oil-importers like the Philippines, Thailand and Singapore were the worst hit among the oil importing developing countries. Oil-producers like Brunei, Indonesia and Malaysia benefited through significant increase in their foreign exchange reserves.

Export subsidies are given to the country's exporters or would-be exporters through direct payments, tax reliefs or subsidized loans. Export subsidies in the form of low-interest rate loans can also be given to foreign buyers to boost the country's exports. In the case of the European Union, the subsidies being poured into the sugar industry have cost the EU taxpayers US$1.7 billion every year.[17] This is in the form of extremely high guaranteed prices for EU sugar producers which lead to overproduction. This has proved to be harmful to the major sugar exporting countries from the developing world including Brazil, Thailand, South Africa and Guatemala. In its study titled "The Great EU Sugar Scam," Oxfam pointed out that European consumers and taxpayers are paying to destroy livelihoods in some of the world's poorest countries and that they are paying for a system that rewards a handful of sugar producers in Europe, while undermining markets and opportunities for farmers and agricultural laborers in the developing world.[18] For their part, the Cairns Group (an informal bloc of big and medium-sized developed and developing country agricultural exporters that includes, among others, Southeast Asian countries, Argentina and New Zealand) has urged for a broader and faster liberalization of agricultural markets via increased market access, an

[15] The Straits Times, "Japan to use Mexico as trade gateway to US, EU," March 15, 2004, p.A15.

[16] Geoffrey Becker, Agricultural Exports: Technical Barriers to Trade, CRS Report for Congress, Oct 21, 1997. (see the National Council for Science and the Environment website http://www.ncseonline.org/NLE/CRSreports/Agriculture/ag-43.cfm)

[17] Asia Times, "Propping up sugar prices a bitter prospect," May 27, 2003. See http://www.atimes.com/atimes/Southeast_Asia/EE27Ae01.html

[18] See Asia Times, "Propping up sugar prices a bitter prospect," May 27, 2003. (http://www.atimes.com/atimes/Southeast_Asia/EE27Ae01.html)

end to export subsidies, and a decrease in production subsidies in the North.[19] Thus, the Southeast Asian governments have taken sides with the United States in pressuring for market opening in Japan and the termination of direct income subsidies for EU farmers.

Dumping is the practice of exporting a good at below cost or selling the good overseas at a lower price than in the home country. For example, the US International Trade Commission has imposed anti-dumping duties on shrimp from Thailand, Brazil, Ecuador, India, China and Vietnam in order "to create fair trading" and protect its American producers.[20] These countries are said to have 'dumped" frozen and canned shrimp and prawn in the US market. Because of the US move, the Thai shrimp exports are expected to fall by 20-30 percent, according to Thiraphong Chansiri, secretary-general of the Thai Frozen Foods Association. Unlike other exporting countries, however, Thailand is not likely to feel the impact because most of the shrimp products have premium quality which commands higher prices. Another country which is affected by the US move is Vietnam which exported US$467 million worth of shrimp to the United States in 2003.[21] Accordingly, the Vietnam Association of Seafood Exporters and Producers (Vasep) estimates that in order to fight US anti-dumping move, it will cost about US$1.2 million to US$1.5 million. In 2003, Vietnam lost against the US anti-dumping case on Vietnam's exports of catfish to the US market. Consequently, the US import tariff on catfish rose to 60 percent. The Vietnamese have temporarily stopped exporting the catfish fillet to the United States and instead diverted their exports of catfish to Asian countries such as Hong Kong, Singapore, European destinations as well as Australia.[22]

INDUSTRIAL PATTERNS OF TRADE

Based on the Standard International Trade Classification (SITC) as shown below, trade classification has enabled analysts and policy makers to determine the changes in the structure of exports and imports that take place overtime, and hence make important policy decisions including diversification policy.

0 Food and live animals
1 Beverage and tobacco
2 Crude materials
3 Minerals and fuels
4 Animal oils and fats
5 Chemicals
6 Basic manufactures
7 Machines, transport and equipment
8 Miscellaneous manufactures
9 Miscellaneous transactions

---

[19] See Walden Bello, "Asia, Asian Farmers and the WTO," Focus on Trade, No.36, Transnational Institute (TNI), July 1999. (http://www.tni.org/archives/bello/asiawto.htm)

[20] *The Nation,* "Are anti-dumping duties justified?" Editorial, Feb 21, 2004.

[21] See Intellasia, "Vietnam ready to tackle possible US antidumping lawsuit," Jan 1, 2004 (http://www.intellasia.com/news_today/2004/020104.htm)

[22] See Asia Times, "Vietnamese catfish firm shifts exports from US," Feb 15, 2003 (http://www.atimes.com/atimes/Southeast_Asia/EB15Ae06.html)

For analysis of trade structure, sectors 0 to 4 are considered primary products and sectors 5 to 8, manufactured products. Tables 6 and 7 shows the composition of Southeast Asian exports and imports, respectively. The structure of exports for all countries shifted away from primary products and towards manufactured goods. Indonesia, the Philippines, Thailand and Malaysia were very much dependent on primary exports as shown by their shares in 1975 at 98 percent, 78 percent, 76 percent and 69 percent, respectively. However, Indonesia showed the fastest change over a 26 year period with its share of manufactured goods rising to 58 percent in 2001. For Singapore, its share of manufactured goods more than doubled to 85 percent in 2001. Southeast Asia's dependence on manufactured imports continued to increase.

Table 6. Composition of Trade: Merchandise Exports

	Indonesia		**Malaysia**		**Philippines**		**Singapore**		**Thailand**	
	1975	**2001**	**1975**	**2001**	**1975**	**2001**	**1975**	**2001**	**1975**	**2001**
Total Exports (US$ mil)	7102	56318	3830	88032	2295	32150	5376	121687	2208	65118
0 Food and live animals	5.2	5.8	6.4	2.0	36.1	4.1	7.2	1.3	59.1	14.9
1 Beverage and tobacco	0.5	0.5	0.3	0.4	1.6	0.2	0.3	0.8	1.3	0.3
2 Crude materials	14.9	7.4	35.0	2.3	28.4	1.3	13.3	0.7	15.1	3.7
3 Mineral fuels, etc.	74.8	25.3	10.5	9.7	1.6	0.8	27.0	7.6	0.6	2.8
4 Animal, vegetable oils and fats	2.3	2.6	16.3	3.7	10.2	1.3	1.9	0.2	0.1	0.2
PRIMARY PRODUCTS	**97.7**	**41.6**	**68.5**	**18.1**	**77.9**	**7.7**	**49.7**	**10.6**	**76.2**	**21.9**
5 Chemicals	0.3	5.0	0.9	4.3	1.0	1.0	3.7	8.1	0.5	5.8
6 Basic manufactures	1.3	19.9	17.6	7.2	10.4	3.9	8.5	3.9	14.3	11.7
7 Machines, transport equipment	0.5	16.2	6.2	60.6	0.5	74.3	22.7	64.4	1.3	42.0
8 Misc. manufactures	0.3	16.5	5.7	8.8	4.4	12.9	6.9	8.7	3.5	15.2
MANUFACTURED PRODUCTS	**2.3**	**57.6**	**30.4**	**80.9**	**16.3**	**92.1**	**41.8**	**85.1**	**19.6**	**74.7**
9 Miscellaneous producs	0.0	0.8	1.1	1.1	5.9	0.2	8.4	4.3	4.3	3.5

Sources: ASEAN Secretariat (www.aseansec.org); Bank of Thailand (www.bot.or.th); UN COMTRADE (unstats.un.org); ADB, Key Indicators of Developing Asian and Pacific Countries 2002 (www.adb.org); IE Singapore (www.iesingapore.gov.sg); Bank of Korea (www.bok.or.kr).

Table 7. Composition of Trade: Merchandise Imports

	Indonesia		**Malaysia**		**Philippines**		**Singapore**		**Thailand**	
	1975	2001	1975	2001	1975	2001	1975	2001	1975	2001
Total Imports (US$ mil)	**4770**	**30962**	**3554**	**73098**	**3756**	**29551**	**8134**	**115919**	**3280**	**62072**
0 Food and live animals	12.1	8.1	16.4	4.4	9.6	7.4	8.6	2.5	2.9	4.0
1 Beverage and tobacco	0.3	0.8	1.4	0.3	0.7	0.7	0.7	0.9	1.1	0.4
2 Crude materials	3.4	10.3	6.5	2.5	4.0	3.3	6.4	0.6	6.0	4.1
3 Mineral fuels	5.4	17.8	12.0	5.3	21.7	11.4	24.6	12.6	21.3	12.0
4 Animal, veg oils and fats	0.1	0.1	0.3	0.3	0.2	0.2	1.3	0.2	0.2	0.1
PRIMARY PRODUCTS	**21.3**	**37.1**	**36.6**	**12.8**	**36.2**	**23.0**	**41.6**	**16.8**	**31.5**	**20.6**
5 Chemicals	16.9	17.4	8.3	7.4	11.3	8.9	5.8	5.9	13.6	10.7
6 Basic manufactures	22.5	13.7	16.3	10.7	13.2	11.9	18.2	7.3	15.8	16.1
7 Machines, transport eqpt	37.2	29.2	32.5	60.3	31.7	52.3	26.2	59.7	34.6	45.3
8 Miscellaneous manufactures	2.1	2.5	5.5	5.7	2.1	3.9	6.9	8.9	3.2	5.3
MANUFACTU -RED PRODS	**78.7**	**62.8**	**62.6**	**84.1**	**58.3**	**77.0**	**57.1**	**81.8**	**67.2**	**77.4**
9 Miscellaneous products.	0.0	0.03	0.8	3.1	5.6	0.1	1.4	1.4	1.3	2.0

Sources: As in Table 6.

Geographical Patterns of Trade

As Table 8 shows, by region, Asia is the top destination of Southeast Asia's exports. Indonesia, Malaysia, the Philippines and Singapore are increasingly more dependent on the Asian region as Asia's share of their exports rose in 2000 relative to 1976. Thailand's exports to Asia fell, but remained high at 46 percent in 2000. Thus, we could see that there is a growing trade between Southeast Asia and the Asian region, particularly with the Northeast Asian region and even within the Southeast Asian region itself, which is an indication of rising intra-ASEAN regional exports. The North American Free Trade Agreement (NAFTA) and the European Union (EU) regions are the other two leading regional destinations of Southeast Asia's exports. Within NAFTA, the US is the largest beneficiary. Within EU, the main export partners are UK, Germany, France and the Netherlands. The UK's major role in Southeast Asia emanates to some extent from the historical relationship between it and its former colonies: Brunei, Malaysia and Singapore. On the other hand, Indonesia and the Philippines have shown decreasing dependence on their former colonial masters, Netherlands and Spain, respectively,[23] which is a reflection of their nationalistic attitudes departing from

[23] Teofilo C. Daquila, 1997, "Obstacles to Closer Trade and Investment Links: An ASEAN Viewpoint," in Chia Siow Yue and Joseph L.H. Tan (eds), *ASEAN and EU: Forging New Linkages and Strategic Alliances*, Singapore: Institute of Southeast Asian Studies, and Paris: OECD, p.104.

the colonial pattern in the past.[24] By country, the major export partners of Southeast Asia are US, Japan, and UK.

Table 8. Direction of Trade: Merchandise Exports (% of Total Exports)

From To	INDONESIA		MALAYSIA		PHILIPPINES		SINGAPORE		THAILAND	
	1976	2000	1976	2000	1976	2000	1976	2000	1976	2000
Total Exports (US$ Million)	**8547**	**62124**	**5297**	**98135**	**2574**	**39783**	**6594**	**137804**	**2980**	**61924**
ASIA	**57.3**	**61.4**	**48.2**	**57.2**	**31.7**	**46.0**	**45.0**	**60.2**	**53.6**	**46.2**
***N.E. Asia**	**43.8**	**40.9**	**25.0**	**27.7**	**28.2**	**30.7**	**19.7**	**28.9**	**34.0**	**25.7**
-Japan	41.7	23.2	21.1	13.0	24.3	14.1	10.3	7.5	25.8	14.8
-South Korea	1.8	7.0	1.8	3.3	9.0	2.9	1.1	3.6	1.0	1.8
-Hong Kong	0.3	2.5	1.2	4.5	1.5	4.8	7.8	7.9	5.0	5.0
-China	...	4.5	0.8	3.1	1.5	1.7	0.6	3.9	2.1	4.1
-Taiwan	...	3.8	...	3.8	...	7.2	...	6.0	...	0.0
***ASEAN-10**	**13.1**	**17.5**	**22**	**26.6**	**2.6**	**15.0**	**21.1**	**27.4**	**18.0**	**18.7**
- Indonesia	-	0.0	-	1.7	...	0.5	-	0.0	5.2	1.9
-Malaysia	0.3	3.2	-	0.0	0.2	3.5	15.2	18.2	4.2	4.2
-Philippines	1.1	1.3	1.5	1.8	...	0.0	7.9	2.5	1.0	1.6
-Singapore	11.7	10.6	18.2	18.4	2.2	7.9	-	0.0	6.8	8.7
-Thailand	...	1.7	1.3	3.6	0.3	3.0	3.0	4.3	-	0.0
-Brunei	...	0.0	0.7	0.3	...	0.0	1.5	0.4	0.1	0.1
-Vietnam	...	0.6	...	0.5	...	0.2	0.2	1.5	...	1.2
-Laos	...	0.0	...	0.0	...	0.0	...	0.0	0.6	0.6
-Myanmar	...	0.1	0.2	0.2	...	0.0	0.3	0.3	0.1	0.0
-Cambodia	...	0.1	...	0.1	...	0.0	...	0.3	...	0.5
South Asia	**0.4**	**2.8**	**1.1**	**2.8**	**0.4**	**0.2**	**1.9**	**3.3**	**1.6**	**1.7**
Other Asia	**0**	**0.2**	**0.1**	**0.1**	**0.5**	**0.1**	**2.3**	**0.6**	**...**	**0.1**
EUROPEAN UNION	**7.5**	**13.0**	**17.3**	**13.7**	**19.6**	**17.2**	**15.4**	**13.2**	**23.0**	**15.7**
-U. Kingdom	0.5	2.4	...	3.1	2.8	3.8	3.7	2.6	1.6	3.4
-Germany	2.4	2.3	4.3	2.5	4.1	3.3	4.0	3.1	3.3	2.4
-Netherlands	2.7	3.0	6.6	4.2	8.2	7.5	1.7	3.0	13.3	3.3
-France	0.4	1.2	1.8	0.7	2.3	0.7	2.5	1.6	1.3	1.3
-Italy	0.9	1.2	2.1	0.6	0.6	0.4	1.3	0.4	1.2	1.2
-Belgium	0.2	1.3	0.9	0.9	0.5	0.3	0.5	0.5	0.7	1.6
-Other EU	0.4	1.5	1.6	1.6	1.1	1.0	1.7	2.1	1.6	2.6
NAFTA	**28.9**	**14.7**	**16.6**	**22.0**	**37.0**	**30.2**	**16.1**	**18.3**	**10.4**	**22.9**
-United States	28.7	13.7	15.6	20.5	36.0	28.7	14.6	17.3	10.0	21.3
-Canada	0.2	0.7	0.8	0.8	1	0.9	1.3	0.4	0.4	1.1
-Mexico	...	0.4	0.2	0.6	...	0.7	0.3	0.6	...	0.6
CER	**0.4**	**2.4**	**2.6**	**2.8**	**2.0**	**0.8**	**6.1**	**2.6**	**1.1**	**2.6**
- Australia	0.4	2.4	2.2	2.5	1.7	0.8	5.1	2.3	1.0	2.3
- New Zealand	...	0.0	0.4	0.4	0.3	0.0	1.0	0.3	0.1	0.3
MERCOSUR	**...**	**0.6**	**0.4**	**0.4**	**...**	**0.1**	**0.9**	**0.3**	**0.1**	**0.4**
Rest of the World	**6.0**	**7.9**	**14.8**	**3.9**	**9.5**	**5.6**	**16.4**	**5.3**	**11.9**	**12.1**

Source: IMF, *Direction of Trade Statistics Yearbook*, Washington D.C.: International Monetary Fund, Various Issues.

[24] Teofilo C. Daquila, 1997, "Obstacles to Closer …," p.122.

Table 9. Direction of Trade: Merchandise Imports (% of Total Imports)

To From	INDONESIA		MALAYSIA		PHILIPPINES		SINGAPORE		THAILAND	
	1976	**2000**	**1976**	**2000**	**1976**	**2000**	**1976**	**2000**	**1976**	**2000**
Total Imports (US$ Million)	5674	33515	3831	82199	3952	33808	9070	134545	3572	61924
ASIA	**49.0**	**54.7**	**45.5**	**62.9**	**37.7**	**51.8**	**41.6**	**58.9**	**43.8**	**56.0**
***NE. Asia**	**30.5**	**33.1**	**27.6**	**37.8**	**30.0**	**36.5**	**22.3**	**33.1**	**36.3**	**34.5**
-Japan	26.2	16.1	21.2	21.1	27.1	17.8	16.0	17.2	32.4	23.8
-South Korea	0.8	6.2	0.7	4.4	0.5	7.0	0.9	3.6	0.8	3.4
-Hong Kong	1.2	1.0	2.2	2.8	1.3	3.6	2.4	2.6	1.0	4.5
-China	2.3	6.0	3.5	3.9	1.0	2.3	2.9	5.3	2.0	2.8
-Taiwan	...	3.8	...	5.6	...	5.8	...	4.4	...	...
***ASEAN-10**	**15.7**	**19.2**	**16.3**	**24.1**	**6.5**	**14.7**	**17.8**	**20.0**	**4.9**	**20.0**
- Indonesia	-	...	-	2.8	3.0	2.0	...	...	0.1	1.8
-Malaysia	0.3	3.4	-	0.0	2.3	3.4	14.3	17.0	0.5	5.4
-Philippines	0.3	0.3	0.3	2.4	-	0.0	0.4	2.5	0.2	1.7
-Singapore	10.0	11.3	8.7	14.3	0.6	6.3	-	-	2.5	9.7
-Thailand	3.7	3.3	4.2	3.9	0.7	2.5	2.3	4.3	-	-
-Brunei	...	0.0	2.0	...	0.1	...	0.2	0.2	1.4	0.8
-Vietnam	0.1	0.9	...	0.6	...	0.5	0.3	0.6	...	0.5
-Laos	...	...	0.7	...	...	0.0	...	...	0.1	0.1
-Myanmar	1.6	...	0.5	0.1	...	...	0.2	0.1	0.1	...
-Cambodia	...	0.0	...	...	...	...	...	0.1	...	...
South Asia	**2.6**	**2.0**	**1.7**	**0.9**	**0.7**	**0.5**	**1.2**	**1.0**	**1.5**	**1.3**
-India	2.2	1.6	1.5	0.9	0.6	0.5	0.8	0.8	1.2	1.0
Other Asia	**0.2**	**0.3**	**0.1**	...	**0.5**	...	**0.3**	**4.8**	**1.1**	**0.2**
EUROPEAN UNION	**21.8**	**12.4**	**18.8**	**10.8**	**12.9**	**8.8**	**11.5**	**10.2**	**14.3**	**10.0**
-U. Kingdom	3.1	1.7	7.4	2.0	3.4	1.0	3.8	2.0	3.6	1.4
-Germany	8.5	3.7	5.6	3.0	3.4	2.2	3.3	3.1	4.8	2.8
-Netherlands	3.0	1.3	0.7	0.7	1.1	1.0	1.0	1.0	1.2	1.5
-France	3.5	1.2	1.6	1.7	2.5	1.0	1.3	1.6	1.3	1.1
-Italy	1.2	1.0	0.9	0.7	0.7	0.5	0.8	0.1	1.3	0.8
-Belgium	1.6	0.7	0.7	0.4	0.6	0.4	0.3	0.5	0.5	1.1
-Other EU	0.9	2.8	1.9	2.4	1.2	2.7	1.0	1.8	1.6	1.3
NAFTA	**18.4**	**12.1**	**13.8**	**17.3**	**23.5**	**16.5**	**13.7**	**15.8**	**14.8**	**11.4**
-United States	17.4	10.1	12.7	16.6	22.2	15.8	13.2	15.1	13.5	10.7
-Canada	1.0	1.9	1.1	0.5	1.2	0.6	0.5	0.4	1.3	0.6
-Mexico	0.1	0.1	...	0.2	0.1	0.1	...	0.3	0.1	0.1
CER	**3.7**	**5.8**	**8.0**	**2.4**	**4.5**	**2.9**	**3.0**	**1.8**	**2.5**	**2.1**
- Australia	3.3	5.1	7.1	2.0	3.5	2.4	2.6	1.7	2.1	1.8
- New Zealand	0.4	0.7	0.9	0.4	1.0	0.5	0.4	0.1	0.4	0.3
MERCOSUR	**0.2**	**1.0**	**0.4**	**0.4**	**0.8**	**0.3**	**0.4**	**0.2**	**0.3**	**0.8**
Rest of the World	**7.0**	**14.0**	**13.5**	**6.2**	**20.7**	**19.0**	**29.8**	**13.0**	**24.2**	**19.7**

Source: IMF, Direction of Trade Statistics Yearbook, Washington D.C.:International Monetary Fund, Various Issues.

Trade Liberalization and AFTA

Economic globalization is broadly defined as the shrinkage of economic distances between nations which consists of two separate but not necessarily mutually exclusive trends:

globalization of production and trade and globalization of finance and capital flows.[25] It is the closer integration of the countries and peoples of the world which has been brought about by the enormous reduction of costs of transportation and communication, and the breaking down of artificial barriers to the flows of goods, services, capital, knowledge, and (to a lesser extent) people across borders.[26] Various international institutions have been responsible in pushing for the global removal of barriers to free trade and the closer integration of national economies. The General Agreement of Tariffs and Trade (GATT) and its successor, the World Trade Organization (WTO) have been in charge of promoting free trade in goods and services on a global scale. The International Monetary Fund (IMF) has been responsible for removing the barriers to global finance and capital.

This section discusses the evolution of trade liberalization in Southeast Asia. The idea of trade liberalization and economic co-operation in Southeast Asia began with the UN team's report whose terms of reference were the promotion of free trade. The UN report recommended a comprehensive action plan which consisted of trade liberalization and industrial co-operation. Trade liberalization can take either a maximal approach which envisaged a free trade area with total elimination of tariff barriers, or a minimal approach which involves a gradual item-by-item approach. The UN recommended the latter.[27]

In 1974, Singapore's former minister, Mr. S. Rajaratnam emphasized that trade was the logical framework for economic activities in Southeast Asia. There was disagreement on the pace and method of trade liberalization. Singapore favored a free trade area via across-the-board tariff cuts to be implemented at a faster pace. This was supported by the Philippines. Indonesia and Malaysia, however, favored a cautious step-by-step approach. Thailand was neutral, but tended to lean towards across-the-board approach.

Following the first ASEAN summit meeting in 1976, trade liberalization measures were implemented since 1977 through a preferential trading arrangement (PTAs) which granted tariff preferences. Items covered were based on voluntary offers and product-by-product negotiations, followed by a sectoral approach. This was then changed to across-the-board approach in 1980 which provided for a minimum preferential tariff cut of 20 percent to all intra-ASEAN imports. The implementation of PTAs, however, was not very effective and had very minimal impact on trade. It covered only 2 percent of of intra-ASEAN trade in 1980 and 5 percent in 1986. Only 337 of 12,783 items offered in the PTA list were granted tariff preferences in 1987. This low utilization rate was commonly attributed to various factors, including a long exclusion list, too detailed dis-aggregation and inclusion of irrelevant items.

Intra-ASEAN Trade

Historically, intra-ASEAN trade has remained very low at around 15-20 percent mainly accounted for by trade between Singapore, Indonesia and Malaysia. This is shown in Tables 10 and 11. It reveals that intra-ASEAN exports as a proportion of global exports increased

---

[25] Rajan, Ramkishen Rajan, Economic Globalization and Asia: Trade, Finance and Taxation, Discussion Paper No.0108, Centre for International Economic Studies, University of Adelaide, 2001, p.1.

[26] Joseph Stiglitz, *Globalization and its Discontents,* England: The Penguin Press, 2002, p.9.

[27] For a discussion of the early attempts at ASEAN economic cooperation, see Marjorie Suriyamongkol, *Politics of ASEAN Economic Cooperation,* Singapore: Institute of Southeast Asian Studies, and Oxford University Press, pp.45-111.

from 12.7 percent in 1970 to 19.7 percent in the year 2000. Intra-ASEAN imports as a proportion of ASEAN's global imports rose from 5.5 percent to 19.1 percent during the same period. However, if we exclude Singapore from the picture, intra-ASEAN exports and imports would be extremely low, rising from 3.3 percent to 7.0 percent for the former and from 4.0 to 8.2 percent for the latter. Thus, the calculations would highlight the significant role of Singapore in intra-ASEAN trade and why Singapore encourages a faster pace of trade liberalization.

Table 10. Intra-ASEAN Exports (% of ASEAN's global exports)

From\To	INDO	MSIA	PHILS	SPORE	THAI	ASEAN-5	ASEAN-4
Indonesia							
1970		…	2.4	15.8	0.02	**18.2**	**2.4**
2000		3.2	1.3	10.6	1.7	**16.8**	**6.2**
Malaysia							
1970	0.6		1.7	21.6	0.9	**24.8**	**3.2**
2000	1.7		1.8	18.4	3.6	**25.5**	**7.1**
Philippines							
1970	0.2	…		0.7	0.3	**1.2**	**0.4**
2000	0.5	3.5		7.9	3.0	**14.9**	**7.0**
Singapore							
1970	n.a.	1.0	0.3		3.3	**4.6**	
2000	n.a.	18.2	2.5		4.3	**25.0**	
Thailand							
1970	2.3	5.6	0.1	6.6		**14.6**	**8.0**
2000	1.9	4.2	1.6	8.7		**16.4**	**7.7**
ASEAN-5							
1970	**3.1**	**6.6**	**4.5**	**44.7**	**4.5**	**12.7**	
2000	**4.1**	**29.1**	**7.2**	**45.6**	**12.6**	**19.7**	
ASEAN-4							
1970	**3.1**	**4.5**	**4.2**		**1.2**		**3.3**
2000	**4.1**	**10.9**	**4.7**		**8.3**		**7.0**

ASEAN-4 excludes Singapore. Source: IMF, Direction of Trade Statistics Yearbook, Washington D.C.:International Monetary Fund, Various Issues.

Other factors were responsible for the low intra-ASEAN trade. First, ASEAN imports from developed countries faced lower tariffs as these were mostly producer/capital goods while imports of manufactured goods from ASEAN faced higher tariffs as these were mainly final consumer goods. Second, ASEAN countries have historically depended on countries outside ASEAN for its trade, FDIs and technology. Third, there were differences in the pace of industrialization. During the 1950s and 1960s, ASEAN countries adopted an import-substitution policy which restricted imports through high tariff rates. The Philippines had the longest IS policy experience while Singapore, the shortest. Given a limited market size, scarce financial resources, massive unemployment, and lack of domestic entrepreneurs, Singapore has shifted to outward-orientation of its economy since the late 1960s through an industrialization policy which relied heavily on export-oriented labor-intensive FDIs. Since 1979, however, Singapore has re-directed its industrialization policy by encouraging more capital-intensive, highly-skilled, high-tech and high-value added industries. Since the 1970s, having learned from the successful experiences of Singapore, other ASEAN countries have switched to export-oriented industrialization policy which is dependent on FDIs.

Table 11. Intra-ASEAN Imports (% of ASEAN's global imports)

To\From	INDO	MSIA	PHILS	SPORE	THAI	ASEAN-5	ASEAN-4
Indonesia							
1970		1.0	0.2	…	1.6	**2.8**	**2.8**
2000		3.4	0.3	11.3	3.3	**18.3**	**7.0**
Malaysia							
1970	4.8		0.2	7.5	3.6	**16.1**	**8.6**
2000	2.8		2.4	14.3	3.9	**23.4**	**9.1**
Philippines							
1970	2.4	…		0.4	0.04	**2.9**	**2.5**
2000	2.0	3.4		6.3	2.5	**14.2**	**7.9**
Singapore							
1970	n.a.	…	0.4		2.0	**2.4**	
2000	n.a.	17.0	2.5		4.3	**23.8**	
Thailand							
1970	1.5	0.5	0.3	1.0		**3.3**	**2.3**
2000	1.8	5.4	1.7	9.7		**18.6**	**8.9**
ASEAN-5							
1970	**8.7**	**1.5**	**1.1**	**8.9**	**7.2**	**5.5**	
2000	**6.6**	**29.2**	**6.9**	**41.6**	**11.4**	**19.1**	
ASEAN-4							
1970	**8.7**	**1.5**	**0.7**		**5.2**		**4.0**
2000	**6.6**	**12.2**	**4.4**		**9.7**		**8.2**

Note: n.a. = not available. ASEAN-4 excludes Singapore. Source: IMF, Direction of Trade Statistics Yearbook, Washington D.C.:International Monetary Fund, Various Issues

Towards the ASEAN Free Trade Area (AFTA)

As Greenaway and Morgan stated, the 1980s and 1990s have seen a remarkable wave of unilateral liberalization which has involved developing countries, newly independent states in Central and Eastern Europe, and even some developed market economies most notably Australia and New Zealand.[28] In the case of Southeast Asia, the idea of free trade was proposed during the Manila summit in 1987 but was not well-received. However, the idea was revived in 1991 by Thailand's former PM Anand Panyarachun and was supported by Singapore's former PM Goh Chok Tong. Some feasibility studies were undertaken by some sectors in the region. The academe recommended the use of a differentiated approach to provide grace periods for countries not ready yet for fast-track liberalization. The private sector proposed a 40-percent ASEAN content rule. On the government side, committees were set up to consider the idea and to develop a practical working scheme. Discussions and deliberations were conducted through formal and informal dialogue sessions.

During the 22nd ASEAN Economic Ministers meeting, Indonesia proposed a trade instrument known as the Common Effective Preferential Tariff or CEPT which was adopted during the 1992 summit meeting in Singapore. The most significant step to promote intra-ASEAN trade was the decision of this summit to establish AFTA by the year 2008. The

[28] See David Greenaway, Wyn Morgan, and Peter Wright, "Trade Liberalization and Growth in Developing Countries: Some New Evidence," *World Development,* Vol.25, No.11, 1997, p.1885.

ASEAN member countries agreed in September 1994 to accelerate the establishment of AFTA by shortening the initial time frame from 15 years to 10 years. The primary objectives of AFTA include the promotion of intra-ASEAN trade, intra-ASEAN investment, greater FDIs in ASEAN, and also to promote ASEAN as a competitive production base.

The achievement of AFTA is not without problems. First, there is a lack of commitment from the private sector. Second, it will generate unemployment from inefficient industries. Third, there is a lack of harmonized safety and technical standard and customs clearance regulation. Fourth, there are differences in tariff structures, with Indonesia, the Philippines and Thailand having higher tariff rates. Moreover, a reduction in tariffs will result in loss of revenues particularly for the poorer countries in Southeast Asia.

To achieve AFTA, the CEPT scheme has been implemented since 1993. It covers manufactured products, capital goods and processed agricultural goods. Under the CEPT scheme, there are two groups of commodities covered, namely, the 'priority goods' and the 'other goods.' The 15 priority products included in the fast-track scheme are pulp, cement, fertiliser, vegetable oil, gems and jewellery, rubber products, pharmaceuticals, copper cathodes, leather products, wooden and rattan furnitures, plastics, textiles, chemicals, electronics, and ceramics and glass products.

For the priority goods, tariffs should be reduced to 0-5 percent at a faster pace than the other goods. The original members of ASEAN are expected to achieve the AFTA required tariff rates of 0-5 percent by the year 2003. The CEPT scheme has provided the most comprehensive coverage with the inclusion of more than 90 percent of total ASEAN tariff lines and the coverage of more than 85 percent of intra-ASEAN trade values and about 86 percent of the overall trade of ASEAN member countries. By the year 2000, more than 95 percent of the total ASEAN tariff lines were placed under CEPT.

Each member of ASEAN has a 10-year time frame of tariff reduction program under AFTA. By 2003, the older ASEAN-6 countries have experienced a tariff regime of not more than 5 percent tariff rate. The newer ASEAN members (Cambodia, Laos, Myanmar and Vietnam) are given a longer period to achieve this reduction in light of their current level of economic development. Vietnam is targeted to fully implement the AFTA in 2006, while the target year for Laos and Myanmar is 2008, and 2010 for Cambodia. Thus, the CEPT has been expected to boost intra-ASEAN trade significantly.

Trade liberalization measures since 1993 have proved to be effective as indicated by the rising level of intra-ASEAN trade. Intra-ASEAN trade grew significantly by 40 percent from US$79 billion in 1993 to US$111 billion in 1994. In 1995, it rose to US$140 billion which is about 25 percent of ASEAN's global trade. The adoption by ASEAN economies of outward-oriented trade policies, and pragmatic exchange rate policies, combined with rapid expansion of exports, have indicated that ASEAN's path replicated that of the newly industrialized countries in the 1960s and the 1970s.

Benefits of AFTA

The formation of AFTA offers several benefits. First, trade creation exists when a member country imports products or inputs from a more efficient exporting member country rather than from a less efficient non-member country. However, a negative effect is also possible in the form of trade diversion which refers to the condition when a member country imports products or inputs from a less efficient exporting member country rather than from a more efficient non-member country.

Second, it provides for a free flow of goods and services. The ASEAN region offers a large market size as it has some 500 million population. Third, AFTA will generate economies of scale. Regional producers will produce commodities according to comparative advantage which will lead to greater specialization, increased production and cost reduction. Fourth, AFTA will attract more foreign direct investments particularly those which are trade-related given that there will be reduced tariffs ranging from 0 to 5 percent. More multinational corporations will invest in the region to avail of the huge consumer base and reduced tariffs.

CONCLUSION

This chapter discusses the various theories and policies of trade with some applications to Southeast Asia. Among the various policies, tariffs are the most commonly used to generate revenues and protect domestic industries. This chapter also provides an analysis of the geographical and industrial patterns of Southeast Asian exports and imports. We have seen that Southeast Asia's major trading partners by region are Asia, North America and the European Union. It is important to note that Asia has increasingly become a significant regional partner of Southeast Asia. By industry, we have seen that Southeast Asia's trade has experienced a structural change away from primary exports towards manufactured exports, and a continuing dependence on manufactured imports. The Southeast Asian region has also implemented various measures aimed at liberalizing trade within the region through schemes like preferential trading arrangements and the Common Effective Preferential Tariffs – aimed at achieving AFTA by 2003 for the older members of the regional grouping and at various stages for other members. AFTA would certainly bring some benefits to the member countries but there will also be costs involved and problems along the way.

QUESTIONS FOR DISCUSSION

1. To what extent are trade theories relevant in the real world? Discuss your answer with reference to Southeast Asia.
2. Intra-ASEAN regional trade has been historically at low levels compared to those with countries/region outside ASEAN mainly, the United States, Japan and the European Union. Why?
3. Would ASEAN's trade dependence on the US, Japan and the EU persist?
4. Trade liberalization policies have resulted in lower tariffs globally. However, non-tariff barriers (NTBs) have risen particularly those which are imposed by the developed world against the developing nations including the ASEAN Asian region. Give examples of these NTBs and discuss their implications on the ASEAN economies.

Suggested Materials for Case Studies

Malaysia and Thailand

Reinhardt, Nola, 2000, "Back to Basics in Malaysia and Thailand: The Role of Resource-Based Exports in Their Export-led Growth," *World Development,* Vol.28, No.1, pp.57-77.

Vietnam

Hill, Hal, 2000, "Export Success Against the Odds: A Vietnamese Case Study," *World Development,* Vol.28, No.2, pp.283-300.

REFERENCES

Alam, Asad, 1995, "The New Trade Theory and its Relevance to the Trade Policies of Developing Countries," *The World Economy,* Vol.18, No.3, pp.367-385.

Azarcon, Chulia, 1997, "Comparative Tariff Policies of ASEAN Member Countries," *Journal of Philippine Development,* Number 43, Vol.24, No.1, pp.93-135.

Boltho, A., 1996, "The Assessment: International Competitiveness," *Oxford Review of Economic Policy,* Vol.12, No.3, pp.1-16.

Daquila, Teofilo C., 1997, "Obstacles to Closer Trade and Investment Links: An ASEAN Viewpoint," in Chia Siow Yue and Joseph L.H. Tan (eds), *ASEAN and EU: Forging New Linkages and Strategic Alliances*, Singapore: Institute of Southeast Asian Studies, and Paris: OECD, pp.103-134.

Daquila, Teofilo C., 2000, "Japanese Economic Policy in Asia: An Asian Perspective," in Verena Blechinger and Jochen Legewie (eds), *Facing Asia – Japan's Role in the Political and Economic Dynamism of Regional Cooperation,* Munich:Germany, Iudicium Verlag, pp.175-198.

Fagerberg, J., 1996, "Technology and Competitiveness," *Oxford Review of Economic Policy,* Vol.12, No.3, pp.39-51

Fukuda, Shin-ichi and Hideki Toya, 1995, "Conditional Convergence in East Asian Countries: The Role of Exports in Economic Growth," in Takatoshi Ito and Anne O. Krueger (eds), *Growth Theories in Light of the East Asian Experience,* Chicago, USA: The University of Chicago Press, pp.247-265.

Greenaway, David and Wyn Morgan, 1998, "Trade Orientation and Economic Development: Theory and Evidence," in David Sapsford and John-ren Chen (eds), *Development Economics and Policy,* London, UK: Macmillan Press, pp.113-132.

Greenaway, David, Wyn Morgan and Peter Wright, 1997, "Trade Liberalization and Growth in Developing Countries: Some New Evidence," *World Development,* Vol.25, No.11, pp.1885-1892.

Hill, Hal, 2000, "Export Success Against the Odds: A Vietnamese Case Study," *World Development,* Vol.28, No.2, pp.283-300.

IMF, Various Issues, *Direction of Trade Statistics Yearbook,* Washington D.C.: International Monetary Fund.

James, William, 1998, "Trade and Financial Market Reforms in ASEAN," *ASEAN Economic Bulletin,* Vol.14, No.3, pp.224-237.

Krugman, Paul, 1994, "Competitiveness: A Dangerous Obsession," *Foreign Affairs,* Vol.73, No.2, pp.28-45.

Lall, Sanjaya, 2001, "Competitiveness Indices and Developing Countries: An Economic Evaluation of the Global Competitiveness Report," *World Development,* Vol.29. No.9, pp.1501-1525.

Le, Quoc-Phuong, Duc-Tho Nguyen, and J.S. Bandara, 1996, "Vietnam's Foreign Trade in the Context of ASEAN and the Asia-Pacific Region," *ASEAN Economic Bulletin,* Vol.13, No.2, pp.185-199.

Lincoln, Edward J., 1987, *Japan's Economic Role in Northeast Asia.* Asian Agenda Report No. 10. Maryland: University Press of America and the Asia Society, pp.xviii-xi.

Porter, Michael, 1990, *The Competitive Advantage of Nations,* New York: The Free Press.

Rajan, Ramkishen, 2001, Economic Globalization and Asia: Trade, Finance and Taxation, Discussion Paper No.0108, Centre for International Economic Studies, University of Adelaide.

Reinhardt, Nola, 2000, "Back to Basics in Malaysia and Thailand: The Role of Resource-Based Exports in their Export-led Growth," *World Development,* Vol.28, No.1, pp.57-77.

Reynolds, Christopher, 2002, "The Southeast Asian Economic Miracle and International Trade Theory," in *Global Logic: The Challenge of Globalization for Southeast Asian Business,* Singapore: Prentice Hall, pp. 89-118.

Sala-I-Martin, Xavier, 2003-2004, "Executive Summary," The Global Competitiveness Report, Switzerland: World Economic Forum, pp.xi-xxiv.

Salvatore, Dominick, 1990, "Trade Restrictions: Tariffs," in *International Economics*, New York: Macmillan Publishing Co., pp.207-286.

Santos-Paulino, Amelia, 2002, "The Effects of Trade Liberalization on Imports in Selected Developing Countries," *World Development,* Vol.30, No.6, pp.959-974.

Singaravelu, Ananda and Loh Shen Lee, 1997, "Competitive Advantage: The US and ASEAN," in Tan Teck Meng, Low Aik Meng, John Williams and John Webster (eds), *US-ASEAN Relations: Implications for Business,* Nanyang Business Report Series, Singapore: Prentice Hall, pp.73-97.

Sodersten, Bo, 1980, "The Theory of Comparative Advantage and the Gains from Trade," *International Economics,* New York: St. Martin's Press, pp.11-27.

Stiglitz, Joseph, 2002, *Globalization and its Discontents,* England: The Penguin Press.

Suriyamongkol, Marjorie, 1988, *Politics of ASEAN Economic Cooperation,* Singapore: Institute of Southeast Asian Studies, and Oxford University.

The Nation, "Are Anti-Dumping Duties Justified?" Editorial, Feb 21, 2004.

The Straits Times, "Japan to use Mexico as trade gateway to US, EU," March 15, 2004, p.A15.

INTERNET SOURCES

ADB, Key Indicators of Developing Asian and Pacific Countries 2002 *(www.adb.org)*.

Asia Times, "Vietnamese catfish firm shifts exports from US," Feb 15, 2003 (http://www.atimes.com/atimes/Southeast_Asia/EB15Ae06.html)

Asia Times, "Propping up sugar prices a bitter prospect," May 27, 2003. (http://www.atimes.com/atimes/Southeast_Asia/EE27Ae01.html)

ASEAN Secretariat *(www.aseansec.org)*.

ASEAN Secretariat, 2003, "Joint Media Statement," released during the 17th meeting of the AFTA Council, Phnom Penh, Cambodia, September 1. (http://www.aseansec.org/15070.htm)

Bank of Korea *(www.bok.or.kr)*.

Bank of Thailand *(www.bot.or.th)*

Becker, Geoffrey, 1997, Agricultural Exports: Technical Barriers to Trade, CRS Report for Congress, October 21. (see the National Council for Science and the Environment website: *http://www.ncseonline.org/NLE/CRSreports/Agriculture/ag-43.cfm*)

Bello, Walden, 1999, "Asia, Asian Farmers and the WTO," Focus on Trade, No.36, Transnational Institute (TNI). (http://www.tni.org/archives/bello/asiawto.htm)

IE Singapore *(www.iesingapore.gov.sg)*

Intellasia, "Vietnam ready to tackle possible US antidumping lawsuit," Jan 1, 2004 *(http://www.intellasia.com/news_today/2004/020104.htm)*

Textile World Asia, "EU and Vietnam sign quota agreement," Spring 2003. *(http://www.textileworldasia.com/News.htm?CD=1846andID=5025)*

UN COMTRADE (unstats.un.org)

In: Asian Economic and Political Issues, Volume 11
Editor: Harvey E. Roth, pp. 191-207
ISBN: 1-60021-192-5

Chapter 9

PUTIN, PETROLEUM, PIPELINES, AND A POLITICAL DYNASTY IN AZERBAIJAN: OPPORTUNITIES AND RISKS FOR THE EUROPEAN UNION AND THE UNITED STATES

Robert C. Rickards
TUI Chair in International Management; The Leipzig Graduate School of Management; Handelshochschule Leipzig; Leipzig, Germany; Email: robert.rickards@hhl.de; and Hochschule Harz, Wernigerode, Germany; Email: rrickards@hs-harz.de

ABSTRACT

This article begins by summarizing President Putin's petroleum-and-pipelines strategy to revitalize Russia and, possibly, the country's imperial ambitions. It then shifts its focus to Azerbaijan, which once made Russia the world's largest petroleum producer. The article reviews key developments there during the czarist, Soviet, and post-independence periods. Next, it describes Baku's second oil and natural gas revolution, together with various pipeline alternatives for exporting Azerbaijani energy. The article goes on to consider several threats to these energy exports. In doing so, it pays particular attention to dangers resulting from the stolen presidential election of 2003 and the establishment of a political dynasty by the Aliyev clan in Baku. After taking note of the international reaction to this situation, the article concludes with a discussion of its consequences for Azerbaijan, Russia, the European Union, and the United States.

Keywords: Azerbaijan, Caspian Sea, European Union, Oil, the United States, Russia

INTRODUCTION

In December 2004, Russia's President Vladimir Putin gave a spikey end-of-the-year Kremlin press conference. He spoke as the leader of a troubled regional power that is in demographic decline, just was downgraded to an "unfree country" by the human rights group Freedom House, had frightened capital markets with the rigged takeover of Yuganskneftegaz's oil assets, and was humiliated when a bald attempt to steal Ukraine's presidential election failed.[1]

The fact that Putin does not think of Russia as part of the West thus has become very explicit. In his view, Ukraine remains a part of Russia's area of "vital concern," the former Soviet republics with deep economic, historical and, in Ukraine's case, cultural, linguistic, and ethnic bonds. Putin's apparent strategy to reverse his country's decline involves uniting Russia, Belarus, Ukraine, and Kazakhstan into an economic and political union. It recognizes what many people seem to have forgotten since the 1980s: oil is a political commodity. Hence, geopolitics and oil markets are fundamentally intertwined. This strategy utilizes Russia's and Kazakhstan's energy resources, together with the pipelines running through Belarus and Ukraine. It relies on Russia's role as the world's second-largest exporter of oil and natural gas to make China, France, Germany, Italy, and Japan more interested in maintaining strong bilateral ties with Moscow than openly questioning Putin's subversion of democratic institutions at home, prosecution of the war in Chechenya, military occupation of Georgian and Moldavan territory, or other forms of heavy-handed interference in the internal affairs of former Soviet republics and satellite countries.[2]

As a recent article suggested, whether Russia's energy policy is a narrowly national, competitive one or internationally more cooperative is the litmus test of Putin's intentions.[3] To date, the huge profits generated by energy exports have not been used to boost retirees' pensions above the poverty level, pay salaries on which school teachers, doctors, nurses, and policemen can live, restructure uncompetitive industries, or repair environmental damage caused by heavy pollution. On the contrary, a large portion of the revenues appears to be flowing into modernizing Russia's strategic weaponry and state security services as well as maintaining oversized conventional military forces and subsidizing a dysfunctional economy.

Even well-meant, indirect criticism of this petroleum-based strategy, such as Polish President Aleksander Kwaniewski's suggestion that Russia would be better off without Ukraine, provokes an angry response. Putin's answer to Kwasniewski evoked a Western plot to limit Russia's ability in developing relations with its neighbors and thus to isolate it.[4] Such paranoia denotes a fear of seeing the West lure away former Soviet republics and satellite countries, which the old KGB and military brass around Putin want to anchor in a Russian sphere of influence. The possibility that, by its actions, the Kremlin just might be isolating itself has not been the subject of public debate in Russia.

This article is the first in a series that analyzes Putin's hardball petroleum-and-pipelines strategy. It does so with regard to economic and political developments in selected countries proximate to Russia. It begins in Azerbaijan, where the czarist and Soviet energy industries originated. After highlighting their history, the article next summarizes petroleum, natural gas, and pipeline developments since Azerbaijan regained its independence. Following brief

---

[1] Myers, Steven Lee, "Just Like Bad Old Days," *International Herald Tribune*, November 24, 2004, pp. 1, 3.

[2] Dempsey, Judy, "EU Needs to Act, Some Say," *International Herald Tribune*, November 23, 2004, pp. 1, 4.

[3] Rickards, Robert C., "Big Oil, bin Laden, and the Great Game: Impressions of Central Asia in 1998 and 2001," *Current Politics and Economics of Asia*, Vol. 10, No. 4, 2002, pp. 239-259. This article also appears in Edward V. Linden (ed.), *Focus on Terrorism*, Vol. 5, (Nova Science, 2002; Chapter 1, pp. 1-21) and in Frank Columbus (ed.), *Asian Economic and Political Issues*, Vol. 6, (Nova Science, 2002; Chapter 5, pp. 83-103).

[4] N.a., "Vladimir Putin's Paranoia Is Isolating Russia," *International Herald Tribune*, December 30, 2004, p. 6

discussion of the dangers discord, environmental degradation, ignorance, and poverty pose for Azerbaijanis, the article then examines the country's recent politics in greater detail. The analysis concludes with a consideration of possible consequences these economic and political developments may have for Azerbaijan, the European Union, Russia, and the United States.

DEVELOPMENTS DURING THE CZARIST AND SOVIET PERIODS

As long as anyone can remember, petroleum has oozed out of Kirmaki Mountain. Even today, it partly covers the light brown sandstone of the mountainside, creating a checkerboard pattern. As a thick rivulet, the oil slowly snakes its way into the valley. In depressions along its course, it forms pools. They turn into natural asphalt, when the lighter parts of the raw petroleum evaporate in summer's glowing heat. The mountain's flat top is covered with holes. One stumbles across these circular openings, which resemble sewer shafts without manhole covers, practically everywhere. The holes, dug into the earth by human hands more than 150 years ago, are all that is left of wells, where workers once bailed oil from the earth with hand-buckets.

Kirmaki Mountain on the Caspian Sea remains a visible symbol for the beginnings of the oil industry in Baku. A host of rotting steel skeletons, thousands of production platforms and slowly nodding pumpjacks, a jungle of gooey pipes, and a despoiled landscape bear silent witness to the rule of black gold over men and nature.

The first oil revolution in Baku, Azerbaijan's capital, began with the law Czar Alexander II signed in St. Petersburg on February 1, 1872. At the time, Azerbaijan belonged to the Russian Empire. This czarist law created the legal framework for a private oil industry in Russia. From then on, wealthy foreigners were welcome as investors.

Large foreign firms soon opened subsidiaries in Baku. In 1874, for example, the Swede Robert Nobel arrived in this city on the Caspian Sea, followed shortly thereafter by his brother Ludwig. A little later, members of the Parisian Rothschild banking family came to Baku. With help from the Rothschilds, the Nobel brothers founded their first stock company there in 1879.

By the beginning of the 20th century, Baku was producing roughly half of the world's petroleum output.[5] Over one hundred foreign enterprises had branches in the city. Their oil flowed through 16 pipelines into 10 large storage areas. Baku, a fortress with centuries-old palaces of the Khans, caravansaries, and moschees, became the Mecca of the oil barons. It quickly grew into a modern metropolis with *Jugendstil* palaces, parks, and industrial districts.

In order to attract clients, Baku's businessmen stuffed their offices full with costly furniture, brocade hangings, and crystal chandeliers. One immediately recognized the oil barons by the giant gold rings and heavy gold belts they wore, richly encrusted in diamonds and rubies.

In those days, the oil king of Baku was Tadschi Tagiyev, a farmer's son, who became an oil billionaire. He also owned grain mills, fisheries, department stores, and cargo ships. In 1920, though, all his property fell to the Soviets. He died at age 105 in 1924 and his widow lived the rest of her life as a beggar.

[5] Siegl, Elfie, "Die neuen Ölbarone von Baku," *Frankfurter Allgemeine Sonntagszeitung*, 23. Juni 2002, p. 38.

Another Azebaijani oil baron, Murtusa Muxtarow, barricaded himself inside his manor house, when he heard Red Army soldiers firing their rifles outside. In 1920, his home was one of the last to be taken. Under heavy battering by the besiegers, the door to his ornate Gothic building groaned, plaster fell from its molded ceiling, and the leaded glass windows rattled. When two soldiers stood in the entry hall, Muxtarow suddenly appeared at the top of the marble staircase, his left hand gripping the banister, his right hand holding a revolver. He shot twice, killing both intruders. Then he fired a final shot into his own temple.[6]

The Soviet state moved into Muxtarov's palace, and the scarcely two-year old country of Azerbaijan lost its independence. Already, the October Revolution had driven the foreign investors away. Now most of the indigenous oil magnates and noble beys also fled to the West, while the oil production sites crumbled under Bolshevik rule. The splendid villas of the oil barons and merchants became schools, clinics, dormitories or administrative buildings. Tagiyev's palace is today the Museum for the History of Azerbaijan.

Baku's expropriated oil industry nevertheless remained an important factor in the Soviet Union's planned economy. At the battle of Stalingrad in the Second World War, about 70 percent of the fuel for Soviet combat troops came from the refineries in Baku. Then, in the late 1950s, oil production began in western Siberia, in the Tyumen area. One of the first state prospectors, who found oil there, was Forman Salmanov from Baku. Following his example, many petroleum specialists subsequently left their homes on the Caspian Sea for the Russian taiga .

Vagit Alekperov was one of them. Born in 1950 in Baku, he grew up there in an atmosphere drenched in oil, receiving his education as a mining engineer, with a specialty in oil and gas production, at the famous Petroleum Institute. At 24 years of age, he went Tyumen. By the time he was 41 years old, he had become president of Lukoil, Russia's largest oil concern. Yet he never has lost his ties to Baku. On the contrary, today Lukoil is among the largest players in the competition to produce and transport Caspian oil.

DEVELOPMENTS SINCE INDEPENDENCE

During Soviet times, when oil fever heated up bitterly cold western Siberia, Baku almost became a backwater. Then, however, the Soviet Empire collapsed, and the capital city of Azerbaijan awoke to new life. Since 1991, Azerbaijan again is independent and is fighting for its young life. In Baku, the old palaces from the turn of the 19th century into the 20th still are standing. Most of them are gray and in disrepair. Several palaces, though, have been beautifully restored to their former glory. The country's new petroleum princes reside in them, along the Boulevard of the Oil Workers, with its unrestricted view of the Caspian Sea. They are not private businessmen with pistols, operating on their own account. On the contrary, they are career civil servants, armed with direct telephone connections to Azerbaijan's president.

Until shortly before his death in December 2003, Azerbaijan's president was Heydar Aliyev. His background as KGB chief in Azerbaijan and one-time sychophant to Leonid Brezhnev formerly epitomized the Soviet way of politics. As a wolf in sheep's clothing, he controlled the Soviet republic's destiny for more than thirty years. When times changed, he

---

[6] Thumann, Michael, "Die Feuer von Baku," *Die Zeit*, 8. Mai 2002, p. 3.

transformed himself from a communist party provincial prince into the feudalistic president of an independent country. As an insider, he was well acquainted with many of the men and women who wielded power in Russia – especially former KGB officers like Putin. He thus knew that they had inherited a Soviet mentality, which regarded all politics as a naked struggle for power. The notion that Azerbaijanis acutally might want to remain independent of Moscow never has dawned on this group of Russian leaders.

Heydar Aliyev no doubt was acutely aware that a resurgent Russia would seek to reincorporate Azerbaijan into its sphere of influence. He also recognized that the same potential oil and natural gas reserves that made Baku attractive to Moscow were the keys to maintaining his country's independence. Heydar Aliyev ruled long enough to see the streams of Caspian oil begin to swell again. While he held office, his son, Ilham, was crown prince and designated heir. As vice president, Ilham Aliyev kept a watchful eye on Azerbaijan's largest state-owned oil company, Socar. Without the Aliyevs' blessing, nothing was possible in the Baku oil business.

The Aliyevs learned a lesson from Czar Alexander II. As he did, they opened the country for foreign investors. During the Soviet period, geologists had discovered oil and gas deposits in the Caspian Sea, possibly indicating reserves of gigantic dimensions. Unfortunately for the U.S.S.R., it didn't have the modern technology necessary to recover oil at great depths in the open sea. The Aliyevs knew that. Foreign know-how for domestic oil became their motto.

At the Aliyevs' behest, Socar therefore started to participate in energy consortia with foreign concerns. The basic principle underlying the consortia was simple: if a test well proved dry, the foreigners bore the costs alone. If it struck oil or natural gas, they were paid with it. Despite the risk involved, Americans, Britons, Frenchmen, Italians, Norwegians, Russians, and Turks stampeded to Baku. The latter-day Nobel brothers are called ExxonMobil, BP/Amoco, Totalfinaelf, Agip, Statoil, (Alekperov's) Lukoil, and Botas, while the contemporary Rothschilds are the World Bank and the European Bank for Recovery and Development (ERBD).

Baku's Second Oil Revolution

The start of Baku's second oil revolution had an exact date. It was September 20, 1994, the birthday of the Aliyevs' "contract of the century," when the first, newly founded international-Azerbaijani consortium, under BP's leadership, was formed to develop the oil fields previously discovered beneath the Caspian Sea. Ever since, Baku has fevered for the black gold. Today, two dozen consortia are at work in Azerbaijan, producing energy or constructing pipelines.

They are in a poker game with uncertain results. Only in six, or eight, or ten years will it be clear, whether their bets ultimately will bring profits. Meanwhile, dreams of vast wealth continue to lure ever more golddiggers and diplomats. The United States has the largest foreign embassy staff in Baku, followed by Turkey.

Whether wildcatter or pinstriper, the high-paid personnel from the West largely avoids contact with the local populace for fear of being denounced as spies. There have been cases like that. Moreover, in the Nobel brothers' day, state civil servants expected foreigners to give them expensive presents for their services. Many newcomers to Baku swear that things are no different today.

Valech Aleskerov has one of the direct telephone connections to Azerbaijan's president. A fancier of naturalistic paintings of oil platforms, he is Socar's general director. Accordingly, he also is one of the most important architects of Azerbaijan's future. Like Salmanov and Alekperov, Aleskerov is an engineer, who gained his work experience in Russia's oil fields. In the neo-classical Socar-Palace the 56-year-old now plans how his country can manage without the Russian government.

President Valdimir Putin's proposals to construct an energy consortium of former Soviet republics under Russian leadership, angered Aleskerov because they promised to destroy free competition in the marketplace. More importantly, through its ownership of the oil and natural gas pipelines necessary to export these resources, Russia would control the transit fees and, hence, reap most of the profits. As a signer of the "contract of the century," Aleskerov's big worry for the next several years therefore was how to get Azerbaijan's offshore oil to market, if possible, without relying on Russia.

Pipeline Alternatives

With an annual capacity of 18 million metric tons, the established Russian pipeline from the Tengis oil field in Kazakhstan to Novorossiisk on Russia's Black Sea coast was one obvious choice. However, it had been riddled with holes, shot by rebels during the Chechenya War. In addition, it had been tapped by local oil barons, who didn't waste time prospecting for black gold in the ground, but simply bored into other people's pipelines instead. In past years, Socar had delivered 50,000 barrels of oil per day via the Russian pipeline network. The oil company complained about the transit fees being too high. Moreover, Novorossiisk's port was navigable only 10 months a year.

The Azerbaijanis thus began, together with the Turks and the Georgians, to plan a big pipeline from Baku to the Georgian Black Sea port of Supsa and the Turkish Mediterranean port of Ceyhan. In contrast to Novorossiisk, Ceyhan's harbor is accessible even to the largest tankers 365 days a year.

With its oil consumption projected to rise from 28 million to 50 million metric tons by 2010, Turkey itself nevertheless will be the most important consumer of Azerbaijani petroleum. Yet the Turks wanted to prevent still more oil being sent through the Dardenelle Straits. That is because every additional 10 million metric tons of oil require another 800 midsize tanker ships to sail through the middle of Istanbul, a megacity. The danger of a catastrohpic oil spill or tanker explosion rises proportionally with increased traffic in the already congested shipping lanes. Besides agreeing to the pipeline deal, the Turkish government consequently issued a construction guarantee for $1.3 billion.[7]

The U.S. government also nurtured the Azeri-Georgian-Turkish plans, but for several other reasons. To begin with, it promised to deliver some Caspian oil to Western markets, while bypassing both Russia and Iran. Next, the investments and transit fees involved would prove particularly beneficial to empoverished Georgia, a country aspiring to join both the European Union and NATO. In addition, the Central Asian republics of Turkmenistan and

[7] Her, "Neue Ölleitung von Baku nach Ceyhan," *Frankfurter Allgemeine Zeitung*, 19. September 2002, p. 16.

Uzbekistan eventually might use this pipleline for a portion of their petroleum exports too, instead of building a shorter one via Iran. Hence, the project promised to bring peace, prosperity, and stability to the Caucasus region. Finally, over and above the other benefits, Caspian undersea reserves would help weaken OPEC's dominance of the world energy market.

Moscow and Teheran ridiculed the pipeline as an economically irrational, geopolitical measure. After all, the southern end of the Caspian Sea, near Baku, was not where the most promising energy reserves had been found. Many oil men furthermore scoffed at the unrealistic assumptions underlying the cost-benefit analysis accountants in Washington and Baku had made. No one possibly could hope to make money using that route with oil costing just $20 a barrel. Moreover, there was considerable skepticism about Azerbaijan's ability to produce enough oil to fill the planned pipeline. As shown in Table 1, in 2001, Azerbaijan was not exactly a petroleum heavyweight.

Table 1. Largest Petroleum Producing Countries

Country	(Millions of Metric Tons in 2001)
Saudi Arabia	379
United States	353
Russia	352
Mexico	177
China	165
Iran	159
Venezuela	157
Norway	154
Canada	127
Great Britain	114
For comparison:	
Azebaijan	15
Total world production 2001	3,414

Source: ExxonMobil; BP/FAZ Grafik Brocker

WHO LAUGHS LAST, LAUGHS BEST

Yet, the pipeline nonetheless could play a significant role in the market. By itself, Azerbaijan's expected output of 850,000 to 1 million barrels a day is not a huge amount. But in the context of world demand, which is growing annually by 100,000 barrels a day, this quantity looks more significant. According to the head of the World Bank office in Baku, Akbar Norman, even relatively modest amounts of new oil reaching world markets from the Caspian Sea could affect how the Organization of Petroleum Exporting Countries sets its production levels - because OPEC might feel that its bargaining position is weakening. Furthermore, if there are major new discoveries in the Caspian Sea, the Azerbaijani output correspondingly could have a much larger impact.

Do the pipeline partners constitute an American conspiracy against the unloved Russians and Iranians? No such thing! Albeit President Bill Clinton first courted the countries involved and then, in 1999, negotiated the treaty between Georgia, Turkey, and Azerbaijan. However, in the construction consortium that built the pipeline there were – an irony of oil history – just two U.S. firms participating, each with exactly 10 percent. The lion's share of the work went to European multinational companies, the Turks, and the Azerbaijanis – out of commercial interests.

As noted earlier, the investor group's leader is the BP-concern. Its managers reside high above the Caspian Sea in an orientally decorated building, formerly the Ilich (i.e., Vladimir Ilich Lenin) Palace of Culture. In the summer of 2001, BP sent 2,000 more men to Azerbaijan to help supervise construction of the pipeline from Baku via Tiflis, Georgia, to the Turkish harbor Ceyhan. Simultaneously, BP is heading another consortium, the one that readied the Azeri-Chirag-Güneschli oil field (out on the open sea) for production.

With each boring, the expected reserves continue to increase. Most recently BP has talked about 5.2 billion instead of 4.7 billion barrels. In any event, there is more than sufficient petroleum to fill the pipeline to Ceyhan to full capacity. Not included in the figure, of course, is what the concern still will discover in coming years in the Caspian Sea. The Kazakhs, for example, discovered the largest oil field in the world outside the Middle East, Kashagan, only after years of drilling on the sea bottom. With oil currently bringing more than $40 per barrel and the pipeline about to begin operation, it is Aleskerov's turn to laugh at the pipeline's critics.

The high-tech pipeline from the oil terminal Sangatschal near Baku to Ceyhan is 1,746 kilometers (1,094 miles) long. It has an annual capacity of 50 million metric tons per year. In 2005, it will begin carrying 375,000 barrels of oil a day and will reach 1 million barrels daily in 2007.[8] Eight pumping stations, each the size of a football field soon will push the raw oil along, until it gushes forth in the Turkish and Georgian port terminals. Its entire length, and also that of the smaller oil pipeline from Baku to Supsa, is protected by local security guards. They wear cute pink shirts and patrol the pipeline on horseback. As an additional precaution, long portions of the stretch to Ceyhan were laid underground.

The pipeline cost $3 billion to build. BP owns 35 percent of it, while Azerbaijan's Socar has the next largest stake at 25 percent. Other partners include Statoil AS of Norway, Unocal Corp. and Amerada Hess Corp. of the United States, TPAO of Turkey, ENI SpA of Italy, TotalFinaElf SA of France, and Impex and Itochu Corp. of Japan. The oil companies have covered a third of the pipeline project's costs, with the rest financed by international credit companies. Turkish firms built much of the pipeline because the government in Ankara promised to cover any unexpected cost overruns.

A Mountain is Burning

On the outskirts of Mamedli, a mountain is on fire. That is nothing unusal. The salt workers' donkey carts and the oil magnates' Jeeps drive past it every day. In contrast, groups of visiting Japanese businessmen regularly make themselves comfortable around the giant hearth. Beneath a decorative canopy they often have themselves served tea and nuts. Ten

[8] Greene, Richard Allen, "Hopes and Risks in Caspian Project," *International Herald Tribune*, September 20, 2002, p. 12.

meters behind them, natural gas issues from the mountainside. The fire can not be put out and so has become a bucolic natural wonder.

This site north of Baku, where in ancient times a Zarathustran temple once stood, fascinates energy managers today just as much as it did fire worshippers centuries ago. As is the case with Azerbaijani oil, though, the largest natural gas deposits no longer are on the mainland, but in the Caspian Sea. Off the coast, a multinational consortium hit upon the rich Schah-Denis gas field in 1998. BP and the Norwegian concern Statoil want to divide the estimated 700 billion cubic meters of gas with Azerbijanis, Turks, the French, Italians, and the Russian Lukoil Group. Commercial production will start here in 2005 too.

Besides oil, natural gas thus also is contributing to Baku's emergence as the Grand Café of the Caspian Sea. It is a place to see and to be seen. In a tea house, the former First Lady of Chechenya, Alla Dudayeva, autographs copies of her late husband's biography. Dchochat Dudayev was killed by the Russians.

In the Hyatt Hotel, the Greek minister for strategic development receives guests for coffee in the presidential suite. Akis Tzochatsopoulos is in town to negoiate with the government about gas deliveries from Azerbaijan to Greece. It is a perfectly reasonable thing to do because, parallel to the oil pipeline from Baku to Ceyhan, another international-Azerbaijani consortium is building a gas pipeline to Turkey. An Iranian company, OIEC Group, participates in the consortium as a minority partner. For the energy market of the region, it is a revolutionary development. Just a decade ago, Greeks and Turks stood on the brink of war. Today they are combining their gas networks. The natural gas will come from Azerbaijan and probably from neighboring countries as well. Tzochatspoulos next is traveling to Iran and Kazakhstan.

The Turks already have been there. Their natural gas imports are growing rapidly. Both the deputy energy minister, Yurdakul Yigitgüden, and the Turkish security council want the country to avoid becoming too dependent on any single source for energy imports. Russia currently is the largest supplier – via a new underwater pipeline in the Black Sea. However, Turkey, the United States' model ally in the Near East, also imports natural gas directly from the "Axis of Evil" – from Iran. According to Yigitgüden, by 2006 the quantity will be three times the amount imported in 2002. In Azerbaijan, the Turks themselves furthermore participate directly in gas production. So, beginning in 2005, a lot of natural gas will flow from Baku via Tiflis, Georgia, to Erzerum, Turkey, and eventually on to Europe[9]

DANGERS

Isn't all that natural gas too much of a good thing for Turkey? Yigitgüden laughs. The big pipelines are not just for Turkey, but also for the rest of Europe. With a finger on the map, the Turk traces the same lines as his Greek colleague did a few days earlier: from the Caspian Sea into Turkey, further on to Greece – and from there across the Balkans or perhaps Italy to Middle Europe.

Glancing at the map, it is immediately obvious that Azerbaijan and Iran are noticeably closer to Europe than most of the Siberian gas fields. The latter location is where, until now, around a third of the energy Europe consumes has originated. Given Russia's high transport

[9] Zdf/heute.de, "Aserbaidschan: Bau von Öl-Pipeline begonnen," 18.09.02.

costs, the proximity of Azerbaijan and Iran is not unimportant. For Europe, the raw materials beneath the Caspian Sea thus represent great economic opportunities. If only it were not for the dangers, in the form of discord, environmental degradation, ignorance, poverty, and politics associated with them.

Discord

At the end of April 2002, the presidents of the Caspian states met in the Turkmen capital Ashkhabad. Their purpose was to negotiate the division of the region's submarine resources. Russia, Kazakhstan, and Azerbaijan largely agreed. However, the "great leader of all Turkmen" Saparmurat Niyasov and the Iranians refused to accept a split clearly defined by the coastline.[10] The resultant argument continues to hinder development of more oil and natural gas fields. Iran even has deployed gunboats to drive off BP geologists looking for oil on the high seas.

Environmental Degradation

The Apscheron-Peninsula is a natural park representative of Azerbaijan's environment. Its visitors see a ruined landscape of reddish-gleaming sea salt and black pools of oil. Baku's suburbs are dotted with countless drilling towers leaning in the wind, above a thick, sticky, oozing mess. Even in densely populated residential areas, the pumpjacks tirelessly swing up and down around the clock. Wherever one walks on the peninsula, one has to be careful to avoid falling into a dark pit. Just as in the anecdote about Kirmaki Mountain recounted earlier, no one has taken the trouble to fill in the thousands of oil wells gone dry on the Apscheron-Peninsula either. In the 19th century, many workers drowned in the mineshafts they had dug. Even today, residual oil gurgles around in the ground and seeps up into daylight - too much to drain away, too little to be worth developing.

Ignorance

Since the 1990s, Azerbaijan and Georgia have been the darlings of the American and Turkish governments. In the West, only Washington and Ankara have spoken of pipelines, and only they have demonstrated an official interest in the region as a future supplier of raw materials. That seems remarkable because for the United States or Turkey, Azerbaijan is just one possible supplier among many energy-exporting countries. For much of nearby Europe, though, petroleum from Baku could be far more important. Yet the EU generally and, above all, Germany have shown scant interest. Albeit Brussels bureaucrats did develop a "Strategy for the Caucasus," and German Foreign Minister Joschka Fischer did come to Baku for a lightening visit in 2001. But there has been no follow-up: no attempts to broker negotiations

[10] For more on Niyasov, see Rickards, "Business, Bureaucratic Reform, and the EU in Turkmenistan," *Current Politics and Economics of Asia*, Vol. 9, No. 1, 2000, pp. 13-34.

among the Caspian states or between the Azerbaijanis and the Armenians, no stability pact. For their part, German entrepreneurs largely have steered clear of Baku. An Azerbaijani, who has lived in Germany under its incumbent social democratic-enviromentalist government, offers his conversation partner the following explanation for that disinterest. "Why should the Germans be interested in the Caspian Sea? They think they don't consume any energy, but only conserve it!"

POVERTY

Baku has been leading a double life again for more than a decade. The city's five-star hotels, Irish pubs, Japanese sushi-restaurants, European luxury boutiques, and office buildings of glass and steel lend a mondane flair to the life well-heeled foreigners lead there. Standing in stark contrast are the unmanicured suburbs with their shoddily-built, rundown, Soviet-era housing projects as well as the cheap bazaars and drafty, ramshackle cottages of the Old City. Together, they comprise the world of the indigenous population. Somewhere in between the vast wealth and the equally vast poverty run threads of a common history. The grain mill of the oil king Tagiyev is one such thread. Located on a prime downtown site, it teetered on the verge of bankruptcy in the Soviet planned economy. Its cellars were home to tens of thousands of rats. For fear of loosing a plague upon the city, the authorities refrained from demolishing the mill. Today it is a well-guarded, luxury office building housing Exxon/Mobil's headquarters in Azerbaijan.

POLITICS

These stark contrasts would be easier to accept, if the political system were transparent and transitioning toward something akin to the Norwegian welfare state. That is not the case.

As is the custom in the region, Azerbaijan is ruled by one family and its cronies. Heydar Aliyev led his country out of Russia's filthy backyard to independence in the 1990s. He won the multinationals as investors. But he did not understand how to let his people share in the prosperity brought by Azerbaijan's energy exports. In this country where natural gas literally leaks out of the earth by itself, most households remain without gas for hours every day because the lines serving them continually break down. Worsening the situation are the IMF's policies forbidding Baku from redirecting a portion of its oil and natural gas revenues from servicing international debt to infrastructure investments outside the energy industry

NEVER TRUST A FAT MAN IN A THIN COUNTRY[11]

A police-state calm ruled over Azerbaijan's fragile, mortgaged stability, when the 78-year-old Heydar Aliyev fell seriously ill in 2002. While everyone, who warmed themselves in his glow, wished him many more years of life, his opponents did not. They rallied in Baku in

[11] An ancient Central Asian proverb with modern relevance.

April 2003 to demand that the former Soviet republic create the proper conditions for democratic presidential elections the following fall. The protest, organized by a coalition of 12 opposition groups and approved by the authorities, attracted 12,000 to 13,000 demonstrators. The demonstrators demanded that the government stop stifling dissent and media freedom. They also called for adoption of an electoral code that fully met democratic principles for free and fair elections. In addition, they sought Heydar Aliyev's immediate resignation.[12]

For his part, the elder Aliyev had announced his intention to run again in the October presidential elections. Just a few days after the demonstration, though, he collapsed twice before reviving to complete a televised speech. Heydar Aliyev had been addressing a military audience in the capital when he suddenly gasped, clutched his heart and collapsed. Live transmission ended. Broadcasting resumed 12 minutes later as the frail-looking leader reappeared to a standing ovation. He continued his speech, but soon collapsed again. Transmission stopped and resumed shortly afterward as he returned to the podium to finish his speech.[13]

After this television appearance, the president was treated for high blood pressure and broken ribs. In early July, he began undergoing further treatment at a military hospital in Ankara. In August, while Heydar Aliyev still was hospitalized in Turkey, the Azerbaijani Parliament elected Ilham Aliyev prime minister. The elder Aliyev engineered the evident succession move. As prime minister, the younger Aliyev, 41, would become interim head of state if his father were to die in office. Opposition figures said the move was an attempt to ensure that the younger Aliyev would win the presidential election on October 15, 2003, and thereby be able to protect the interests of the Aliyev clan.[14]

The Election

By early October, President Heydar Aliyev was on his deathbed in a hospital in Cleveland, Ohio. There, less than two weeks before the election, he pulled out of the presidential race in favor of his son.[15] So, across the pale hills and parched flatlands of Azerbaijan, people cast their votes in a tightly controlled presidential election that aimed at cementing a ruling dynasty for years to come.

Soon after the polls opened, the opposition parties, which had fought an uphill battle against government control, began to complain of irregularities at almost every step of the voting process. Opposition observers were barred from a number of polling stations. They furthermore charged that some votes had been marked and ballot boxes stuffed before the polls opened. Moreover, many people found that their names were not on the voting rolls even as busloads of unregistered voters moved from one polling station to the next. In addition, independent human rights groups had been asserting for weeks that the government of Ilham Aliyev was manipulating election procedures, repressing opposition parties, and

[12] AP, "Demonstrators Seek Fair Elections and Resignation of the President," *International Herald Tribune*, April 14, 2003, p. 9.

[13] Reuters, "President Collapses Twice During Speech," *International Herald Tribune*, April 14, 2003, p. 5.

[14] Reuters, "President's Son Is Put in Line of Succession," *International Herald Tribune*, August 5, 2003, p. 8.

[15] Mydans, Seth, "Political Dynasty in Azerbaijan," *International Herald Tribune*, October 15, 2003, p. 6.

restricting their access to television. The authorities obstructed or violently dispersed opposition rallies, intimidated, beat, or arrested numerous opposition activists, and stacked election commissions. In interviews before and during election day, large numbers of ordinary citizens showed anger and contempt both for the Aliyev government and for its manipulation of the election.[16] Consequently, some opposition leaders said they planned to protest an outcome that they admitted was a foregone conclusion.

On the other hand, anyone visiting the country could have witnessed the careful registration of voters. On election day, one also could have seen the clear plastic voting boxes and the row of opposition observers sitting by the curtained booths in most polling stations. While these voting sites may have constituted Potemkin villages for international observers, far from every vote for Aliyev was fraudulent. The military, the government, the civil service, and other institutions that were doing well in the current regime certainly supported him. Other Azerbaijanis, for example many farmers, were pleased to embrace Aliyev's campaign promises to increase their pensions. Still other citizens expressed skepticism about the opposition candidates, asserting that they thought only of themselves. Once in power, they would just help their own families. Because Aliyev was young and already had everything, he would be more likely to try to help the country than those candidates would.

POLITICAL DYNASTY

Ilham Aliyev won the election contest hands down. So, for the first time in the vast former Soviet bloc, a son inherited his father's presidency. That strong-arm election illustrated once again the failure of democracy and political feedom to take root throughout most of the old Soviet Union.

Apart from the Baltic states – Latvia, Lithuania, and Estonia, which in October 2003 were set to join NATO and the European Union – there had been only one genuinely democratic transition in the 15 former republics since the Soviet Union came apart in 1991. That was in the small nation of Moldova, which an occupying Russian army nevertheless has assured will remain an authoritarian state. Even following the subsequent Rose Revolution in Georgia in November 2003 and the Orange Revolution in Ukraine in December 2004, there is no consolidated liberal democracy in the former Soviet Union except for the Baltic countries. Instead, there is the legacy of the state dominating politics. It's not a level playing field, and Azerbaijan is an absurd example of that.

After the election, the battle to subdue Azerbaijan's political opposition moved into the streets and it was as intense, harsh, and definitive as the dynastic victory in the presidential election the previous day. Again, the chief weapon was the big stick as thousands of well-drilled soldiers, police officers, and special security units charged through the streets, banging on their metal shields and clubbing both protesters and bystanders. According to various reports, at least one person was killed and dozens were injured among both protesters and the security forces.[17]

The central election commission announced preliminary results that gave Ilham Aliyev about 80 percent of the vote. The commission said the chief opposition candidate, Isa

[16] Mydans, "Aliyev Foes Cite Irregularities at Polls," *International Herald Tribune*, October 16, 2003, p. 5.
[17] Mydans, "Aliyev Wins in Voting and Brawls," *International Herald Tribune*, October 17, 2003, p. 3.

Gambar, had won about 12 percent of the vote in an election that observers from the Organization for Security and Cooperation in Europe (OSCE) primly said fell short of international standards. The observers listed such practices as violence, excessive use of force, intimidation of opposition supporters, journalists, and others, prohibitive restrictions on political rallies and meetings, severely imbalanced media coverage, and manipulation of the voting, counting, and tabulation processes.

The anger on the streets was explosive. Crowds of men supporting the opposition charged the police and soldiers, hurling volleys of stones and swinging their own batons. As in the election itself, the government forces were far better organized – deployed and commanded as if on a battlefield. These brief riots following the voting – quickly crushed by the police and the military – were the first major outbreak of political violence in Azerbaijan during the past decade.

The fraudulent presidential election ensured that the current, dynastic government would maintain its control over the country's significant oil reserves. Many individuals in Western policy circles viewed this transition as critical to the stability of billions of dollars of investments in Azerbaijan's energy sector. The violent events subsequent to the election should make them think otherwise.

The government clearly stole the election, and then brutally beat hundreds of people who poured out onto the streets in protest. Afterward, the riot police raised their shields to the sky and turned their batons into drumsticks, celebrating the victory of intimidation. Hundreds of people were arrested, while Gambar, the opposition leader, effectively was under house arrest and activists from his Musavat party were detained all over the country.

The violence surrounding the election was shocking yet predictable, because the government for years had shut the opposition out of the political process. In the months leading up to the poll, Azerbaijani authorities blatantly had manipulated the electoral process to guarantee that Ilham Aliyev would inherit his father's presidency. The opposition had nowhere to go but the streets.

International Reaction

More astonishing, however, were the public assessments of the election made by the OSCE and the Council of Europe. Their election-monitoring missions in Azerbaijan took due note of the violence and election irregularities, but their overall appraisals were alarmingly upbeat. The OSCE mission chief, Giovanni Kessler, said the election showed "an increased vitality of political life and serious efforts in Azerbaijan towards democracy and international standards." Meanwhile, the head of the Council of Europe's parliamentary delegation, Guillermo Martínez Casañ, said he hoped the election could "mark the beginning of a new era in Azerbaijan, in which progress could be achieved through cooperation of all democratic forces in the country."[18]

The Aliyev government has a terrible human rights record, and a long history of imprisoning its opponents, rigging elections, and breaking up public protests with excessive violence. Futhermore, international and local observers already had charged that the country's previous national election, the parliamentary election of 2000, was a farce.

[18] Bouckhaert, Peter, "A Stolen Election and Oil Stability," *International Herald Tribune*, October 20, 2003, p. 8.

The international community is well aware of this sorry history, but it seems to want to wish it away so it can continue doing business with the oil-rich country's government. Europe's foremost human rights body, the Council of Europe, admitted Azerbaijan in 2000 despite the country's disastrous parliamentary election. The Council of Europe did establish a body that monitors the country's democratic development and requires the government to report back on charges of election fraud. But this measure did little to restrain the government from repeating election fraud in the presidential election.

The crackdown may have reflected the relatively weaker political position of the new president, Ilham Aliyev. In any event, during its first three months in office, the new government of Azerbaijan continued to conduct a campaign of repression marked by arbitrary arrests, beatings, torture, and the dismissal of dissenters from government jobs, according to a report by the international rights group Human Rights Watch. The detailed 55-page report described a wave of up to 1,000 arrests of opposition leaders and party members, pro-democracy activists, journalists, and election officials and observers, who had challenged widespread electoral fraud. It said that more than 10 detainees remained in custody and that police harassment of opposition supporters was ongoing.[19]

The experience left the opposition and pro-democracy groups broken and demoralized. The thorough manipulation of the election, the crushing of opposition protests that followed it, the continuing crackdown, and the absence of strong condemnation from Brussels and Washington left opponents of the goverment with few options and little hope in the near future. No doubt it will be difficult to motivate the people of Azerbaijan to participate in future elections. Basically they have lost faith in the process. They now have all the evidence they need to show that there is no opportunity for them to change their government peacefully.

The successful crushing of dissent and the muted response from Washington contrast sharply with the situation in neighboring Georgia and in Ukraine. In those countries, pro-democracy groups were fostered with American aid, Washington spoke out in criticism of a flawed parliamentary election in November 2003 and an attempted theft of a presidential election in December 2004, respectively.

In January 2004, Secretary of State Colin Powell attended the inauguration of Georgia's new president, Mikhail Saakashvili, who was elected after driving his predecessor, Eduard Shevardnadze, from office in a peaceful popular uprising on November 23, 2003. Secretary of Defense Donald Rumsfeld also paid a courtesy visit to the new leaders of Georgia. By contrast, on a visit to Azerbaijan on December 4, 2003, to discuss military cooperation, Rumsfeld congratulated Aliyev on his election victory, but refused to answer questions from the international press about whether the election had met international standards.

CONSEQUENCES

Both Georgia and Azerbaijan are of strategic interest to the European Union and the United States because of their location between Russia and key Islamic nations and because they offer access to oil from the Caspian Sea. The political equations in the two countries differ, however. In Azerbaijan, pro-democracy groups have not been allowed to flourish, the

[19] Mydans, "Rights Group Pillories New Azerbaijani Regime," International Herald Tribune, January 23, 2004, p. 3.

press is under tighter control, and nascent democratic institutions have been demolished. Accordingly, aside from Gambar, no really attractive political opposition figures have emerged as alternatives to the Aliyev regime. There simply can be no fair elections in Azerbaijan when there is only one institution of power, namely the presidency, which controls everything in the country (just as Putin does in Russia!). The very idea of democracy now is under threat in Azerbaijan, which it wasn't in the past. Azerbaijanis justifiably are tired of the corruption and arbitrariness of years of rule under the current government. They are growing increasingly suspicious of the West, its passive acceptance of violently stolen elections, and its unwillingness to be tough on the Aliyev clan.

Moreover, allowing the Azerbaijani government to steal its presidential election merely emboldens other governments to do the same. Similar elections meanwhile have occurred in Armenia, Kazakhstan, Ukraine (the first two rounds of the presidential election), Kyrgyzstan, and Uzbekistan. In the long run, these stolen elections will contribute to more public discontent and destabilize this oil-rich region. Western leaders need to be every bit as supportive of the other struggling civil societies in the region, as they were of the Georgian and Ukrainian oppositions, before there is nothing left to support.

At least for the near term, though, Azerbaijan will continue to be ruled by a corrupt regime. Powerful economic clans, the armed forces, bureaucracy, and state security apparatus will support it. To a certain extent, foreign companies and institutions with vested interests in the country's energy resources will do so too. Aliyev likely will resist any Western attempts to lay the groundwork for a Rose or Orange Revolution (Gambar flew to Kiev in December 2004) by investing a portion of Azerbaijan's new wealth in his means of repression. That very well may include substantial expansion and modernization of the armed forces. A larger, better-equipped military potentially could be useful for quelling internal unrest or defending the country's economic zone in the Caspian Sea. In a worst case scenario, Aliyev also could employ it to resume the dormant war with Armenia over Nagorno-Karabakh. By appealing to Azerbaijanis' patriotism, such a conflict could shift popular attention away from dissaffection with Aliyev and refocus it on regaining lost territory. Armed conflict in the region, especially one pitting a Muslim country against a Christian one, certainly would create a difficult situation for Western governments and investors.

Like Azerbaijan, for the foreseeable future, Russia will continue to experience increasing authoritarianism, disdain for the rule of law, and suppression of an independent civil society. Domestically, Putin will trade on the popular perception that people from the East are patronized as a lower order by the West. Admittedly, there is plenty to feed this powerful source of Russian resentment. All the debates about expanding the European Union and NATO eastward, or about American military bases in Central Asia, or about assisting the revolutions in Georgia and Ukraine have been full of talk about constraining the Kremlin's imperial ambitions. The United States has campaigned for oil pipelines that skirt Russia. New European Union members (most notably Poland and Lithuania) have sought to make Ukraine a buffer between them and Russia. Without Ukraine or Caspian oil, Putin's dream of restoring Russia to major power status will be much harder to realize. What Putin probably fears most, however, is that the peaceful uprisings along Russia's borders may prove contagious. That kind of encirclement eventually could threaten his bankrupt *nomenklatura*-oligarchy as well. Recent events are putting Putin to a real test. He already has begun to destroy what he created with such effort – trust between between Russia and the world. Will he stop short of the abyss? Will the Russian bear acquiesce, adapt, or start destroying everything within reach? We shall see soon.

NATO and European Union expansion pose problems for Brussels too. It still is unclear about where Europe ends.[20] Moreover, the latest round of enlargement occurred without the EU reforming its internal structures. It is both tired and frightened of its own courage with regard to accepting more new members. With Turkey's membership in the pipeline, the EU finds it even more difficult to discuss Ukraine, let alone Georgia or Azerbaijan. The EU has a "New Neighborhood Policy" for Ukraine, Moldova, and Belarus, but it offers no perspective of membership for them. Yet, history won't wait. It is in the European Union's interest to bring its Eastern neighbors closer to the West by assisting them in building open and prosperous societies. With their small defense establishments, the EU's member countries lack a "big stick" to back up their diplomacy. Instead, they must rely solely on their "soft power" to help resolve political crises in countries the Kremlin tends to view as a continuation of Russia. If Europe succeeds in Kiev, next on the agenda might be Georgia's regions of Abkhazia and South Ossetia, the Trans-Dniestr region of Moldova, Armenia, and Azerbaijan. Doing so will involve persuading Putin that the "near abroad" is useful to Russia not as a *cordon sanitaire*, but as a bridge to Europe. Whether Europe is ready, willing, and able to play this new role in a way that will not enrage the Russians remains to be seen. The fact that the EU to date has taken no action to ameliorate conditions for Azerbaijanis living under the Aliyev regime, despite the report by Human Rights Watch, suggests it is not. The EU, therefore, more likely will continue to be a free rider on American policy initiatives, risking little politically, while profiting economically wherever it can.

The United States government and American investors have made considerable inroads into southeastern Europe and Central Asia. At least in Central Asia and Azerbaijan, these advances have led to dangerous entanglements with unsavory regimes. Justifiably or not, they also have contributed to Russia's sense of isolation. The United States, though, needs Russian cooperation in a variety of areas, most notably the fight against Islamic fundamentalist terrorism. Hence, it behooves President George W. Bush to convince Putin that the West really wants to engage Russia broadly in ways that are mutually beneficial. Even assuming Putin were so convinced, the possibility nevertheless would remain that America's substantial energy investments in the Caucasus and Central Asia could draw it into a conflict there. This possibility is not the only reason why the United States needs to become much more concerned about energy conservation. But it is a compelling one.

PROFESSIONAL BIOGRAPHY

Prof. Dr. Robert C. Rickards is the acting director of the TUI Chair in International Management at the Leipzig Graduate School of Management, Handelshochschule Leipzig, in Leipzig, Germany. He teaches controlling, accounting, and international management there and at the Hochschule Harz, in Wernigerode, Germany.

[20] Rickards, "The EU's Eastward Expansion," in Frank Columbus (ed.), *European Economic and Political Issues*, Vol. 3, (Nova Science, 2001; Chapter 1, pp. 1-18).

INDEX

A

B

C

D

E

F

G

H

I

J

K

L

M

N

O

P

Q

R

S

T

U

V

W

Y